Beyond Words

Beyond Words

Daily Readings in the ABC's of Faith

Frederick Buechner

 HarperSanFrancisco
A Division of HarperCollins*Publishers*

BEYOND WORDS: *Daily Readings in the ABC's of Faith.* Copyright © 2004 by
Frederick Buechner. All rights reserved. Printed in the United States of America. No
part of this book may be used or reproduced in any manner whatsoever without
written permission except in the case of brief quotations embodied in critical articles
and reviews. For information address HarperCollins Publishers, Inc., 10 East 53rd
Street, New York, NY 10022.

HarperCollins books may be purchased for educational, business, or sales promo-
tional use. For information please write: Special Markets Department, HarperCollins
Publishers, Inc., 10 East 53rd Street, New York, NY 10022.

HarperCollins Web site: http://www.harpercollins.com

HarperCollins®, ☷®, and HarperSanFrancisco™ are trademarks of HarperCollins
Publishers, Inc.

FIRST EDITION

Book design by Ralph L. Fowler

Library of Congress Cataloging-in-Publication Data
    Buechner, Frederick.
        Beyond words : daily readings in the ABC's of faith / Frederick
    Buechner.—1st ed.
            p.   cm.
        A compilation of three of the author's previously published works,
    Wishful thinking, 1973, Peculiar treasures, 1979, and Whistling in the
    dark, 1988, with 19 new entries.
    Includes index.
    ISBN 0–06–057446–1
    1. Devotional calendars.   I. Title.
    BV4811.B824   2004
    242'.2—dc22   2003056947

        07 08 ❖RRD(H) 10 9 8 7 6 5 4

For
my grandson
Douglas

Introduction

My three ABC books—*Wishful Thinking* (1973), *Peculiar Treasures* (1979), and *Whistling in the Dark* (1988)—have been in print for so long now that I'm encouraged to think there continue to be people who find them useful and might find them more useful still if combined into a single handy volume. So that is what I have done here—tweaking some of the original entries a little and adding enough new ones to bring the grand total up to 366 in the hope that maybe a word a day will help keep the demons at bay.

In *Wishful Thinking,* the words I dealt with were mostly religious words like *God, sin, salvation, repentance,* and in that book I was as much concerned to show what they don't mean as what I think they do. I made no attempt to define them in any comprehensive, scholarly way, but to show how much less boring, banal, and irrelevant they are than the way they all too often sound in church or Sunday school or on the lips of some televangelistic vaudevillian. I tried to suggest something of the true richness and vitality of the realities they point to. I tried to have some fun with them.

In *Whistling in the Dark*, I turned to just plain, everyday words like *good-bye, marriage, animals,* and *remember* in the effort to show that they too have a religious dimension and that, just like the plain, everyday events of our lives, speak to us of holy things if we have our eyes and ears open. It is less a theological ABC like its predecessor than an ABC theologized.

Peculiar Treasures deals not with words, but with biblical characters all the way from Aaron to Zaccheus. Far from the moral exemplars and stained-glass superstars they are usually taken to be, they are just such a conglomeration of saints and scoundrels, oddballs and screwballs, apostles and apostates, as we are ourselves, so that to look at them as they move through the pages of Scripture is not unlike looking into a mirror.

I have called the collection *Beyond Words* because in one way or another all the words it contains point to the realm of mystery and depth that lies beyond our ordinary experience and thus could be called beyond-words. To say something is beyond words is also to say that it is beyond the power of even beyond-words to convey adequately. Beethoven's last string quartets, falling in love, the death of a friend—how can we possibly describe such things other than to say that they are ultimately indescribable? You can know them only by experiencing them for yourself, and maybe that is the final message of a gallimaufry like this: Be alive to your life! Observe! *Pay attention!*

Beyond Words

AARON

MOSES WAS THREE YEARS YOUNGER than his brother, Aaron, but starting with the day Pharaoh's daughter fished him out of the bulrushes and adopted him, Moses was the one who always got the headlines while Aaron got the short end of the stick. Even when Moses had to clear out of Egypt for doing in an Egyptian Jew-baiter, he landed on his feet by marrying the daughter of a well-heeled sheep rancher across the border.

Aaron, in the meanwhile, went quietly off into the ministry, where in the long run he didn't do so badly either, except that the only people who ever heard about him were the ones who turned to the religion section on the back pages. Moses, on the other hand, was forever making the cover. The payoff came around the time Moses hit eighty, and out of a burning bush God himself voted him Man of the Year. As usual, Aaron had to be content with playing second fiddle, which he did well enough until he got the break he'd been waiting for at last, and then he blew it.

With Moses lingering so long on Mt. Sinai that some thought he'd settled down and gone into real estate, the people turned to Aaron for leadership, and in no time flat—despite an expensive theological education and all those years in denominational head-quarters—he had them dancing around the Golden Calf like a bunch of aborigines.

Nobody knows whether this was Aaron's way of getting even with his kid brother for all those years of eating humble pie, or whether he actually believed with the rest of humankind that a God in the hand is worth two in the bush.   *Exodus 32:1–4*

ABISHAG

DAY 2   WHEN KING DAVID was nearing the end of his days, not even his electric blanket could fend off the ominous chill he felt rising in his bones. The fires of life were all but out, and in an effort to rekindle them for the old man and at the same time preserve their own jobs, the establishment enlisted the aid of a beautiful young woman named Abishag. In the hope that she, if anybody, could start his blood coursing again, they persuaded her to join him in the sack. By this time, however, the old man was past rising to the occasion, and not long afterward—perhaps as the result of his unsuccessful attempts to do so—he died. When one of his sons offered to make an honest woman of Abishag by marrying her, the establishment turned him down on the grounds that by taking over his father's girlfriend, he was just making a play for taking over his father's throne. What finally became of Abishag is not recorded, and perhaps it is just as well.

This sad story makes it clear that in peace as well as in war there's no tragic folly you can't talk a nation's youth into simply by calling it patriotic duty.   *1 Kings 1–2*

ABORTION

Speaking against abortion, someone has said, "No one should be denied access to the great feast of life," to which the rebuttal, obviously enough, is that life isn't much of a feast for children born to people who don't want them or can't afford them or are one way or another incapable of taking care of them and will one way or another probably end up abusing or abandoning them. DAY 3

And yet, and yet. Who knows what treasure life may hold for even such children as those, or what treasures even such children as those may grow up to become? To bear a child even under the best of circumstances, or to abort a child even under the worst—the risks are hair-raising either way and the results incalculable.

How would Jesus himself decide, he who is hailed as Lord of Life and yet who says that it is not the ones who, like an abortionist, can kill the body we should fear, but the ones who can kill body and soul together the way only the world into which they are born can kill unloved, unwanted children (Matthew 10:28)?

There is perhaps no better illustration of the truth that in an imperfect world there are no perfect solutions. All we can do, as Luther said, is *sin bravely*, which is to say, (a) know that neither to have the child nor not to have the child is without the possibility of tragic consequences for everybody, yet (b) be brave in knowing also that not even that can put us beyond the forgiving love of God.

ABRAHAM

If a schlemiel is a person who goes through life spilling soup on people and a *schlemozzle* is the one it keeps getting spilled on, then Abraham was a *schlemozzle*. It all began when God told him to DAY 4 go to the land of Canaan, where he promised to make him the father of a great nation, and he went.

The first thing that happened was that his brother-in-law Lot took over the rich bottomland, and Abraham was left with the scrub country around Dead Man's Gulch. The second thing was that the prospective father of a great nation found out his wife couldn't have babies. The third thing was that when, as a special present on his hundredth birthday, God arranged for his wife, Sarah, to have a son anyway, it wasn't long before he told Abraham to go up into the hills and sacrifice him. It's true that at the last minute God stepped in and said he'd only wanted to see if the old man's money was where his mouth was, but from that day forward Abraham had a habit of breaking into tears at odd moments, and his relationship with his son Isaac was never close.

In spite of everything, however, he never stopped having faith that God was going to keep his promise about making him the father of a great nation. Night after night, it was the dream he rode to sleep on—the glittering cities, the up-to-date armies, the curly-bearded kings. There was a group photograph he had taken not long before he died. It was a bar mitzvah, and they were all there down to the last poor relation. They weren't a great nation yet by a long shot, but you'd never know it from the way Abraham sits enthroned there in his velvet yarmulke with several great-grandchildren on his lap and soup on his tie.

Even through his thick lenses, you can read the look of faith in his eye, and more than all the kosher meals, the ethical culture societies, the shaved heads of the women, the achievements of Maimonides, Einstein, Kissinger, it was that look that God loved him for and had chosen him for in the first place.

"They will all be winners, God willing. Even the losers will be winners. They'll all get their names up in lights," say the old schlemozzle's eyes.

"Someday—who knows when?—I'll be talking about my son, the Light of the World."   *Genesis 12–18; 22*

See also faith, Hagar, Isaac, Lot, Sarah.

ABSALOM

ALMOST FROM THE START, Absalom had a number of strikes against him. For one thing, he was much too handsome for his own good, and his special pride was such a magnificent head of hair that once a year when he had it trimmed, the trimmings alone tipped the scales at three and a half pounds. For another thing, his father, King David, was always either spoiling him rotten or reading him the riot act. This did not promote stability of character. He murdered his lecherous brother Amnon for fooling around with their sister, Tamar, and when the old war-horse Joab wouldn't help him patch things up with David afterward, he set fire to his hay field. All Israel found this kind of derring-do irresistible, of course, and when he eventually led a revolt against his father, a lot of them joined up.

On the eve of the crucial battle, David was a wreck. If he was afraid he might lose his throne, he was even more afraid he might lose Absalom. The boy was the thorn in his flesh, but he was also the apple of his eye, and before the fighting started, he told the chiefs of staff till they were sick of hearing it that, if Absalom fell into their clutches, they must promise to go easy on him for his father's sake. Remembering what had happened to his hay field, old Joab kept his fingers crossed, and when he found Absalom caught in the branches of an oak tree by his beautiful hair, he ran him through without blinking an eye. When they broke the news to David, it broke his heart, just as simple as that, and he cried out in

DAY 5

words that have echoed down the centuries ever since. "O my son Absalom, my son, my son," he said. "Would I had died instead of you, O Absalom, my son, my son" (2 Samuel 18:33).

He meant it, of course. If he could have done the boy's dying for him, he would have done it. If he could have paid the price for the boy's betrayal of him, he would have paid it. If he could have given his own life to make the boy alive again, he would have given it. But even a king can't do things like that. As later history was to prove, it takes the King himself.

2 Samuel 13–19

ADAM

DAY 6

HE LET THE *Times* fall to the carpet beside him. It was the usual recital—a new tax plan, the danger of oral contraceptives to women over forty, the mayor's special committee on child abuse. He pushed his glasses back on his forehead and with his thumb and forefinger massaged the loose flesh under his eyes. Through the club window he could see a fat woman in slacks waiting for a bus, a boy with a ponytail walking a dog. Somebody had the TV on in another room, and he could hear the rise and fall of canned laughter. He lit a cigarette and let the smoke drift out of his mouth without exhaling it. The city sky was turning brown with the approach of dusk. Then suddenly, as if it had been only yesterday, he remembered Eden.

The leopard . . . the starling . . . the rose—he remembered giving each its name, remembered the green river, the shy, green girl. He could no longer remember why it was he had felt compelled to leave it except that it had something to do with asserting his independence. Beyond that, he had only the dim sense that somehow a terrible injustice had been done, or possibly a terrible justice.

He saw the flame of what must have been the sunset flash like a sword in the upper-story windows across the street. When the old steward brought him his third martini, he called him Pete. Actually, his name was Angelo.

Genesis 2–3

See also Eve.

ADOLESCENCE

THE ANCIENT DRUIDS are said to have taken a special interest in in-between things like mistletoe, which is neither quite a plant nor quite a tree, and mist, which is neither quite rain nor quite air, and dreams, which are neither quite waking nor quite sleep. They believed that in such things as those they were able to glimpse the mystery of two worlds at once.

DAY 7

Adolescents can have the same glimpse by looking in the full-length mirror on back of the bathroom door. The opaque glance and the pimples. The fancy new nakedness they're all dressed up in with no place to go. The eyes full of secrets they have a strong hunch everybody is on to. The shadowed brow. Being not quite a child and not quite a grown-up either is hard work, and they look it. Living in two worlds at once is no picnic.

One of the worlds, of course, is innocence, self-forgetfulness, openness, playing for fun. The other is experience, self-consciousness, guardedness, playing for keeps. Some of us go on straddling them both for years.

The rich young ruler of the Gospels comes to mind (Matthew 19:16–22). It is with all the recklessness of a child that he asks Jesus what he must do to be perfect. And when Jesus tells him to give everything to the poor, it is with all the prudence of a senior vice-president of Morgan Guaranty that he walks sadly away.

We become fully and undividedly human, I suppose, when we discover that the ultimate prudence is a kind of holy recklessness, and our passion for having finds peace in our passion for giving, and playing for keeps is itself the greatest fun. Once this has happened and our adolescence is behind us at last, the delight of the child and the sagacity of the Supreme Court justice are largely indistinguishable.

ADVENT

DAY 8

THE HOUSE LIGHTS GO OFF and the footlights come on. Even the chattiest stop chattering as they wait in darkness for the curtain to rise. In the orchestra pit, the violin bows are poised. The conductor has raised the baton.

In the silence of a midwinter dusk there is far off in the deeps of it somewhere a sound so faint that for all you can tell it may be only the sound of the silence itself. You hold your breath to listen.

You walk up the steps to the front door. The empty windows at either side of it tell you nothing, or almost nothing. For a second you catch a whiff in the air of some fragrance that reminds you of a place you've never been and a time you have no words for. You are aware of the beating of your heart.

The extraordinary thing that is about to happen is matched only by the extraordinary moment just before it happens. Advent is the name of that moment.

The Salvation Army Santa Claus clangs his bell. The sidewalks are so crowded you can hardly move. Exhaust fumes are the chief fragrance in the air, and everybody is as bundled up against any sense of what all the fuss is really about as they are bundled up against the windchill factor.

But if you concentrate just for an instant, far off in the deeps of yourself somewhere you can feel the beating of your heart. For all its madness and lostness, not to mention your own, you can hear the world itself holding its breath.

AGAG

DAY 9

A CCORDING TO THE PROPHET SAMUEL, God wanted King Saul to wipe out every last one of the Amalekites—not just the men, but the women and children, the babies and the residents of the old folks home. When he heard that Saul had decided to spare the Amalekite king, Agag, he was so enraged that he tore the royal robe from Saul's back and told him to consider it a mild foretaste of how God would tear the kingdom of Israel from him next. He then had them drag out poor Agag, who was quick to size up the situation. With something less than total conviction, he said, "Surely the bitterness of death is past" (1 Samuel 15:32). Within seconds Samuel had personally hacked him to pieces to prove that God meant what Samuel said that he said.

Since Agag had hacked quite a few people to pieces himself in his day, he may well have been dismayed by the experience, but can hardly have been surprised. What was perhaps new to him was the length to which the friends of God will go to make God enemies.

1 Samuel 15

AGING

DAY 10

W HEN YOU HIT SIXTY or so, you start having a new feeling about your own generation. Like you, they can remember the Trilon and Perisphere, Lum and Abner, ancient Civil War veterans riding in open cars at the rear of Memorial Day parades, the Lindbergh kidnapping, cigarettes in flat fifties which nobody believed then could do any more to you than cut your wind. Like you, they know about blackouts, bond rallies, A-stickers, "Kilroy Was Here." They remember where they were when the news came through that FDR was dead of a stroke in Warm Springs, and they could join you in singing *"Bei Mir Bist Du Schön"* and "The Last Time I Saw Paris." They wept at Spencer Tracy with his legs bitten off in *Captains Courageous.*

As time goes by, you start picking them out in crowds. There aren't as many of them around as there used to be. More likely than not, you don't say anything, and neither do they, but something seems to pass between you anyhow. They have come from the same beginning. They have seen the same sights along the way. They are bound for the same end and will get there about the same time you do. There are some who by the looks of them you wouldn't invite home for dinner on a bet, but they are your *compagnons de voyage* even so. You wish them well.

It is sad to think that it has taken you so many years to reach so obvious a conclusion.

AGNOSTIC

DAY 11 AN AGNOSTIC IS SOMEBODY who doesn't know for sure whether there really is a God. That is some people all of the time and all people some of the time.

There are some agnostics who don't know simply because they've never taken pains to try to find out—like the bear who didn't know what was on the other side of the mountain.

There are other agnostics who have taken many pains. They have climbed over the mountain, and what do you think they saw? Only the other side of the mountain. At least that was all they could be sure of. That faint glimmer on the far horizon could have been just Disneyland.

AGRIPPA

T HERE'S SOMETHING A LITTLE SAD about seeing anybody for the last time, even somebody you were never particularly crazy about to begin with. Agrippa, for instance. He was the last of the Herods, and after him that rather unsavory dynasty came to an end.

DAY 12

When Saint Paul was on his way to Rome to stand trial, King Agrippa granted him a hearing, and Paul, who was seldom at a loss for words, put up a strong defense. He described how on the road to Damascus he had come to believe Jesus was the Messiah and how all he had been doing since was trying to persuade other people to believe he was right. He said the fact the Jews were out to get him showed only that they didn't understand their own Scriptures, because the whole thing was right there, including the prediction that the Messiah would suffer and rise from the dead just the way Jesus had.

After Paul finished, Agrippa came out with the only remark he ever made that has gone down in history. "Almost thou persuadest me to become a Christian," he said (Acts 26:28).

Almost is apt to be a sad word under the best of circumstances, and here, on the lips of the last of his line the last time you see him, it has a special poignance. If only Paul had been a little more eloquent. If only Agrippa had been a little more receptive, a little braver, a little crazier. If only God weren't such a stickler for letting people make up their own minds without forcing their hands. But things are what they are, and *almost* is the closest Agrippa ever got to what might have changed his life. It's sad enough to miss the boat at all, but to miss it by inches, with a saint right there to hand you aboard, is sadder still.

Acts 26:1–28, KJV

See also Felix, Herod Antipas, Herod the Great, Paul.

AHAB

DAY 13

WHEREAS JUST ABOUT EVERYBODY has a cross to bear, King Ahab had two. One cross was the prophet Elijah. If, generally speaking, a prophet to a king was like ants at a picnic, Elijah was like a swarm of bees. The other cross was his foreign-born wife, Jezebel, who had gotten religion in a big way back in the old country and was forever trying to palm it off on the Israelites, who had a perfectly good religion of their own. Unfortunately for Ahab, the two of them sometimes got to working on him at the same time, one from one side, the other from the other. A case in point was the Naboth affair.

To make a sordid story short, Naboth had a vineyard that Ahab wanted so much he could taste it, and when Naboth refused either to sell or to swap, Ahab went into a sulk. "He laid him down upon his bed, and turned away his face, and would eat no food" (1 Kings 21:4). It was the kind of opening Jezebel was always on the lookout for. Was he a king or a cup custard, she asked and proceeded to take charge. Found guilty of a trumped-up charge, Naboth got stoned to death, and Ahab got the vineyard. He also, needless to say, got a visit from Elijah.

Down through the years they'd kept meeting like that, usually in secluded places, always at critical moments. Ahab arrived incognito—the dark glasses, the Panama hat, the business suit—and Elijah with a ten-day growth of beard. Ahab addressed him in his usual informal way as a royal pain in the neck (1 Kings 21:20), and then Elijah let him have it with both barrels. When God got through with him, Elijah said, there wouldn't be enough left of Ahab to scrape off the sidewalk, and what there was the dogs would take care of. As for Jezebel, not only because of Naboth but because of all her imported witch doctors and totem poles, she would end up the same way.

Ahab at least said he was sorry, and as a result was allowed to die honorably in battle, the part about the dogs coming true only in the sense that they got to lap the water up that his bloody chariot was hosed off with afterward. Jezebel, on the other hand, continued unrepentant to the end. When the time finally came, they threw her out of the window, and when the dogs got finished, all that was left for the undertaker was "the skull and the feet and the palms of her hands" (2 Kings 9:35).

God is merciful, and if Jezebel and Ahab and Elijah all eventually met up again in paradise, you can only assume that Ahab said if it weren't for the honor of the thing, he'd as soon take his chances in a warmer climate, and immediately put in for a transfer.

1 Kings 21–22; 2 Kings 9:30–36

ALCOHOLICS ANONYMOUS

Alcoholics Anonymous, or A.A., is the name of a group of men and women who acknowledge that addiction to alcohol is ruining their lives. Their purpose in coming together is to give it up and help others do the same. They realize they can't pull

DAY 14

this off by themselves. They believe they need each other, and they believe they need God. The ones who aren't so sure about God speak instead of their Higher Power.

When they first start talking at a meeting, they introduce themselves by saying, "I am John. I am an alcoholic," "I am Mary. I am an alcoholic," to which the rest of the group answers each time in unison, "Hi, John," "Hi, Mary." They are apt to end with the Lord's Prayer or the Serenity Prayer. Apart from that they have no ritual. They have no hierarchy. They have no dues or budget. They do not advertise or proselytize. Having no buildings of their own, they meet wherever they can.

Nobody lectures them, and they do not lecture each other. They simply tell their own stories with the candor that anonymity makes possible. They tell where they went wrong and how day by day they are trying to go right. They tell where they find the strength and understanding and hope to keep trying. Sometimes one of them will take special responsibility for another—to be available at any hour of day or night if the need arises. There's not much more to it than that, and it seems to be enough. Healing happens. Miracles are made.

You can't help thinking that something like this is what the church is meant to be and maybe once was before it got to be big business. Sinners Anonymous. "I can will what is right but I cannot do it," is the way Saint Paul put it, speaking for all of us. "For I do not do the good I want, but the evil I do not want is what I do" (Romans 7:19).

"I am me. I am a sinner."

"Hi, you."

Hi, every Sadie and Sal. Hi, every Tom, Dick, and Harry. It is the forgiveness of sins, of course. It is what the church is all about.

No matter what far place alcoholics end up in, either in this country or virtually anywhere else, they know that there will be an A.A. meeting nearby to go to and that at that meeting they will find strangers who are not strangers to help and to heal, to listen to the truth and to tell it. That is what the Body of Christ is all about.

Would it ever occur to Christians in a far place to turn to a church nearby in hope of finding the same? Would they find it? If not, you wonder what is so big about the church's business.

See also Lord's Prayer.

ALGEBRAIC PREACHING

$x + y = z$. If you know the value of one of the letters, you know something. If you know the value of two, you can probably figure out the whole thing. If you don't know the value of any, you don't know much.

DAY 15

Preachers tend to forget this. "Accept Jesus Christ as your personal Lord and Savior and be saved from your sins," or something like that, has meaning and power and relevance only if the congregation has some notion of what, humanly speaking, sin is, or being saved is, or who Jesus is, or what accepting him involves. If preachers make no attempt to flesh out these words in terms of everyday human experience (maybe even their own) but simply repeat with variations the same old formulas week after week, then the congregation might just as well spend Sunday morning at home with the funnies.

The blood atonement. The communion of saints. The Holy Ghost. If people's understanding of theological phrases goes little deeper than their dictionary or catechetical definitions, then to believe in them has just about as much effect on their lives as to believe that Columbus discovered America in 1492 or $E = mc^2$.

Coming home from church one snowy day, Emerson wrote, "The snow was real but the preacher spectral." In other words, nothing he heard from the pulpit suggested that the preacher was a human being more or less like everybody else with the same dark secrets and high hopes, the same doubts and passions, the same weaknesses and strengths. Undoubtedly he preached on matters like sin and salvation but without ever alluding to the wretched, lost moments or the glad, liberating moments of his own life or anybody else's.

There is perhaps no better proof for the existence of God than that year after year the whole God enterprise survives despite the way the professionally godly promote it. If there are people who remain unconvinced, let them tune in their TVs to almost any of the big-time pulpit pounders almost any Sunday morning of the year.

AMOS

DAY 16

WHEN THE PROPHET AMOS walked down the main drag, it was like a shoot-out in the Old West. Everybody ran for cover. His special target was the "beautiful people," and shooting from the hip, he never missed his mark. He pictures them sleek and tanned at Palm Beach, Acapulco, St. Tropez. They glisten with Bain de Soleil. The stereo is piped out over the marble terrace. Another tray of Bloody Marys is on the way. A vacationing bishop plunges into the heated pool.

With one eye cocked on them, he has his other cocked on the unbeautiful people—the varicose veins of the old waiter, the pasty face of the starch-fed child, the Indian winos passed out on the railroad siding, the ragged woman fumbling for food stamps at the check-out counter.

When justice is finally done, Amos says, there will be hell to pay. The happy hour will be postponed indefinitely, because the sun will never make it over the yardarm. The cashmere sweaters, the tangerine-colored slacks, the flowered Lillys will all fade like grass. Nothing but a few chicken bones will mark the place where once the cold buffet was spread out under the royal palms.

But according to Amos, it won't be the shortage of food and fun that will hurt. It will be the shortage "of hearing the words of the Lord" (Amos 8:11). Toward the end, God will make himself so scarce that the world won't even know what it's starving to death for.

Amos 6–8

ANANIAS

IT WASN'T BECAUSE ANANIAS held back from the poor box some of the proceeds of his real-estate deal that Saint Peter came down on him so hard. The poor would get by somehow. They always had. What got the old saint's goat was that Ananias let on he was handing over his whole pile instead of only as much as he thought he wouldn't be needing himself.

DAY 17

"You do not lie to us but to God," Peter said (Acts 5:4), and the undeniable truth of the charge together with the unbearable shame of it were more than Ananias could take, so he dropped dead. His wife, Sapphira, had been in on the real-estate deal with him, and when she turned up three hours later and found out what had happened, she dropped dead too.

Lying to God is like sawing the branch you're sitting on. The better you do it, the sooner you fall.

Acts 5:1–11

ANGELS

SLEIGHT-OF-HAND MAGIC is based on the demonstrable fact that as a rule people see only what they expect to see. Angels are

DAY 18

powerful spirits whom God sends into the world to wish us well. Since we don't expect to see them, we don't. An angel spreads its glittering wings over us, and we say things like, "It was one of those days that made you feel good just to be alive," or "I had a hunch everything was going to turn out all right," or "I don't know where I ever found the courage."

ANGER

DAY 19

OF THE SEVEN DEADLY SINS, anger is possibly the most fun. To lick your wounds, to smack your lips over grievances long past, to roll over your tongue the prospect of bitter confrontations still to come, to savor to the last toothsome morsel both the pain you are given and the pain you are giving back—in many ways it is a feast fit for a king. The chief drawback is that what you are wolfing down is yourself. The skeleton at the feast is you.

ANIMALS

DAY 20

OUT OF THE GROUND the Lord God formed every beast of the field and every bird of the air, and brought them to the man to see what he would call them; and whatever the man called every living creature, that was its name" (Genesis 2:19). Following Adam's lead, we say *that* is the elephant and the albatross, *that* is the weasel and the goldfish. What or who they really are we do not know because they do not tell. They do not tell because they lack what is either the gift or the curse of speech, depending on your point of view. Perhaps another reason they do not tell is that they do not know. The marmalade cat dozing among the nasturtiums presumably doesn't think of herself as a marmalade cat or as anything else for that matter. She simply is what she is and what she does. Whether she's mating under the moon or eviscerating a mouse or gazing into empty space, she seems to make herself up from moment to moment as she goes along.

Humans live largely inside their heads, from which they tell the rest of their bodies what to do, except for occasional passionate moments when the tables are turned. Animals, on the other hand, do not seem compartmentalized that way. Everything they are is in every move they make. When a dachshund takes a shine to you, it is not likely to be because he has thought it over ahead of time. Or in spite of certain reservations. Or in expectation of certain benefits. It seems to be just because it feels to him like a good idea at the time. Such as he is, he gives himself to you hook, line, and sinker, the bad breath no less than the frenzied tail and the front paws climbing the air. Needless to say, the whole picture can change in a flash if you try to make off with his dinner, but for the moment his entire being is an act of love bordering on the beatific.

"Ask the animals, and they will teach you," Job says to his foul-weather friends. Innocence, as above, is one of their lessons, but the one Job has in mind is another, that is, that "in [the Lord's] hand is the life of every living thing and the breath of every human being" (Job 12:7, 10). When the ravens came and fed Elijah bread and meat by the brook Cherith (1 Kings 17:6), we're told they did it because the Lord commanded them to. However, I suspect that since, in spite of Poe, ravens are largely nonverbal, the Lord caused the sight of the old man to be itself the command the way the smell of breakfast is a command to be hungry or the sound of your best friend on the stair a command to rejoice.

Elijah sat there all by himself—bald, on the run, in danger of starving to death. If the ravens could have talked, they would probably have tried to talk either the Lord or themselves out of doing anything about it. As it was, there was simply nothing for it but to bring him two squares a day till he moved on somewhere else. The sleek, black birds and the bony, intractable prophet—since all life is one life, to save another is to save yourself, and with their wings, and beaks, and throbbing birds' hearts all working at once, the ravens set about doing it.

ANNUNCIATION

DAY 21

MARY COULDN'T SAY she wasn't warned. The angel came with an Easter lily in his hand and stood so still he could have been one of the columns in the loggia where they met. Mary had trouble hearing what he said and afterward thought it might have been just a dream. Even so, it troubled her.

It was not until later that the real trouble came. The real trouble came when what the angel announced would happen happened, but in a way she couldn't have dreamed: squatting there in the straw with her thighs wrenched apart, while out of her pain she dropped into the howling world something that looked like nothing so much as raw beefsteak: who was the one the angel had said was to be called Holy, the Son of the Most High: who was the Word itself fleshed with—of all flesh—hers.

ANOREXIA

DAY 22

NOTHING FOR BREAKFAST. A diet soda for lunch. Maybe a little lettuce with low-calorie dressing for supper. Or once in a while, when everybody has gone to bed, a binge on ice cream, which you get rid of in the bathroom later. Relentless exercise.

Obsession with food, cooking great quantities of it for everybody except yourself. In time you come to look like a victim of Dachau—the sunken eyes and hollow cheeks, the marionette arms and calfless legs. If you are a woman, you stop menstruating. If you are told your life itself is in jeopardy, it makes no difference, because not even dying is as fearsome as getting fat, a view that the combined industries of fashion, dietetic food, and advertising all endorse. In every respect but this, you may be as sane as everybody else. In this, you are mad as a hatter.

Anorexia seems to be a modern disease, but old phrases like *pining away* and *wasting away* suggest it may have been around unnamed for a long time. Nobody seems to know what it's all about, though there are endless theories. Young anorexics want to strike free of parental control, they say, and where does it assume a more elemental form than in "Take a bite for Mummy, a bite for Daddy"? So that is where they draw the battle line. The more desperately they are urged to eat, the more desperately they resist. Their bodies are their last citadel, and they are prepared to defend them literally to the death. Yet on the other side of it, of course, they desperately need Mummy and Daddy and are scared stiff of the very independence they are fighting to achieve.

The craving to be free and independent. The craving to be taken care of and safe. The magic of the sickness is that it meets both these cravings at once. By not eating you take your stand against the world that is telling you what to do. By not eating you make your body so much smaller, lighter, weaker that in effect it becomes a child's body again, and the world flocks to your rescue. Is something like this at the heart of it?

Most anorexics are young women. Feeling that a male-dominated world has given them no models for what full womanhood means, do they believe that the golden key to that Wonderland garden is to make themselves as little as Alice had to in order to pass through the tiny curtained door? Who can say for sure?

But at least one thing is sure. By starving themselves, anorexics are speaking symbolically, and by trying above all else to make them start eating again, their families are in their own fashion speaking back the same way. Far beneath the issue of food there are, on both sides, unspoken issues of love, trust, fear, loss, separation. Father and mother, brother and sister, they are all of them afflicted together, acting out in pantomime a complex, subterranean drama whose nature they are at best only dimly aware of. And so, one way or another, are we all.

"So then, putting away falsehood, let all of us speak the truth to our neighbors, for we are members one of one another," says the author of Ephesians (4:25), and that is the heart of the matter.

"I need you." "I need to be myself." "I am afraid." "I am angry." "I am in pain." "Hear me." "Help me." "Let me try to help you." "Let us love one another." If we would only speak the truth to one another—parents and children, friends and enemies, husbands and wives, strangers and lovers—we would no longer have to act out our deepest feelings in symbols that none of us understand.

In our sickness, stubbornness, pride, we starve ourselves for what we hunger for above all else. "Speaking the truth in love" is another phrase from Ephesians (4:15). It is the only cure for the anorexia that afflicts us all.

ANXIETY

DAY 23

"HAVE NO ANXIETY about anything," Paul writes to the Philippians. In one sense it is like telling a woman with a bad head cold not to sniffle and sneeze so much or a lame man to stop dragging his feet. Or maybe it is more like telling a wino to lay off the booze or a compulsive gambler to stay away from the track.

Is anxiety a disease or an addiction? Perhaps it is something of both. Partly, perhaps, because you can't help it, and partly because for some dark reason you choose not to help it, you torment yourself with detailed visions of the worst that can possibly happen. The nagging headache turns out to be a malignant brain tumor. When your teenage son fails to get off the plane you've gone to meet, you see his picture being tacked up in the post office among the missing and his disappearance never accounted for. As the latest Mideast crisis boils, you wait for the TV game show to be interrupted by a special bulletin announcing that major cities all over the country are being evacuated in anticipation of a terrorist attack. If Woody Allen were to play your part on the screen, you would roll in the aisles with the rest of them, but you're not so much as cracking a smile at the screen inside your own head.

Does the terrible fear of disaster conceal an even more terrible hankering for it? Do the accelerated pulse and the knot in the stomach mean that, beneath whatever their immediate cause, you are acting out some ancient and unresolved drama of childhood? Since the worst things that happen are apt to be the things you don't see coming, do you think there is a kind of magic whereby, if you only *can* see them coming, you will be able somehow to prevent them from happening? Who knows the answer? In addition to Novocain and indoor plumbing, one of the few advantages of living in the twenty-first century is the existence of psychotherapists, and if you can locate a good one, maybe one day you will manage to dig up an answer that helps.

But answer or no answer, the worst things will happen at last even so. "All life is suffering" says the first and truest of the Buddha's

Four Noble Truths, by which he means that sorrow, loss, death await us all and everybody we love. Yet "the Lord is at hand. Have no anxiety about anything," Paul writes, who was evidently in prison at the time and with good reason to be anxious about everything, "but in everything by prayer and supplication with thanksgiving let your requests be made known to God."

He does not deny that the worst things will happen finally to all of us, as indeed he must have had a strong suspicion they were soon to happen to him. He does not try to minimize them. He does not try to explain them away as God's will or God's judgment or God's method of testing our spiritual fiber. He simply tells the Philippians that in spite of them—even in the thick of them—they are to keep in constant touch with the One who unimaginably transcends the worst things and also unimaginably transcends the best.

"In everything," Paul says, they are to keep on praying. Come hell or high water, they are to keep on asking, keep on thanking, above all keep on making themselves known. He does not promise them that as a result they will be delivered from the worst things any more than Jesus himself was delivered from them. What he promises them instead is that "the peace of God, which passes all understanding, will keep your hearts and your minds in Christ Jesus."

The worst things will surely happen no matter what—that is to be understood—but beyond all our power to understand, he writes, we will have peace both in heart and in mind. We are as sure to be in trouble as the sparks fly upward, but we will also be "in Christ," as he puts it. Ultimately not even sorrow, loss, or death can get at us there.

That is the sense in which he dares say without risk of occasioning ironic laughter, "Have no anxiety about anything." Or, as he puts it a few lines earlier, "Rejoice in the Lord always. Again I will say, Rejoice!" (Philippians 4:4–7).

APOLOGISTS

C. S. LEWIS once said something to the effect that no Christian doctrine ever looked so threadbare to him as when he had just finished successfully defending it. The reason is not hard to find.

DAY 24

In order to defend the faith successfully—which is the business of apologists—they need to reduce it to a defendable size. It is easier to hold a fortress against the enemy than to hold a landscape. They try to make each doctrine as it comes along sound as logical and plausible as they can. The trouble, of course, is that by and large logic and plausibility are not the heart of the matter, and therefore apologists are apt to end up proclaiming a faith that may be quite persuasive on paper, but is difficult to imagine either them or anyone else getting very excited about.

The other danger is that apologists put so much effort into what they do that they may end up not so much defending the faith because they believe it is true as believing the faith is true because they have worked so hard and long to defend it.

ART

"AN OLD SILENT POND. / Into the pond a frog jumps. / Splash! Silence again." It is perhaps the best known of all Japanese haiku. No subject could be more humdrum. No language could be more pedestrian. Basho, the poet, makes no comment on what he is describing. He implies no meaning, message, or metaphor. He simply invites our attention to no more and no less than just this: the old pond in its watery stillness, the kerplunk of the frog, the gradual return of the stillness.

DAY 25

In effect he is putting a frame around the moment, and what the frame does is enable us to see not just something about the moment, but the moment itself in all its ineffable ordinariness and particularity. The chances are that if we had been passing by when the frog jumped, we wouldn't have noticed a thing or, noticing it, wouldn't have given it a second thought. But the frame sets it off from everything else that distracts us. That is the nature and purpose of frames. The frame does not change the moment, but it changes our way of perceiving the moment. It makes us *notice* the moment, and that is what Basho wants above all else. It is what literature in general wants above all else too.

From the simplest lyric to the most complex novel and densest drama, literature is asking us to pay attention. Pay attention to the frog. Pay attention to the west wind. Pay attention to the boy on the raft, the lady in the tower, the old man on the train. In sum, pay attention to the world and all that dwells therein and thereby learn at last to pay attention to yourself and all that dwells therein.

The painter does the same thing, of course. Rembrandt puts a frame around an old woman's face. It is seamed with wrinkles. The upper lip is sunken in, the skin waxy and pale. It is not a remarkable face. You would not look twice at the old woman if you found her sitting across the aisle from you on a bus. But it is a face so remarkably *seen* that it forces you to see it remarkably, just as Cézanne makes you see a bowl of apples or Andrew Wyeth a muslin curtain blowing in at an open window. It is a face unlike any other face in all the world. All the faces in the world are in this one old face.

Unlike painters, who work with space, musicians work with time, with note following note as second follows second. Listen! say Vivaldi, Brahms, Stravinsky. Listen to this time that I have framed between the first note and the last and to these sounds in time. Listen to the way the silence is broken into uneven lengths between the sounds and to the silences themselves. Listen to the scrape of bow against gut, the rap of stick against drumhead, the rush of breath through reed and wood. The sounds of the earth are like music, the old song goes, and the sounds of music are also like the sounds of the earth, which is of course where music comes from. Listen to the voices outside the window, the rumble of the furnace, the creak of your chair, the water running in the kitchen sink. Learn to listen to the music of your own lengths of time, your own silences.

Literature, painting, music—the most basic lesson that all art teaches us is to stop, look, and listen to life on this planet, including our own lives, as a vastly richer, deeper, more mysterious business than most of the time it ever occurs to us to suspect as we bumble along from day to day on automatic pilot. In a world that for the most part steers clear of the whole idea of holiness, art is one of the few places left where we can speak to each other of holy things.

Is it too much to say that to stop, look, and listen is also the most basic lesson that the Judeo-Christian tradition teaches us? Listen to history, is the cry of the ancient prophets of Israel. Listen to social injustice, says Amos; to head-in-the-sand religiosity, says Jeremiah; to international treacheries and power plays, says Isaiah; because it is precisely through them that God speaks his word of judgment and command.

And when Jesus comes along saying that the greatest command of all is to love God and to love our neighbor, he too is asking us to pay attention. If we are to love God, we must first stop, look, and listen for him in what is happening around us and inside us. If we are to love our neighbors, before doing anything else we must *see* our neighbors. With our imagination as well as our eyes, that is to say like artists, we must see not just their faces, but the life behind and within their faces. Here it is love that is the frame we see them in.

In a letter to a friend Emily Dickinson wrote that "Consider the lilies of the field" was the only commandment she never broke. She could have done a lot worse. Consider the lilies. It is the sine qua non of art and religion both.

See also music.

ATHEIST

DAY 26

A TRUE ATHEIST is one who is willing to face the full consequences of what it means to say there is no God.

To say there is no God means among other things that there are no absolute standards. For instance, if you are an atheist who believes with all your heart that murder is wrong and you run into somebody else who believes with all her heart that murder isn't wrong as long as she can get away with it, there is no absolute standard by which it can be shown that one view is better than the other, just as there is no absolute standard by which it can be shown that vanilla is better than chocolate.

If you are an atheist who says that murder is wrong because it works against the good of society in general, then you are saying that the good of society in general is gooder than the good of the murderer in particular, and, having thrown out all absolute standards, you can't say that. All you can say is that vanilla is better than chocolate because you like it better and so do most of your friends.

If you say, "In the absence of absolute standards, I declare that murder is wrong in the name of *common sense*," then you have simply made common sense your absolute standard. What is in accord with common sense is right and what isn't is wrong.

What is American is right and what is un-American is wrong. What is ethical is right and what is unethical is wrong. What works

is right and what doesn't work is wrong. These all bring God back
under different names: nationalism, ethics, pragmatism. To be a
true atheist is to acknowledge no rule except the rule of thumb.

Thus many an atheist is a believer without knowing it, just as
many a believer is an atheist without knowing it. You can sincerely
believe there is no God and live as though there is. You can sincerely believe there is a God and live as though there isn't. So it goes.

Lots of the time atheism isn't bad fun. I do what seems right to
me and you do what seems right to you, and if we come into conflict with each other, society has human judges to invoke human
laws and arbitrate between us. Who needs a Divine Judge and a
Cosmic Law? We can learn to live in lower case.

Except sometimes. Sometimes it's almost as hard to believe God
doesn't exist as to believe he does. I don't mean a baby's smile,
which is probably gas. I don't mean the beauty of nature, which is
always soon followed by the indifferent cruelty and ugliness of nature. I mean an atheist is about as likely as anybody else to walk
into a newsstand someday and pick up a copy of the *National
Enquirer* or some such paper. On the front page is a picture of a
dead child. The bare back is covered with welts. The eyes are
swollen shut. Both arms are broken. The full story is on page three
if you have the stomach for it.

To be consistent with the atheistic creed, the atheist can say no
more than that to beat a child to death is wrong with a small *w*.
Wrong because it is cruel, ugly, inhuman, pointless, illegal, and
makes the gorge rise. But what is apt to rise along with the gorge is
the suspicion that it is wrong also with a capital *W*—the suspicion
that the law that has been broken here is not just a human law, but
a law as immutable as the law of gravity, one by which even if there
were no children in the universe and no grown-ups to beat them, it
would be written into the very fabric of reality itself that such an
act is wrong.

The atheist holds the tabloid in hand and asks the question, "Why should such things happen?" Atheism can reply only, "Why *shouldn't* such things happen?" But the atheist keeps on asking.

What makes it hard to be an atheist is the feeling you sometimes get in the pit of your stomach that there must be after all, mad as it seems, an absolute good in terms of which such an act as this can be denounced as absolutely evil. Thus the problem of good is a major stumbling block for atheism, just as the problem of evil is a major stumbling block for religious faith. Both must learn how to live with their doubts.

A true atheist takes human freedom very seriously. With no God to point the way, humans must find their own way. With no God to save the world, humans must save their own world if it's going to be saved. They must save it from themselves, if nothing else. A true atheist does not dance on the grave of God.

The laughter of faith in God is like Abraham's laughter when God says his ninety-year-old wife is in a family way. The laughter of faith in no-God is heard in Sartre's story "The Wall": A man is threatened with death if he doesn't betray the whereabouts of his friend to the enemy. The man refuses to do this and sends the enemy on a wild goose chase to a place where he knows his friend isn't. By chance it turns out to be the very place where his friend is. The friend is captured and executed and the man given his freedom. Sartre ends the story by saying that the man laughed till he cried.

See also evil, faith, idolatry.

AVARICE

DAY 27   AVARICE, GREED, CONCUPISCENCE, and so forth are all based on the mathematical truism that the more you get, the more you have. The remark of Jesus that it is more blessed to give than to receive (Acts 20:35) is based on the human truth that the more you give away in love, the more you are. It is not just for the sake of other people that Jesus tells us to give rather than get, but for our own sakes too.

AWE

I REMEMBER SEEING a forest of giant redwoods for the first time. There were some small children nearby, giggling and chattering and pushing each other around. Nobody had to tell them to quiet down as we entered. They quieted down all by themselves. Everybody did. You couldn't hear a sound of any kind. It was like coming into a vast, empty room.

DAY 28

Two or three hundred feet high the redwoods stood. You had to crane your neck back as far as it would go to see the leaves at the top. The trees made their own twilight out of the bright California day. There was a stillness and stateliness about them that seemed to become part of you as you stood there stunned by the sight of them. They had been growing in that place for going on two thousand years. With infinite care they were growing even now. You could feel them doing it. They made you realize that all your life you had been mistaken. Oaks and ashes, maples and chestnuts and elms you had seen for as long as you could remember, but never until this moment had you so much as dreamed what a Tree really was.

"Behold the man," Pilate said when he led Jesus out where everybody could see him. He can't have been much to look at after what they'd done to him by then, but my guess is that, even so, there suddenly fell over that mob a silence as awed as ours in the forest when for the first time in their lives they found themselves looking at a Human Being.

B

BALAAM

DAY 29 THE LEGEND OF SOLOMON'S RING, the adventures of Dr. Doolittle, the attempt to decipher the dots and dashes of dolphins, and the attempt to teach chimpanzees to type out their thoughts on computers all reflect our ancient dream of being able to talk with the animals. As fascinating as a message from outer space would be a message from the inner space of a great blue heron or a common house cat sunning herself on the kitchen linoleum. Their mute gaze suggests a vision of reality beyond our imagining. What do they see in their ignorance that we in our wisdom are mostly blind to?

In the book of Numbers, Balaam's ass sees an angel of the Lord barring the way with a drawn sword in his hand and thereupon lies down in the middle of the road with Balaam still on his back. When Balaam clobbers him over the head with a stick, the ass speaks out reproachfully in fluent Hebrew, and then Balaam sees the angel too.

This is perhaps a clue to the mystery. Whereas people as a rule see only what they expect to see and little more, animals, innocent of expectation, see what is there. The next time the old mare looks up from her browsing and lets fly with an exultant whinny at the empty horizon, we might do well to consider at least the possibility that the horizon may not be quite as empty as we think.

Numbers 22:22–31

BAPTISM

BAPTISM CONSISTS OF GETTING DUNKED or sprinkled. Which technique is used matters about as much as whether you pray kneeling or standing on your head. Dunking is a better symbol, however. Going under symbolizes the end of everything about your life that is less than human. Coming up again symbolizes the beginning in you of something strange and new and hopeful. You can breathe again.

Question: How about infant baptism? Shouldn't you wait until the child grows up enough to know what's going on?

Answer: If you don't think there is as much of the less-than-human in an infant as there is in anybody else, you have lost touch with reality.

When it comes to the forgiving and transforming love of God, one wonders if the six-week-old screecher knows all that much less than the archbishop of Canterbury about what's going on.

DAY 30

BARABBAS

PILATE TOLD THE PEOPLE that they could choose to spare the life of either a murderer named Barabbas or Jesus of Nazareth, and they chose Barabbas. Given the same choice, Jesus, of course, would have chosen to spare Barabbas too.

DAY 31

To understand the reason in each case would be to understand much of what the New Testament means by saying that Jesus is the Savior, and much of what it means too by saying that, by and large, people are in bad need of being saved.   *Mark 15:6–15*

BATHSHEBA

DAY 32

EVEN WHEN KING DAVID lay on his deathbed and she was there with the rest of them to nag him about the succession, he still remembered the first time he had ever seen her. The latest round of warfare with the Syrians had just ended, and his victory had left him feeling let down. He drank too much at lunch and went upstairs for a long nap afterward. It was almost twilight when he awoke. The palace was unusually quiet, and he felt unusually solemn and quiet inside his own skin. There were no servants around for some reason, nobody to remind him that he was anointed king, victorious general, all that. He bathed, made himself a drink, and with just a towel wrapped around his waist, walked out onto the terrace on the roof where he looked down over the parapet in a kind of trance.

If the whole Syrian army had been drawn up in battle dress, he would have simply noted their presence and passed on. There was a bay gelding tethered to a tree, sweeping the flies away with his tail. In the servants' court, a cistern had overflowed onto the cobbles leaving a puddle the shape of Asia. Beyond a wall, a naked girl stood in a shallow pool dipping water over her shoulders with a shell. In as detached a way as he saw the girl, he saw both that he had to have her at any cost and that the cost would be exorbitant. Her husband's murder, the death of their first child—like actors awaiting their cues, the fatal consequences lurked just out of sight in the wings.

A long time afterward, when the chill was in his bones and, rattling with beads, Bathsheba came to pester him about Solomon, he could hardly see her the way she looked there at his bedside, but saw her instead glimmering in the dusk like a peeled pear as he'd first gazed down at her from the roof with his glass in his hand all those years earlier. Raising it first to eye level, he had drained it off in a single swallow like a toast, but it was only on his deathbed that he caught a glimpse of why.

It wasn't just Bathsheba he'd been toasting or the prospect of their life together, but a much more distant prospect still. He had been drinking, he realized, to the child of their child of their child a thousand years thence, who he could only pray would find it in his heart to think kindly someday of the beautiful girl and the improvident king who had so recklessly and long ago been responsible for his birth in a stable and his death just outside the city walls.

2 Samuel 11–12

See also Uriah the Hittite.

BEATITUDES

IF WE DIDN'T ALREADY KNOW but were asked to guess the kind of people Jesus would pick out for special commendation, we might be tempted to guess one sort or another of spiritual hero— men and women of impeccable credentials morally, spiritually, humanly, and every which way. If so, we would be wrong. Maybe those aren't the ones he picked out because he felt they didn't need

DAY 33

the shot in the arm his commendation would give them. Maybe they're not the ones he picked out because he didn't happen to know any. Be that as it may, it's worth noting the ones he did pick out.

Not the spiritual giants, but the "poor in spirit," as he called them, the ones who, spiritually speaking, have absolutely nothing to give and absolutely everything to receive, like the Prodigal telling his father "I am not worthy to be called thy son," only to discover for the first time all he had in having a father.

Not the champions of faith who can rejoice even in the midst of suffering, but the ones who mourn over their own suffering because they know that for the most part they've brought it down on themselves, and over the suffering of others because that's just the way it makes them feel to be in the same room with them.

Not the strong ones, but the meek ones in the sense of the gentle ones, that is, the ones not like Caspar Milquetoast but like Charlie Chaplin, the little tramp who lets the world walk over him and yet, dapper and undaunted to the end, somehow makes the world more human in the process.

Not the ones who are righteous, but the ones who hope they will be someday and in the meantime are well aware that the distance they still have to go is even greater than the distance they've already come.

Not the winners of great victories over evil in the world, but the ones who, seeing it also in themselves every time they comb their hair in front of the bathroom mirror, are merciful when they find it in others and maybe that way win the greater victory.

Not the totally pure, but the "pure in heart," to use Jesus' phrase, the ones who may be as shopworn and clay-footed as the next one, but have somehow kept some inner freshness and innocence intact.

Not the ones who have necessarily found peace in its fullness, but the ones who, just for that reason, try to bring it about wherever and however they can—peace with their neighbors and God, peace with themselves.

Jesus saved for last the ones who side with heaven even when any fool can see it's the losing side and all you get for your pains is pain. Looking into the faces of his listeners, he speaks to them directly for the first time. "Blessed are you," he says.

You can see them looking back at him. They're not what you'd call a high-class crowd—peasants and fisherfolk for the most part, on the shabby side, not all that bright. It doesn't look as if there's a hero among them. They have their jaws set. Their brows are furrowed with concentration.

They are blessed when they are worked over and cursed out on his account he tells them. It is not his hard times to come but theirs he is concerned with, speaking out of his own meekness and mercy, the purity of his own heart.   *Matthew 5:1–12*

BEAUTY

B EAUTY IS TO THE SPIRIT what food is to the flesh. A glimpse   DAY 34
of it in a young face, say, or an echo of it in a song fills an emptiness in you that nothing else under the sun can. Unlike food, however, it is something you never get your fill of. It leaves you always aching with longing not so much for more of the same as for whatever it is, deep within and far beyond both it and yourself, that makes it beautiful.

"The beauty of holiness" is how the Psalms name it (29:2), and "As the hart panteth after the water brooks, so panteth my soul after thee" (42:1) is the way they describe the ache and the longing.

BELIEVING

DAY 35

PREPOSITIONS CAN BE VERY ELOQUENT. A man is "in" architecture or a woman is "in" teaching, we say, meaning that is what they do weekdays and how they make enough money to enjoy themselves the rest of the time. But if we say they are "into" these things, that is another story. "Into" means something more like total immersion. They live and breathe what they do. They take it home with them nights. They can't get enough of it. To be "into" books means that just the sight of a signed first edition of *Alice's Adventures in Wonderland* sets your heart pounding. To be "in" books means selling them at B. Dalton's.

Along similar lines, New Testament Greek speaks of believing "into" rather than believing "in." In English we can perhaps convey the distinction best by using either "in" or no preposition at all.

Believing in God is an intellectual position. It need have no more effect on your life than believing in Freud's method of interpreting dreams or the theory that Sir Francis Bacon wrote *Romeo and Juliet*.

Believing God is something else again. It is less a position than a journey, less a realization than a relationship. It doesn't leave you cold like believing the world is round. It stirs your blood like believing the world is a miracle. It affects who you are and what you do with your life like believing your house is on fire or somebody loves you.

We believe in God when for one reason or another we choose to do so. We believe God when somehow we run into God in a way that by and large leaves us no choice to do otherwise.

When Jesus says that whoever believes "into" him shall never die, he does not mean that to be willing to sign your name to the

Nicene Creed guarantees eternal life. Eternal life is not the result of *believing in*. It is the experience of *believing*.

BELSHAZZAR

T HERE WERE BLOCKS OF ICE carved into peacocks, gods, galleons in full sail. There were mounds of peeled shrimp and caviar, whole lambs roasted with their forepaws crossed like crusaders, suckling pigs cradled in lilies-of-the-valley and watercress. There were doves of whipped cream and meringue, a huge silver cake in the shape of a six-pointed star. Dwarfs and Nubians waited on a thousand guests. The sound of cymbals shivered across the teak floor, where a sixteen-year-old virgin disported herself with a Barbary ape, while the flames from basins of scented oil threw their shadows on the whitewashed walls of Belshazzar's palace.

DAY 36

It was all for the Persian ambassadors, who sat there with their absurd bonnets and their beards stiff with pomade. Belshazzar tried to read some clue to their secret thoughts in their little wedge-shaped smiles, but the smiles were as hard to decipher as their cuneiform inscriptions. He hadn't had a decent sleep for a week. His head was splitting. One of the eunuchs was nickering behind him like a mare in heat.

When the handwriting started to appear on the flame-lit wall, most people thought it was more of the floor show, and when Belshazzar offered an extravagant reward to anyone who could translate it properly, several senior ministers proposed various comic obscenities before they saw the king was serious as death. So finally he had them summon Daniel, his late father's pet Jew and an expert on evil omens.

Daniel pointed out that, among other things, the tables were laden with sacred vessels that had been looted from the Temple in Jerusalem. Some of them were clogged with cigarette butts. A big golden one inscribed with a name too holy to be spoken had been used by a concubine who had made herself sick on too much shrimp. A magenta-wigged creature of indeterminate sex was wearing another as a hat.

Like worshiping gods made of wood and stone, Daniel said, all this was another example of Belshazzar's fatal habit of getting the sacred and the profane hopelessly confused. Pointing to the ice-carved idols whose faces had already started running down their shirtfronts, Daniel said that what the handwriting on the wall meant in a nutshell was: the party is over.

Sure enough, that very night, not long after the last guest had staggered home, Belshazzar was stabbed to death in sight of the Persian ambassadors with their wedge-shaped smiles, and just as the dwarfs were leading the exhausted ape home, Darius the Great, King of Persia, took Belshazzar's Babylon the way Grant took Richmond.

Daniel 5

See also Daniel.

BIBLE

DAY 37   THERE ARE PEOPLE WHO SAY we should read the Bible as literature. The advice has a pleasantly modern and reasonable ring to it. We are all attracted. Read the Bible for the story it tells. Read the King James Version especially for the power of its prose and the splendor of its poetry. Read it for the history it contains and for its insights into ancient ways. Don't worry about whatever it's supposed to mean to religious faith. Don't bother about the hocus-pocus. Read it like any other book.

The trouble is it's not like any other book. To read the Bible as literature is like reading *Moby Dick* as a whaling manual or *The Brothers Karamazov* for its punctuation.

Like *The Divine Comedy, Don Quixote, Paradise Lost,* or Proust, the Bible hangs heavy on many a conscience. One ought to have read it—if not for religious reasons, then simply because it has left so deep a mark on Western civilization. One usually hasn't. Some parts of Genesis maybe, a handful of Psalms, a sampling or two from the Gospels. And that's about it.

There are good reasons for not reading it. Its format is almost supernaturally forbidding: the binding rusty black like an old tuxedo, the double columns of a timetable, the print of a phone book, cluttered margins, and a text so overloaded with guides to pronunciation ("Je'-sus came from Naz'-a-reth of Gal'-i-lee and was baptized of John in Jôr'-dan") and so befouled with inexplicable italics ("Nô'-ah only remained *alive,* and they that *were* with him in the ark") that reading it is like listening to somebody with a bad stutter. More often than not the poetry is printed as prose, and poetry and prose alike are chopped up into entirely arbitrary chapters and verses, so that one of the major poems in the Old Testament, for instance, begins toward the end of Isaiah 52 with (in some versions) nothing to suggest that Isaiah 53 is a continuation of it or that it is a poem at all.

There are other reasons for not reading the Bible. It not only looks awfully dull, but some of it is. The prophets are wildly repetitious and almost never know when to stop. There are all the *begats.* There are passages that even Moses must have nodded over, like the six long chapters in Exodus (25–30) that describe the tabernacle and its workings all the way from the length, breadth, and composition of the curtains down to the color and cut of the priest's ephod and a recipe for anointing oil. There are the lists of kings, dietary laws, tribes, and tribal territories. There is the book of Leviticus and most of the book of Numbers. There are places where the parallelism of Hebrew poetry ("Pour out thy indignation upon them / and let thy burning anger overtake them. / May their camp be a desolation, / let no one dwell in their tents") becomes irresistibly soporific. There is the sense you have that you know what the Bible is going to say before it says it. There are all those familiar quotations. There is the phrase "the Good Book." Give me a bad book any day.

There are still more reasons. The barbarities, for instance. The often fanatical nationalism. The passages where the God of Israel is depicted as interested in other nations only to the degree that he can use them to whip Israel into line. God hardening Pharaoh's heart and then clobbering him for hard-heartedness. The self-righteousness and self-pity of many of the Psalms, plus their frequent vindictiveness. The way the sublime and the unspeakable are always jostling each other. Psalm 137, for example, which starts out "By the waters of Babylon, there we sat down and wept" and ends "Happy shall he be who takes your little ones and dashes them against the rock!" Or Noah, the one man left worth saving, God's blue-eyed old sailorman, getting drunk in port and passing out in a tent where his son Ham beholds his shame. Or the book of Deuteronomy, where there are laws thousands of years ahead of their time, like the one that says a newly married man is exempt from military service for a year so "he can be happy with the wife whom he has taken," side by side with laws that would make Genghis Khan blush, like the one that says Israel is to destroy conquered peoples utterly, making no covenants with them and showing no mercy. Or even Jesus of Nazareth, the same Jesus who in one place uses a Samaritan of all people—a member of a hated tribe—as the example of a man who truly loves his neighbor, and in another place is quoted as telling a Canaanite woman who came to him for help that it was not fair for him to throw the children's food to the dogs.

In short, one way to describe the Bible, written by many different people over a period of three thousand years and more, would be to say that it is a disorderly collection of sixty-odd books, which are often tedious, barbaric, obscure, and teem with contradictions and inconsistencies. It is a swarming compost of a book, an Irish stew of poetry and propaganda, law and legalism, myth and murk, history and hysteria. Over the centuries it has become hopelessly associated with tub-thumping evangelism and dreary piety, with superannuated superstition and blue-nosed moralizing, with ecclesiastical authoritarianism and crippling literalism. Let them who try to start out at Genesis and work their way conscientiously to Revelation beware.

And yet—

And yet just because it is a book about both the sublime and the unspeakable, it is a book also about life the way it really is. It is a book about people who at one and the same time can be both believing and unbelieving, innocent and guilty, crusaders and crooks, full of hope and full of despair. In other words, it is a book about us.

And it is also a book about God. If it is not about the God we believe in, then it is about the God we do not believe in. One way or another, the story we find in the Bible is our own story.

But we find something else in it too. The great Protestant theologian Karl Barth says that reading the Bible is like looking out of the window and seeing everybody on the street shading their eyes with their hands and gazing up into the sky toward something hidden from us by the roof. They are pointing up. They are speaking strange words. They are very excited. Something is happening that we can't see happening. Or something is about to happen. Something beyond our comprehension has caught them up and is seeking to lead them on "from land to land for strange, intense, uncertain, and yet mysteriously well-planned service."*

To read the Bible is to try to read the expression on their faces. To listen to the words of the Bible is to try to catch the sound of the queer, dangerous, and compelling word they seem to hear.

Abraham and Sarah with tears of incredulous laughter running down their ancient cheeks when God tells them that he is going to keep his promise and give them the son they have always wanted. King David, all but naked as the day he was born, dancing for joy in front of the ark. Paul struck dumb on the road to Damascus. Jesus of Nazareth stretched out between two crooks, with dried Roman spit on his face. They are all of them looking up. And listening.

How do twenty-first-century men and women, with all their hang-ups, try to see what they were looking at and hear what it was they heard? What follows are some practical suggestions on how to read the Bible without tears. Or maybe with them.

1. Don't start at the beginning and try to plow your way straight through to the end. At least not without help. If you do, you're almost sure to bog down somewhere around the twenty-fifth chapter of Exodus. Concentrate on the high points at first. There is much to reward you in the valleys too, but at the outset keep to the upper elevations. There are quite a few.

   There is the vivid eyewitness account of the reign of

*Karl Barth, *The Word of God and the Word of Men* (New York: Harper Torchbooks, 1957), 63.

King David, for instance (2 Samuel through 1 Kings 1–2), especially the remarkable chapters that deal with his last years, when the crimes and blunders of his youth have begun to catch up with him. Or the Joseph stories (Genesis 39–50). Or the book of Job. Or the Sermon on the Mount (Matthew 5–7). Or the seventh chapter of Paul's Letter to the Romans, which states as lucidly as it has ever been stated the basic moral dilemma of humankind, and then leads into the eighth chapter, which contains the classic expression of Christianity's basic hope.

2. The air in such upper altitudes is apt to be clearer and brighter than elsewhere; but if you nevertheless find yourself getting lost along the way, try a good Bible commentary that gives the date and historical background of each book, explains the special circumstances it was written to meet, and verse by verse tries to illumine the meaning of the difficult sections. Even when the meaning seems perfectly clear, a commentary can greatly enrich your understanding. The book of Jonah, for instance—only two or three pages long and the one genuine comedy in the Old Testament—takes on added significance when you discover its importance in advancing the idea that God's love is extended not just to the children of Israel, but to all humankind.

3. If you have even as much as a nodding acquaintance with a foreign language, try reading the Bible in that. Then you stand a chance of hearing what the Bible is actually saying instead of what you assume it must be saying because it is the Bible. Some of it you may hear in such a new way that it is as if you had never heard it before. "Blessed are the meek" is the way the English version goes, whereas in French it

comes out, "*Heureux sont les débonnaires*" ("Happy are the debonair"). The *debonair* of all things! Doors fly open. Bells ring out.

4. If you don't know a foreign language, try some English version you've never tried before—the more far-out the better. Nothing could be further out than the Bible itself. The trouble with the King James, or Authorized Version, is that it is too full of familiar quotations. The trouble with familiar quotations is that they are so familiar you don't hear them. When Jesus was crucified, the Romans nailed over his head a sign saying "King of the Jews" so nobody would miss the joke. To get something closer to the true flavor, try translating the sign instead: "Head Jew."

5. It may sound like fortune-telling, but don't let that worry you: Let the Bible fall open in your lap and start there. If you don't find something that speaks to you, let it fall open to something else. Read it as though it were as exotic as the *I Ching* or the tarot deck. Because it is.

6. If people claim that you have to take the Bible literally, word for word, or not at all, ask them if you have to take John the Baptist literally when he calls Jesus the Lamb of God.

   If people claim that no rational person can take a book seriously that assumes the world was created in six days and humankind in an afternoon, ask them if they can take Shakespeare seriously, whose scientific knowledge would send a third-grader into peals of laughter.

7. Finally this. If you look *at* a window, you see flyspecks, dust, the crack where Junior's Frisbee hit it. If you look *through* a window, you see the world beyond.

Something like this is the difference between those who see the Bible as a holy bore and those who see it as the Word of God, which speaks out of the depths of an almost unimaginable past into the depths of ourselves.

BIRDS

WHEELING THROUGH THE SUMMER SKY, perching in the treetops, feeding their young, birds go about their business as generally unconcerned with the human race as the human race is generally unconcerned with them. But every so often they do something that catches our attention. Canada geese heading south in the shape of a *V.* A white-throated sparrow grieving over poor Sam Peabody, Peabody, Peabody. A cardinal darting through the shrubbery like a flame. For a moment or two even the dullest of us dimly realizes the world would be a poorer place without them.

DAY 38

One wonders if from time to time birds feel the same way about us. A man with an umbrella walking in the rain. A woman in a bathing suit picking peas. The patter song of a two-year-old in the sandbox. Do birds every once in a while see us as we see them, as basically irrelevant but occasionally worth the cocking of a beady eye, the flicker of a wing, the first few notes of a song?

BLESSING

THE WORD *blessing* has come to mean more often than not a pious formality such as ministers are continually being roped into giving at high-school graduations, Rotarian wienie roasts, and the like, and to say "God bless you" to a person, unless that person

DAY 39

happens to have just sneezed, is generally regarded as a pious eccentricity. It was not always so.

In the biblical sense, if you give me your blessing, you irreversibly convey into my life not just something of the beneficent power and vitality of who you are, but something also of the life-giving power of God, in whose name the blessing is given. Even after old, half-blind Isaac discovered that he had been hoodwinked into blessing the wrong twin, he could no more take the blessing back and give it to Esau than he could take the words of it out of the air and put them back into his mouth again.

Religious language has come to such a pass that perhaps "luck," of all words, suggests the reality of this better than "blessing." Everybody knows that luck has magic in it and that when you have it, you really have something. It may see you through hard times. It may win you the sweepstakes. A blessing, on the other hand, has come to seem something on the order of a Hallmark friendship card.

BOOKS

DAY 40

BOOKS ARE TO READ, but that is by no means the end of it. The way they are bound, the paper they are printed on, the smell of them (especially if they are either very new or very old), the way the words are fitted to the page, the look of them in the bookcase—sometimes lined up straight as West Point cadets, sometimes leaning against each other for support or lying flat so you have to tip your head sideways to see them properly. Bede's *Ecclesiastical History of the English Nation,* the plays of Beaumont and Fletcher, the Pléiade edition of Saint Simon, Chesterfield's letters, the Qur'an. Even though you suspect you will probably never get around to them, it is an honor just to have them on your shelves.

Something of what they contains gets into the air you breathe. They are like money in the bank, which is a comfort even though you never spend it. They are prepared to give you all they've got at a moment's notice, but are in no special hurry about it. In the meanwhile they are holding their tongues, even the most loquacious of them, even the most passionate.

They are giving you their eloquent and inexhaustible silence. They are giving you time to find your way to them. Maybe they are giving you time, with or without them, just to find your *way*.

BOREDOM

B OREDOM OUGHT TO BE ONE of the seven deadly sins. It de-   DAY 41
serves the honor.

You can be bored by virtually anything if you put your mind to it, or choose not to. You can yawn your way through *Don Giovanni* or a trip to the Grand Canyon or an afternoon with your dearest friend or a sunset. There are doubtless those who nodded off at the coronation of Napoleon or the trial of Joan of Arc or when Shakespeare appeared at the Globe in *Hamlet* or when Lincoln delivered himself of a few remarks at Gettysburg. The odds are that the Sermon on the Mount had more than a few of the congregation twitchy and glassy-eyed.

To be bored is to turn down cold whatever life happens to be offering you at the moment. It is to cast a jaundiced eye at life in general, including most of all your own life. You feel nothing is worth getting excited about because you are yourself not worth getting excited about.

To be bored is a way of making the least of things you often have a sneaking suspicion you need the most.

To be bored to death is a form of suicide.

BORN AGAIN

DAY 42 THE PHRASE *born again* comes, of course, from a scene in John's Gospel in which Jesus tells a Pharisee named Nicodemus that he will never see the Kingdom of God unless he is born again. Somewhat testily prodded by Nicodemus to make himself clearer, Jesus says, "That which is born of the flesh is flesh, and that which is born of the Spirit is spirit." In other words, spiritual rebirth by the power of the Holy Spirit is what Jesus is talking about.

He then goes one step further, playing on the word *pneuma*, which means both "spirit" and "wind" in Greek. "The wind blows where it will, and you hear the sound of it, but you do not know whence it comes or whither it goes; so it is with everyone who is born of the Spirit," he says (John 3:1–8). The implication seems to be that the kind of rebirth he has in mind is (a) elusive and mysterious and (b) entirely God's doing. There's no telling when it will happen or to whom.

Presumably those to whom it does happen feel themselves filled, as a sheer gift, with the love, joy, and peace that Saint Paul singles out as the principal fruits of the experience. In some measure, however fleetingly, it is to be hoped that most Christians have had at least a taste of them.

Some of those who specifically refer to themselves as "born-again Christians," however, seem to use the term in a different sense. You get the feeling that to them it means Super-Christians. They are apt to have the relentless cheerfulness of car salesmen. They tend to be a little too friendly a little too soon, and the women to wear more makeup than they need. You can't imagine any of them ever having had a weak moment or a lascivious thought or used a nasty word when they bumped their head getting out of the car. They speak a great deal about "the Lord" as if they have him in their hip pocket and seem to feel that it's no harder to figure out what he wants them to do in any given situation than to look up in *Fanny Farmer* how to make brownies. The whole shadow side of human existence—the suffering, the doubt, the frustration, the ambiguity—appears as absent from their view of things as litter from the streets of Disneyland. To hear them speak of God, he seems about as elusive and mysterious as a Billy Graham rally at Madison Square Garden, and on their lips the born-again experience often sounds like something we can all make happen anytime we want to, like fudge, if only we follow their recipe.

It is not for anybody to judge the authenticity of the born-again's spiritual rebirth or anybody else's, but my guess is that by the style and substance of their witnessing to it, the souls they turn on to Christ are apt to be fewer in number than the ones they turn off.

See also Nicodemus.

BREAD

WE DON'T LIVE BY BREAD ALONE, but we also don't live long without it. To eat is to acknowledge our dependence—both on food and on each other. It also reminds us of other kinds of emptiness that not even the blue-plate special can touch.

DAY 43

See also gluttony.

BROTHERS

CAIN MURDERED ABEL. Jacob cheated Esau. Joseph's brothers sold him for twenty shekels and would probably have paid twice that to get him out of their hair. The Prodigal's elder brother

DAY 44

couldn't stand being in the same room with him even with a fatted calf for inducement. As the Bible presents it, one of the closest of all relationships is also one of the saddest.

Envy and fear are apparently near to the heart of it—one brother is afraid the other is loved more, favored more, given and forgiven more, gets away with more—but that doesn't seem enough of an explanation somehow. You have a sense of signals crossed, of opportunities missed, of messages unheard or unheeded, in short of love gone wrong. You can't help thinking what friends they might have been if they hadn't been enemies. Cain giving Abel a hand with the spring lambing. Jacob letting Esau have his pottage just for the hell of it.

We all have the same dark secrets and the same bright hopes. We come from the same place and are headed in the same direction. Above everything else maybe, we all want to be known by each other and to know each other. Iraq and the United States, the Arabs and the Israelis, the terrorists and the terrorized—we are all of us brothers, all of us sisters.

Yet from the way we manage things most of the time, who in a million years would ever guess it? Who can remain unmoved by the thought of how the world might be if we only managed things right?

BUECHNER

DAY 45

BUECHNER IS MY NAME. It is pronounced Beekner. If somebody mispronounces it in some foolish way, I have the feeling that what's foolish is me. If somebody forgets it, I feel that it's I who am forgotten. There's something about it that embarrasses me in just the same way that there's something about me that embarrasses me. I can't imagine myself with any other name—Held, say, or

Merrill, or Hlavacek. If my name were different, I would be different. When I tell you my name, I have given you a hold over me that you didn't have before. If you call it out, I stop, look, and listen whether I want to or not.

In the book of Exodus, God tells Moses that his name is Yahweh, and God hasn't had a peaceful moment since.

C

CAESAR AUGUSTUS

DAY 46

CAESAR WAS ONLY ONE of the titles Augustus bore. Others were *rex, imperator, princeps, pontifex maximus,* and so on. He ruled Rome and thus virtually the whole civilized world. He was worshiped as a god. People burned incense to him. Insofar as he is remembered at all, most people remember him mainly because at some point during his reign, in a rundown section of one of the more obscure imperial provinces, out behind a cheesy motel among cowflops and moldy hay, a child was born to a pair of up-country rubes you could have sold the Brooklyn Bridge to without even trying. *Luke 2:1*

CAIAPHAS

DAY 47

THE HIGH PRIEST CAIAPHAS was essentially a mathematician. When the Jews started worrying that they might all get into hot water with the Romans because of the way Jesus was carrying on,

Caiaphas said that in that case they should dump him like a hot potato. His argument ran that it is better for one man to get it in the
neck for the sake of many than for many to get it in the neck for the
sake of one man. His grim arithmetic proved unassailable.

The arithmetic of Jesus, on the other hand, was atrocious. He
said that heaven gets a bigger kick out of one sinner who repents
than out of ninety-nine saints who don't need to. He said that God
pays as much for one hour's work as for one day's. He said that the
more you give away, the more you have.

It is curious that in the matter of deciding his own fate, he
reached the same conclusion as Caiaphas and took it in the neck
for the sake of many, Caiaphas included. It was not, however, the
laws of mathematics that he was following.   *John 11:47–50*

CAIN

A BEL WAS LIKE HIS SHEEP—the same flat, complacent gaze,   DAY 48
the thick curls low on the forehead, a voice like the creak of
new shoes when he prayed. The prayers were invariably answered.
His flocks fattened, and the wool fetched top price. His warts disappeared overnight. His advice to his brother, Cain, was invariably ex-
cellent. Cain took it about as long as he could and then let him have
it with his pitchfork one afternoon while they were out tedding hay.

When God asked Cain where Abel was, Cain said, "I don't
know," which didn't fool God for a minute, and "Am I my brother's
keeper?" which didn't even rate an answer (Genesis 4:9). Even so,
God let the crime be its own punishment instead of trying to think
up anything worse: with no stomach for haying that field anymore,
Cain took up traveling instead, but lived in continual fear that he'd
be spotted as a fratricide and lynched.

When he complained to God about this, God gave him some kind of severe facial twitch that marked him as the sort of man you don't kick because he's down already and thus ensured him a long life in which to remember that last incredulous bleat, the glazing over of that flat, complacent gaze. The justice and mercy of God have seldom been so artfully combined in a single act.

Genesis 4:1–16

CHANTING

DAY 49

CHANTING IS A FORM of high-church popery that is supposed to set mainline Protestant teeth on edge. It shouldn't.

Words wear out after a while, especially religious words. We've said them so many times. We've listened to them so often. They are like voices we know so well we no longer hear them.

When a prayer or a psalm or a passage from the Gospels is chanted, we hear the words again. We hear them in a new way. We remember that they are not only meaning, but music and mystery. The chanting italicizes them. The prose becomes poetry. The prosaic becomes powerful.

Of course, chanting wears out after a while too.

CHARISMATIC

DAY 50

MOST OF THE TIME WHEN WE SAY people are charismatic, we mean simply that they have presence. Maya Angelou, Tony Blair, and Desmond Tutu all have it in varying degrees and forms. So did Benito Mussolini and Mae West. You don't have to be famous to have it either. You come across it in children and nobodies. Even if you don't see such people enter a room, you can feel them enter. They shimmer the air like a hot asphalt road. Without so much as raising a finger, they make you sit up and take notice.

On the other hand, if you took Mother Teresa, or Francis of Assisi, or Mahatma Gandhi, or Nelson Mandela, and dressed them up to look like everybody else, nobody would probably notice them any more than they would the woman who can make your day just by dropping by to borrow your steam iron, or the high-school commencement speaker who without any eloquence or special intelligence can bring tears to your eyes, or the people who can quiet a hysterical child or stop somebody's cracking headache just by touching them with their hands. These are the true charismatics, from the Greek word *charis,* meaning "grace." According to Saint Paul, out of sheer graciousness God gives certain men and women extraordinary gifts, or *charismata,* such as the ability to heal, to teach, to perform acts of mercy, to work miracles.

These people are not apt to have presence, and you don't feel any special vibrations when they enter a room. But they are all in their own ways miracle workers, and even if you don't believe in the God who made them that way, you believe in them.

CHASTITY

MARK TWAIN SPEAKS SOMEWHERE of "a good man in the worst sense of the word." A chaste person in the worst sense of the word is one whose chastity is fear and prudery masquerading as moral one-upmanship. A chaste person in the best sense of the word is somebody on the order of a priest who gives up sex in general and marriage in particular so that the church can be his better half and the whole parish his children.

DAY 51

CHILDREN

DAY 52 WHEN THE DISCIPLES, overearnest as ever, asked Jesus who was the greatest in the kingdom of heaven, Jesus pulled a child out of the crowd and said the greatest in the kingdom of heaven were people like this (Matthew 18:1–4). Two thousand years of homiletic sentimentalizing to the contrary notwithstanding, Jesus was not being sentimental. He was saying that the people who get into heaven are people who, like children, don't worry about it too much. They are people who, like children, live with their hands open more than with their fists clenched. They are people who, like children, are so relatively unburdened by preconceptions that if somebody says there's a pot of gold at the end of the rainbow, they are perfectly willing to go take a look for themselves.

Children aren't necessarily better than other people. Like the child in "The Emperor's New Clothes," they are just apt to be better at telling the difference between a phony and the real thing.

CHILDREN'S BOOKS

DAY 53 TO STEP THROUGH THE LOOKING GLASS, to pass through the wardrobe into Narnia, to attend the birthday party of Bilbo Baggins is to reenter the world of childhood more fully than is possible any other way. It is not just a matter of being reminded how strange and new and promising everything was back then, but of experiencing it all over again.

Regardless of how many times you have read the books you loved as a child, the elements of surprise and suspense are always present, so that right up to the last minute you can believe that Scrooge will go on being miserly in spite of everything and that Dorothy may never find her way home.

To us, as to the child, the happy ending always comes as an unexpected gift from on high. It is the deepest truth that children's books have to tell. Possibly it is the deepest truth there is.

CHRISTIAN

SOME THINK A CHRISTIAN is one who necessarily *believes* certain things. That Jesus was the son of God, say. Or that Mary was a virgin. Or that the pope is infallible. Or that all other religions are all wrong.

DAY 54

Some think a Christian is one who necessarily *does* certain things. Such as going to church. Getting baptized. Giving up liquor and tobacco. Reading the Bible. Doing a good deed a day.

Some think a Christian is just a nice person.

Jesus said, "I am the way, and the truth, and the life; no one comes to the Father, but by me" (John 14:6). He didn't say that any particular ethic, doctrine, or religion was the way, the truth, and the life. He said that he was. He didn't say that it was by believing or doing anything in particular that you could "come to the Father." He said that it was only by him—by living, participating in, being caught up by the way of life that he embodied, that was his way.

Thus it is possible to be on Christ's way and with his mark upon you without ever having heard of Christ, and for that reason to be on your way to God though maybe you don't even believe in God.

A Christian is one who is on the way, though not necessarily very far along it, and who has at least some dim and half-baked idea of whom to thank.

A Christian isn't necessarily any nicer than anybody else. Just better informed.

CHRISTMAS

DAY 55 THE LOVELY OLD CAROLS played and replayed till their effect is like a dentist's drill or a jackhammer, the bathetic banalities of the pulpit and the chilling commercialism of almost everything else, people spending money they can't afford on presents you neither need nor want, "Rudolph, the Red-Nosed Reindeer," the plastic tree, the cornball crèche, the Hallmark Virgin. Yet for all our efforts, we've never quite managed to ruin it. That in itself is part of the miracle, a part you can see. Most of the miracle you can't see, or don't.

The young clergyman and his wife do all the things you do on Christmas Eve. They string the lights and hang the ornaments. They supervise the hanging of the stockings. They tuck in the children. They lug the presents down out of hiding and pile them under the tree. Just as they're about to fall exhausted into bed, the husband remembers his neighbor's sheep. The man asked him to feed them for him while he was away, and in the press of other matters that night he forgot all about them. So down the hill he goes through knee-deep snow. He gets two bales of hay from the barn and carries them out to the shed. There's a forty-watt bulb hanging by its cord from the low roof, and he turns it on. The sheep huddle in a corner watching as he snaps the baling twine, shakes the squares of hay apart, and starts scattering it. Then they come bumbling and shoving to get at it with their foolish, mild faces, the puffs of their breath showing in the air. He is reaching to turn off the bulb and leave when suddenly he realizes where he is. The winter darkness.

The glimmer of light. The smell of the hay and the sound of the animals eating. Where he is, of course, is the manger.

He only just saw it. He whose business it is above everything else to have an eye for such things is all but blind in that eye. He who on his best days believes that everything that is most precious anywhere comes from that manger might easily have gone home to bed never knowing that he had himself just been in the manger. The world is the manger. It is only by grace that he happens to see this other part of the miracle.

Christmas itself is by grace. It could never have survived our own blindness and depredations otherwise. It could never have *happened* otherwise. Perhaps it is the very wildness and strangeness of the grace that has led us to try to tame it. We have tried to make it habitable. We have roofed it in and furnished it. We have reduced it to an occasion we feel at home with, at best a touching and beautiful occasion, at worst a trite and cloying one. But if the Christmas event in itself is indeed—as a matter of cold, hard fact—all it's cracked up to be, then even at best our efforts are misleading.

The Word become flesh. Ultimate Mystery born with a skull you could crush one-handed. Incarnation. It is not tame. It is not touching. It is not beautiful. It is uninhabitable terror. It is unthinkable darkness riven with unbearable light. Agonized laboring led to it, vast upheavals of intergalactic space/time split apart, a wrenching and tearing of the very sinews of reality itself. You can only cover your eyes and shudder before it, before *this:* "God of God, Light of Light, very God of very God . . . who for us and for our salvation," as the Nicene Creed puts it, "came down from heaven."

Came down. Only then do we dare uncover our eyes and see what we can see. It is the Resurrection and the Life she holds in her arms. It is the bitterness of death he takes at her breast.

CHURCH

DAY 56   THE VISIBLE CHURCH is all the people who get together from time to time in God's name. Anybody can find out who they are by going to church to look.

The invisible church is all the people God uses for his hands and feet in this world. Nobody can find out who they are except God.

Think of them as two circles. The optimist says they are concentric. The cynic says they don't even touch. The realist says they occasionally overlap.

In a fit of high inspiration, the author of the book of Revelation states that there is no temple in the New Jerusalem, thus squelching once and for all the tedious quip that since heaven is an endless church service, anybody with two wits to rub together would prefer hell.

The reason for there being no temple in the New Jerusalem is presumably the same as the reason for Noah's leaving the ark behind when he finally makes it to Mt. Ararat.

COINCIDENCE

DAY 57   I THINK OF A PERSON I haven't seen or thought of for years, and ten minutes later I see her crossing the street. I turn on the radio to hear a voice reading the biblical story of Jael, which is the story that I have spent the morning writing about. A car passes me on the road, and its license plate consists of my wife's and my initials side by side. When you tell people stories like that, their usual reaction is to laugh. One wonders why.

I believe that people laugh at coincidence as a way of relegating it to the realm of the absurd and of therefore not having to take seriously the possibility that there is a lot more going on in our lives than we either know or care to know. Who can say what it is that's going on? But I suspect that part of it, anyway, is that every once and so often we hear a whisper from the wings that goes something like this: "You've turned up in the right place at the right time. You're doing fine. Don't ever think that you've been forgotten."

COMEDY

"B LESSED ARE YOU that weep now, for you shall laugh," Jesus says (Luke 6:21). That means not just that you shall laugh when the time comes, but that you can laugh a little even now in the midst of the weeping because you know that the time is coming. All appearances to the contrary notwithstanding, the ending will be a happy ending. That is what the laughter is about. It is the laughter of faith. It is the divine comedy.

DAY 58

In the meantime you weep, because if you have a heart to see it with, the world you see is in a thousand ways heartbreaking. Only the heartless can look at it unmoved, and that is presumably why Jesus says, "Woe to you that laugh now, for you shall mourn and weep," meaning a different sort of laughter altogether—the laughter of callousness, mockery, indifference (Luke 6:25). You can laugh like that only if you turn your back on the suffering and need of the world, and perhaps for you the time for weeping comes when you see the suffering and need too late to do anything about them, like the specters of the dead that Jacob Marley shows old Scrooge as they reach out their spectral hands to try to help the starving woman and her child, but are unable to do so now because they are only shadows.

The happiness of the happy ending—what makes the comedy so rich—is the suggestion that ultimately even the callous and indifferent will take part in it. The fact that Jesus says they too will weep and mourn before they're done seems to mean that they too will grow hearts at last, the hard way, and once that happens, the sky is the limit.

COMMUNION OF SAINTS

DAY 59

A T THE ALTAR TABLE, the overweight parson is doing something or other with the bread as his assistant stands by with the wine. In the pews, the congregation sits more or less patiently waiting to get into the act. The church is quiet. Outside, a bird starts singing. It's nothing special, only a handful of notes angling out in different directions. Then a pause. Then a trill or two. A chirp. It is just warming up for the business of the day, but it is enough.

The parson and his assistant and the usual scattering of senior citizens, parents, and teenagers are not alone in whatever they think they're doing. Maybe that is what the bird is there to remind them. In its own slapdash way the bird has a part in it too. Not to mention "angels and archangels and all the company of heaven," if the prayer book is to be believed. Maybe we should believe it. Angels and archangels. Cherubim and seraphim. They are all in the act together. It must look a little like the great *jeu de son et lumière* at Versailles when all the fountains are turned on at once and the night is ablaze with fireworks. It must sound a little like the last movement of Beethoven's *Choral Symphony* or the Atlantic in a gale.

And "all the company of heaven" means everybody we ever loved and lost, including the ones we didn't know we loved until we lost them or didn't love at all. It means people we never heard of. It means everybody who ever did—or at some unimaginable time in the future ever will—come together at something like this table in search of something like what is offered at it.

Whatever other reasons we have for coming to such a place, if we come also to give each other our love and to give God our love, then together with Gabriel and Michael, and the fat parson, and Sebastian pierced with arrows, and the old lady whose teeth don't fit, and Teresa in her ecstasy, we are the communion of saints.

COMPASSION

COMPASSION IS THE SOMETIMES FATAL CAPACITY for feeling what it's like to live inside somebody else's skin. DAY 60

It is the knowledge that there can never really be any peace and joy for me until there is peace and joy finally for you too.

CONFESSION

TO CONFESS YOUR SINS TO GOD is not to tell God anything God doesn't already know. Until you confess them, however, they are the abyss between you. When you confess them, they become the Golden Gate Bridge. DAY 61

CONVERSION

THERE ARE A NUMBER OF CONVERSIONS described in the New Testament. You think of Paul seeing the light on the road to Damascus (Acts 9:1–19), or the Ethiopian eunuch getting Philip DAY 62 to baptize him on the way from Jerusalem to Gaza (Acts 8:28–40). There is also the apostle Thomas saying, "My Lord and my God!" when he is finally convinced that Jesus is alive and whole again (John 20:26–29), not to mention the Roman centurion who witnessed the crucifixion saying, "Truly this man was the Son of God" (Luke 23:47). All these scenes took place suddenly, dramatically, when they were least expected. They all involved pretty much of an about-face, which is what the word *conversion* means. We can only imagine that they all were accompanied by a good deal of emotion.

But in this same general connection there are other scenes that we should also remember. There is the young man who, when Jesus told him he should give everything he had to the poor if he really wanted to be perfect as he said he did, walked sorrowfully away because he was a very rich man. There is Nicodemus, who was sufficiently impressed with Jesus to go talk to him under cover of darkness and later to help prepare his body for burial, but who never seems to have actually joined forces with him. There is King Agrippa, who, after hearing Paul's impassioned defense of his faith, said, "Almost thou persuadest me to be a Christian" (Acts 26:28, KJV). There is even Pontius Pilate, who asked, "What is truth?" (John 18:38) under such circumstances as might lead you to suspect that just possibly, half without knowing it, he really hoped Jesus would be able to give him the answer, maybe even become for him the answer.

Like the conversions, there was a certain amount of drama about these other episodes too and perhaps even a certain amount of emotion, though for the most part unexpressed. But of course in the case of none of them was there any about-face. Presumably all these people kept on facing more or less the same way they had been right along. King Agrippa, for instance, kept on being King Agrippa just as he always had. And yet you can't help wondering if somewhere inside himself, as somewhere also inside the rest of them, the "almost" continued to live on as at least a sidelong glance down a new road, the faintest itching of the feet for a new direction.

We don't know much about what happened to any of them after their brief appearance in the pages of Scripture, let alone what happened inside them. We can only pray for them, not to mention also for ourselves, that in the absence of a sudden shattering event, there was a slow underground process that got them to the same place in the end.

COVENANT

DAY 63

OLD TESTAMENT means "Old Covenant," which means the old agreement that was arrived at between God and Israel at Mt. Sinai with Moses presiding. "I shall be your God and you shall be my people" (Leviticus 26:12) sums it up—that is, if you obey God's commandments, God will love you.

New Testament means "New Covenant," which means the new agreement that was arrived at by God alone in an upstairs room in Jerusalem with Jesus presiding. Jesus sums it up by raising his wine and saying, "This cup is the new covenant in my blood" (1 Corinthians 11:25).

Like Moses, Jesus believed that if you obey God, God will love you, but here he is saying something beyond that. He is saying if you don't obey God, that doesn't mean that God won't love you. It means simply that God's love becomes a suffering love: a love that suffers because it is not reciprocated, a love that suffers because we who are loved suffer and suffer precisely *in* our failure to reciprocate. By giving us the cup to drink, Jesus is saying that in loving us God "bleeds" for us—not "even though" we don't give a damn, but precisely *because* we don't. God keeps his part of the covenant whether we keep our part or not; it's just that one way costs him more.

This idea that God loves people whether or not they give a damn isn't new. In the Old Testament book of Hosea, for instance, the prophet portrays God as lashing out at the Israelites for their disobedience and saying that by all rights they should be wiped off the face of the earth, but then adding, "How can I hand you over, O Israel? . . . My heart recoils within me. . . . I will not execute my fierce anger . . . for I am God and not man, the Holy One in your midst, and I will not come to destroy" (Hosea 11:8–9).

What *is* new about the New Covenant, therefore, is not the idea that God loves the world enough to bleed for it, but the claim that here he is actually putting his money where his mouth is. Like a father saying about his sick child, "I'd do anything to make you well," God finally calls his own bluff and does it. Jesus Christ is what God does, and the cross where God did it is the central symbol of New Covenant faith.

So what? *Does* the suffering of the father for the sick child make the sick child well? In the last analysis, we each have to answer for ourselves.

Like the elderly Christ Church don who was heard muttering over his chop at high table, "This mutton is as hard to swallow as the Lamb of God," there are some who find the whole idea simply unswallowable—just the idea of *God*, let alone the idea of God in Christ submitting to the cross for love's sake. Yet down through the centuries there have been others—good ones and bad ones, bright ones and stupid ones—who with varying degrees of difficulty have been able to swallow it and have claimed that what they swallowed made the difference between life and death.

Such people would also tend to claim that, whereas to respond to the Old Covenant is to become righteous, to respond to the New

Covenant is to become new. The proof, they might add, is in the pudding.

See also Lord's Supper.

CREATION

To MAKE SUGGESTS MAKING SOMETHING out of something else the way a carpenter makes wooden boxes out of wood. To *create* suggests making something out of nothing the way an artist makes paintings or poems. It is true that artists, like carpenters, have to use something else—paint, words—but the beauty or meaning they make is different from the material they make it out of. To create is to make something essentially new.

When God created the creation, God made something where before there had been nothing, and as the author of the book of Job puts it, "the morning stars sang together, and all the sons of God shouted for joy" (38:7) at the sheer and shimmering novelty of the thing. "New every morning is the love / Our wakening and uprising prove" says the hymn. Using the same old materials of earth, air, fire, and water, every twenty-four hours God creates something new out of them. If you think you're seeing the same show all over again seven times a week, you're crazy. Every morning you wake up to something that in all eternity never was before and never will be again. And the you that wakes up was never the same before and will never be the same again either.

DAY 64

CROSS

TWO OF THE NOBLEST PILLARS of the ancient world—Roman law and Jewish piety—together supported the necessity of

DAY 65

putting Jesus Christ to death in a manner that even for its day was peculiarly loathsome. Thus the cross stands for the tragic folly of human beings, not just at their worst but at their best.

Jesus needn't have died. Presumably he could have followed the advice of friends like Peter and avoided the showdown. Instead, he chose to die because he believed that he had to if the world was to be saved. Thus the cross stands for the best that human beings can do as well as for the worst.

"My God, my God, why hast thou forsaken me?" (Matthew 27:46). Jesus died in the profoundest sense alone. Thus the cross stands for the inevitable dereliction and defeat of the best and the worst indiscriminately.

For those who believe that Jesus Christ rose from the dead early on a Sunday morning, and for those also who believe that he provided food for worms just as the rest of us will, the conclusion is inescapable that he came out somehow the winner. What emerged from his death was a kind of way, of truth, of life, without which the last two thousand years of human history would have been even more tragic than they were.

A six-pointed star, a crescent moon, a lotus—the symbols of other religions suggest beauty and light. The symbol of Christianity is an instrument of death. It suggests, at the very least, hope.

DANIEL

NEBUCHADNEZZAR was in such a state when Daniel arrived at about four in the morning with a raincoat thrown over his pajamas that all the customary grovelings and mumbo-jumbo were dispensed with, and he received him the way any man might receive another at that hour—any man, that is, who'd just been scared out of his wits. The guards with their leash of panthers were dismissed, the slatted ivory blinds were pulled shut, and, sitting bolt upright in the middle of his bed with the covers clutched in a knot at his throat, the king stammered out his appalling dream.

He said there was this enormous tree so heavy with leaves and fruit that it gave shade for miles around and all the beasts of the field came to take their ease in it.

"That's you," Daniel said.

He said there was this creature who came down from heaven bearing orders that the tree was to be chopped down, its branches lopped off, and all its leaves and fruit scattered.

"I guess you know where those orders came from," Daniel said.

He said the mutilated stump that was Nebuchadnezzar had its heart changed to a beast's heart, and ate grass with oxen, and its hair got all matted like feathers, and its nails grew long and yellow like an owl's.

"That's to help you get back in touch with reality," Daniel said. "You've gotten so used to being treated like a god, you've started believing you are one."

When the thing finally happened, everybody was very tactful. Nebuchadnezzar would come grazing across the lawn on all fours, and they'd look the other way. He'd lift his leg on the marble balustrade, and business would go on as usual. He'd squat out there in the hanging gardens howling into the dusk as naked as the day he was born, but from everybody's polite expressions, you would have thought it was just the court musicians tuning up for the evening cotillion.

He was still lying out there on the grass one morning when the sun started to come up, and by the time it had cleared the tops of the tallest palms, he was back on two feet again and behaving quite normally. The way he explained it was that as he'd lain there watching the golden rays fan out across the sky, he'd suddenly realized that even a great king like himself must look pretty cheap compared with a god who could put on a show like that once a day and kept putting it on whether the audience was worth it or not because that was the kind of god he was.

"Now you're starting to talk sense," Daniel said.

It wasn't long after this that Nebuchadnezzar got back to the office again, full time, with Daniel as his right-hand man. Except for a certain uneasiness in the presence of ruminants and an occasional friendly chat with his psychiatrist, it was comparatively clear sailing from there on out.

Daniel 4

See also Nebuchadnezzar, Susanna.

DARKNESS

DAY 67

THE OLD TESTAMENT begins with darkness, and the last of the Gospels ends with it.

"Darkness was upon the face of the deep," Genesis says. Darkness was where it all started. Before darkness, there had never been anything other than darkness, void and without form.

At the end of John, the disciples go out fishing on the Sea of Tiberias. It is night. They have no luck. Their nets are empty. Then they spot somebody standing on the beach. At first they don't see who it is in the darkness. It is Jesus.

The darkness of Genesis is broken by God in great majesty speaking the word of creation. "Let there be light!" That's all it took.

The darkness of John is broken by the flicker of a charcoal fire on the sand. Jesus has made it. He cooks some fish on it for his old friends' breakfast. On the horizon there are the first pale traces of the sun getting ready to rise.

All the genius and glory of God are somehow represented by these two scenes, not to mention what Saint Paul calls God's foolishness.

The original creation of light itself is almost too extraordinary to take in. The little cookout on the beach is almost too ordinary to take seriously. Yet if Scripture is to be believed, enormous stakes were involved in them both, and still are. Only a saint or a visionary can begin to understand God setting the very sun on fire in the heavens, and therefore God takes another tack. By sheltering a spark with a pair of cupped hands and blowing on it, the Light of the World gets enough of a fire going to make breakfast. It's not apt to be your interest in cosmology or even in theology that draws you to it so much as it's the empty feeling in your stomach. You don't have to understand anything very complicated. All you're asked is to take a step or two forward through the darkness and start digging in.

DAVID

DAY 68   To see what there was about David that made Israel adore him like no other king it ever had, as good a place to look as any is the account of how he captured Jerusalem and brought in the ark.

Jerusalem was a major plum for the new young king, a hill town considered so untakeable that the inhabitants had a saying to the effect that a blind man and a cripple could hold it against the U.S. Marines (2 Samuel 5:6). Just to remind people who it was that had nevertheless finally taken it, David's first move was to change its name to the City of David. His second move was a brilliant maneuver for giving his victory the stamp of divine approval by trotting out that holy box of acacia wood overlaid with gold that was known as the ark and contained who knows what but was as close as Israel ever officially got to a representation in space of their God, who dwelled in eternity. David had the ark loaded onto a custom-built cart and made a regular circus parade of it, complete with horns, harps, cymbals, and psalteries, not to mention himself high-stepping out front like the mayor of Dublin on Saint Patrick's Day. When they finally made it into town, he set up a big tent to keep out the weather, had refreshments passed around on the house, and, just so nobody would forget who was picking up the tab, did the lion's share of the praying himself and personally took up the collection afterward.

So far it was none of it anything a good public-relations department couldn't have dreamed up for him, but the next thing was something else again. He stripped down to his skivvies, and then with everybody looking on, including his wife—a high-class girl named Michal, who gave his administration tone as the late King Saul's daughter—he did a dance. Maybe it started out as just another Madison Avenue ploy, but not for long.

With trumpets blaring and drums beating, it was Camelot all over again, and for once that royal young redhead didn't have to talk up the bright future and the high hopes, because he was himself the future at its brightest and there were no hopes higher than the ones his people had in him. And for once he didn't have to drag God in for politics' sake either, because it was obvious to everybody that this time God was there on his own. How they cut loose together, David and Yahweh, whirling around before the ark in such a passion that they caught fire from each other and blazed up in a single flame of such magnificence that not even the dressing-down David got from Michal afterward could dim the glory of it.

He had feet of clay like the rest of us, if not more so—he was self-serving and deceitful, lustful and vain—but on the basis of that dance alone, you can see why it was David more than anybody else that Israel lost its heart to and why, when Jesus of Nazareth came riding into Jerusalem on his flea-bitten mule a thousand years later, it was as the Son of David that they hailed him.

2 Samuel 5–6

See also Abishag, Absalom, Bathsheba, Goliath, Jonathan, Mephibosheth, Nathan, Ruth, Saul.

DEBORAH

DEBORAH WAS ISRAEL'S ONLY WOMAN JUDGE. She looked like Golda Meir and did business under a palm tree. Her

DAY 69

business consisted of more than just stepping in and settling things when people got in a wrangle. Like all the other judges of Israel, she was loaded with charisma, and whenever there was any fighting to be done, she was the one who was in charge. Even generals jumped when she snapped her fingers. Barak, for instance.

She summoned him to the palm tree and told him she wanted him to take ten thousand of his best men and beat the stuffing out of the Canaanite forces under a general named Sisera. Barak said he'd do it but indicated he'd feel more secure if Deborah came along. She said she would. She also said it was only fair to warn him, however, that the main glory of the day was going to be not his but a woman's because a woman was going to be the one to wipe out Sisera. In addition to her other hats, Deborah was also something of a prophet and had pronounced feminist sympathies.

Her prediction turned out to be correct, of course. Barak won the battle, but Sisera was disposed of by a lady named Jael in a rather spectacular way, which can be read about later in this book, and to make sure that Jael got all the credit that was coming to her, Deborah wrote a song to help spread the word around.

It is a wonderful song, full of blood and thunder with a lot of hair-raisingly bitter jibes at the end of it about how Sisera's old mother sits waiting at the window for her son to come home, not knowing that Jael has already made mincemeat of him. Deborah composed it, but she got Barak to sing it with her. Barak looked like Moshe Dayan, and it must have been quite a duet. The song brushes by Barak's role rather hastily, but it describes Jael's in lavish detail and must have gotten her all the glory a girl could possibly want. Yahweh himself gets a plug at the end—"So perish all thine enemies, O Lord!" (Judges 5:31)—but by and large the real hero of Deborah's song is herself. Everything was going to pot, the lyrics say, "until you arose, Deborah, arose as a mother in Israel" (5:7), and you can't help feeling that Deborah's basic message was that Mother was the one who really saved the day. And of course, with Yahweh's help, she was.

It's hard not to bridle a little at the idea of her standing under the palm tree belting out her own praises like that, but after all, she had a country to run and a war to fight, and she knew that without good press she was licked from the start. Besides, maybe the more self-congratulatory parts of her song were the ones that she assigned to Barak.

Judges 4–5

See also Jael.

DELILAH

DELILAH KNEW FROM THE START that all she had to do to ruin Samson was cut off his gorgeous mop. It wasn't for nothing that she'd lain in bed watching him brush it in the mirror like a girl, the self-conscious way he tossed it out of his eyes on the dance floor, the silk bandanna he tied it back with when he went gunning for Philistines. It was only to give them a few more days together that she pretended to swallow his clumsy fibs about how the way to get the better of him was with new rope, bowstrings, and so on.

But Philistine headquarters got tough with her finally, so one night when he was asleep with his head in her lap, she slipped out her scissors, and by the time she was through with him he looked like Mr. Clean. Even the Philistine goon squad had some qualms about jumping a man who was crying like a baby when they came in to get him, and after the look she saw him give his reflection in the dresser mirror as they dragged him out, she had the feeling that it was almost a relief to him when they put out his eyes.

Judges 16

DAY 70

DENOMINATIONS

DAY 71   THERE ARE BAPTISTS, Methodists, Episcopalians. There are Presbyterians, Lutherans, Congregationalists. There are Disciples of Christ. There are Seventh-day Adventists and Jehovah's Witnesses. There are Moravians. There are Quakers. And that's only for starters. New denominations spring up. Old denominations split up and form new branches. The question is not, Are you a Baptist? but, What kind of a Baptist? It is not, Are you a member of the Presbyterian church? but Which Presbyterian church? A town with a population of less than five hundred may have churches of three or four denominations and none of them more than a quarter full on a good Sunday.

There are some genuine differences between them, of course. The methods of church government differ. They tend to worship in different forms all the way from chanting, incense, and saints' days to a service that is virtually indistinguishable from a New England town meeting with musical interludes. Some read the Bible more literally than others. If you examine the fine print, you may even come across some relatively minor theological differences among them, some stressing one aspect of the faith, some stressing others. But if you were to ask the average member of any congregation to explain those differences, you would be apt to be met with a long, unpregnant silence. By and large they all believe pretty much the same things and are confused about the same things and keep their fingers crossed during the same parts of the Nicene Creed.

However, it is not so much differences like these that keep the denominations apart as it is something more nearly approaching team spirit. Somebody from a long line of Congregationalists would no more consider crossing over to the Methodists than a Red Sox fan would consider rooting for the Mets. And even bricks and mortar have a lot to do with it. Your mother was married in this church building and so were you, and so was your oldest son. Your grandparents are buried in the cemetery just beyond the Sunday school wing. What on earth would ever persuade you to leave all that and join forces with the Lutherans in their building down the street? So what if neither of you can pay the minister more than a pittance and both of you have as hard a time getting more than thirty to fill the sanctuary built for two hundred as you do raising money to cover the annual heating bill?

All the duplication of effort and waste of human resources. All the confusion about what the church is, both within the ranks and without. All the counterproductive competition. All the unnecessarily empty pews and unnecessary expense. Then add to that picture the Roman Catholic Church, still more divided from the Protestant denominations than they are from each other, and by the time you're through, you don't know whether to burst into laughter or into tears.

When Jesus took the bread and said, "This is my body which is broken for you" (1 Corinthians 11:24), it's hard to believe that even in his wildest dreams he foresaw the tragic and ludicrous brokenness of the church as his body. There's no reason why everyone should be Christian in the same way and every reason to leave room for differences, but if all the competing factions of Christendom were to give as much of themselves to the high calling and holy hope that unite them as they do now to the relative inconsequentialities that divide them, the church would look more like the Kingdom of God for a change and less like an ungodly mess.

See also chanting.

DEPRESSION

ONE OF THE MOST PRECIOUS of the Psalms seems to be one of the least known as well as one of the shortest. It is Psalm 131. "O Lord, my heart is not lifted up," is the way it begins, "my eyes are not raised too high; / I do not occupy myself with things too great and too marvelous for me."

To be in a state of depression is like that. It is to be unable to occupy yourself with anything much except your state of depression. Even the most marvelous thing is like music to the deaf. Even the greatest thing is like a shower of stars to the blind. You do not raise either your heart or your eyes to the heights, because to do so only reminds you that you are yourself in the depths. Even if, like the Psalmist, you are inclined to cry out "O Lord," it is a cry like Jonah's from the belly of a whale.

"But I have calmed and quieted my soul," he continues then, and you can't help thinking that, although maybe that's better than nothing, it's not much better. Depression is itself a kind of calm, as in becalmed, and a kind of quiet, as in a quiet despair.

Only then do you discover that he is speaking of something entirely different. He says it twice to make sure everybody understands. "Like a child quieted at its mother's breast," he says, and then again "like a child that is quieted is my soul." A kind of blessed languor that comes with being filled and somehow also fulfilled; the sense that no dark time that has ever been and no dark time that will ever be can touch this true and only time; *shalom*—something like that is the calm and quiet he has found. And the Lord in whom he has found it is the Lady Mother of us all. It is from her breast that he has drunk it to his soul's quieting.

Finally he tells us that hope is what his mouth is milky with, hope, which is to the hopelessness of depression what love is to the lovesick and lovelorn. "O Israel, hope in the Lord," he says, "from this time forth and for evermore." Hope like Israel. Hope for deliverance the way Israel hoped and you are already half delivered. Hope beyond hope, and—like Israel in Egypt, in Babylon, in Dachau—you hope also beyond the bounds of your own captivity, which is what depression is.

Hope in the Father who is the Mother, the Lady who is the Lord. Do not raise your eyes too high, but lower them to that holy place within you where you are fed and quieted, to that innermost manger where you are yourself the Child.

DESCENT INTO HELL

There is an obscure passage in the First Letter of Peter where the old saint writes that after the crucifixion, Jesus went and preached to "the spirits in prison, who formerly did not obey" (3:19–20), and it's not altogether clear just what spirits he had in mind. Later on, however, he is not obscure at all. "The gospel was preached even to the dead," he says, "that though judged in the flesh like men, they might live in the spirit like God" (4:5–6). DAY 73

"He descended into hell," is the way the Apostles' Creed puts it, of course. It has an almost blasphemous thud to it, sandwiched there between the muffled drums of "was crucified, dead, and buried" and the trumpet blast of "the third day he rose again from the dead." Christ of all people, in hell of all places! It strains the imagination to picture it, the Light of the World making his way through the terrible dark to save whatever ones he can. Yet in view of what he'd seen of the world during his last few days in the thick of it, maybe the transition wasn't as hard as you might think.

The fancifulness of the picture gives way to what seems, the more you turn it over in your mind, the inevitability of it. Of course that is where he would have gone. Of course that is what he would have done. Christ is always descending and redescending into hell.

"Come unto me, all ye that labor and are heavy laden" is spoken to *all,* whatever they've done or left undone, whichever side of the grave their hell happens to be on.

DESPAIR

DAY 74   Despair has been called the unforgivable sin—not presumably because God refuses to forgive it, but because it despairs of the possibility of being forgiven.

DEVIL

DAY 75   To take the Devil seriously is to take seriously the fact that the total evil in the world is greater than the sum of all its parts. Likewise the total evil in yourself. The murderer who says, "I couldn't help it," isn't necessarily just kidding.

To take the Devil seriously is also to take seriously our total and spine-tingling freedom. Lucifer was an angel who even in paradise itself was free to get the hell out.

DIARY

DAY 76   Even the most cursory of diaries can be of incalculable value. What the weather was doing. Who we ran into on the street. The movie we saw. The small boy at the dentist's office. The dream.

Just a handful of the barest facts can be enough to rescue an entire day from oblivion—not just what happened in it, but who we were when it happened. Who the others were. What it felt like back then to be us.

"Our years come to an end like a sigh . . . ," says Psalm 90, "so teach us to number our days that we may get a heart of wisdom" (vv. 9, 12).

It is a mark of wisdom to realize how precious our days are, even the most uneventful of them. If we can keep them alive by only a line or so about each, at least we will know what we're sighing about when the last of them comes.

DINAH

EVERYBODY AGREED that Jacob's daughter, Dinah, had some-   DAY 77
thing special about her.

She was off visiting friends in Canaan when young Shechem the Hivite was so dazzled that he couldn't control himself and took advantage of her. Considering the degree of the temptation, you could hardly blame him in a way, but when Dinah's brothers got wind of it, they hit the roof.

Shechem by this time had fallen head over heels in love, but even when he wanted to make an honest woman of her and came to beg Jacob for her hand in marriage, the brothers were not mollified. On the contrary, they felt he was only adding insult to injury.

Shechem would not take no for an answer. He said that if Jacob would give his permission, he would make it worth his while by arranging some advantageous trade agreements between their two tribes with some personal gifts of cash and real estate thrown in for good measure. It was the kind of offer Jacob always found hard to refuse, but at the urging of his sons, he agreed to make one more condition.

If Shechem wanted to marry a nice Jewish girl like Dinah, he said, then he and all his fellow tribesmen would have to get themselves circumcised. It was the custom. Shechem didn't find it the easiest thing in the world to sell his fellow tribesmen, but somehow he managed it, and that was the break Dinah's brothers had been waiting for.

While the Hivites were still recovering from surgery, the brothers appeared out of nowhere and mowed them down to the last Hivite. When Jacob chided them about it afterward, they seemed quite nonplussed. For Dinah's sake, who would have done less?

Dinah herself had done nothing except be who she was, which was the kind of woman men naturally want to die for or kill for, but that was enough. "Terrible as an army with banners" is the way Solomon describes beauty in his Song of Songs, and you picture her standing there with downcast eyes before her brothers' butchery, totally innocent of the knowledge that there were glittering battalions in her mildest smile and that if she wanted to take the world on single-handed, the world wouldn't stand a chance.   *Genesis 34*

DISASTER

DAY 78   ON THE EVENING OF THE DAY the World Trade Center was destroyed by terrorists, a service was hastily improvised in one of the largest New York churches, where crowds of both believers and nonbelievers came together in search of whatever it is people search for at such times—some word of reassurance, some glimmer of hope.

"At times like these," the speaker said, "God is useless."

When I first heard of it, it struck me as appalling, and then it struck me as very brave, and finally it struck me as true.

When horrors happen we can't use God to make them unhappen any more than we can use a flood of light to put out a fire or Psalm 23 to find our way home in the dark.

All we can do is to draw close to God and to each other as best we can, the way those stunned New Yorkers did, and to hope that, although God may well be useless when all hell breaks loose, there is nothing that happens, not even hell, where God is not present with us and for us.

DOCTRINE

N<small>O MATTER HOW FANCY</small> and metaphysical a doctrine sounds, it was a human experience first. The doctrine of the divinity of Christ, for instance. The place it began was not in the word processor of some fourth-century Greek theologian, but in the experience of basically untheological people who had known Jesus of Nazareth and found something happening to their lives that had never happened before.

DAY 79

Unless you can somehow participate yourself in the experience that lies behind a doctrine, simply to subscribe to it doesn't mean much. Sometimes, however, simply to subscribe to a doctrine is the first step toward experiencing the reality that lies behind it.

DOUBT

W<small>HETHER YOUR FAITH</small> is that there is a God or that there is not a God, if you don't have any doubts, you are either kidding yourself or asleep. Doubts are the ants in the pants of faith. They keep it awake and moving.

DAY 80

There are two principal kinds of doubt, one of the head and the other of the stomach.

In my head there is almost nothing I can't doubt when the fit is upon me—the divinity of Christ, the efficacy of the sacraments, the significance of the church, the existence of God. But even when I am at my most skeptical, I go on with my life as though nothing untoward has happened.

I have never experienced stomach doubt, but I think Jesus did. When he cried out, "My God, my God, why hast thou forsaken me!" I don't think he was raising a theological issue any more than he was quoting Psalm 22. I think he had looked into the abyss itself and found there a darkness that spiritually, viscerally, totally engulfed him. I think God allows that kind of darkness to happen only to God's saints. The rest of us aren't up to doubting that way—or maybe believing that way either.

When our faith is strongest, we believe with our hearts as well as with our heads, but only at a few rare moments, I think, do we feel in our stomachs what it must be like to be engulfed by light.

DREAMS

DAY 81

NO MATTER HOW PROSAIC, practical, and ploddingly unimaginative we may be, we have dreams like everybody else. All of us do. In them even the most down-to-earth and pedestrian of us leave earth behind and go flying, not walking, through the air like pelicans. Even the most respectable go strolling along crowded pavements naked as truth. Even the confirmed disbelievers in an afterlife hold converse with the dead just as the most dyed-in-the-wool debunkers of the supernatural have adventures that would make Madame Blavatsky's hair stand on end.

The tears of dreams can be real enough to wet the pillow and the passions of them fierce enough to make the flesh burn. There are times we dream our way to a truth or an insight so overwhelming that it startles us awake and haunts us for years to come. As easily as from room to room, we move from things that happened so long ago we had forgotten them to things lying ahead that may be waiting to happen or trying to happen still. On our way we are as likely to meet old friends as perfect strangers. Sometimes, inexplicably, we meet casual acquaintances who for decades haven't so much as once crossed our minds.

Freudians and Jungians, prophets and poets, philosophers, fortune-tellers, and phonies all have their own claims about what dreams mean. Others claim they don't mean a thing. But there are at least two things they mean that seem incontrovertible.

One of them is that we are in constant touch with a world that is as real to us while we are in it, and has as much to do with who we are, and whose ultimate origin and destiny are as unknown and fascinating, as the world of waking reality. The other one is that our lives are a great deal richer, deeper, more intricately interrelated, more mysterious, and less limited by time and space than we commonly suppose.

People who tend to write off the validity of the religious experience in general and the experience of God in particular on the grounds that in the real world they can find no evidence for such things should take note. Maybe the real world is not the only reality, and even if it should turn out to be, maybe they are not really looking at it realistically.

DYING

THE AIRPORT IS CROWDED, NOISY, FRENETIC. There are yowling babies, people being paged, the usual ruckus. Outside, a DAY 82 mixture of snow and sleet is coming down. The runways show signs of icing. Flight delays and cancellations are called out over the PA system together with the repeated warning that in view of recent events any luggage left unattended will be immediately impounded. There are more people than usual stepping outside to smoke. The air is blue with it. Once aboard, you peer through the windows for traces of ice on the wings and search the pancaked faces of the flight attendants for anything like the knot of anxiety you feel in your own stomach as they run through the customary emergency procedures. The great craft lumbers its way to the take-off position, the jets shrill. As it picks up speed, you count the seconds till you feel liftoff. More than so many, you've heard, means trouble. Once airborne, you can hardly see the wings at all through the gray turbulence scudding by. The steep climb is as rough as a Ford pickup. Gradually it starts to even out. The clouds thin a little. Here and there you see tatters of clear air among them. The pilot levels off slightly. Nobody is talking. The calm and quiet of it are almost palpable. Suddenly, in a rush of light, you break out of the weather. Beneath you the clouds are a furrowed pasture. Above, no sky in creation was ever bluer.

Possibly the last takeoff of all is something like that. When the time finally comes, you're scared stiff to be sure, but maybe by then you're just as glad to leave the whole show behind and get going. In a matter of moments, everything that seemed to matter stops mattering. The slow climb is all there is. The stillness. The clouds. Then the miracle of flight as from fathom upon fathom down you surface suddenly into open sky. The dazzling sun.

E

EARTH

FOR THOUSANDS UPON THOUSANDS of years people couldn't see the earth whole—only as much of it at a time as there was between wherever they happened to be and the horizon. For most of them, the question of flatness or roundness must have seemed altogether irrelevant. Either way, it was plainly enormous. Beyond the fields and the mountains there was the sea, and beyond the sea more fields, more mountains. Whatever wild ideas they had about how it came into being or who made it, they knew it had been around more or less forever. Just by looking at it you could tell that—the ancient rocks, the vast deserts. Nothing less than God himself could ever bring it to an end, and God didn't seem to be in any special hurry about it. In the meanwhile, though time and change eventually carried off everybody and everything else, it was as clear as anything was clear that at least the place they were carried off from was for keeps. Spring would follow winter like the ebb and flow of the tides. Life in one odd shape or another would keep going on and on, the old ones dying and the new ones being born.

Then suddenly pictures were taken from miles away, and we saw it at last for what it truly is. It is about the size of a dime. It is blue with swirls of silver. It shines. The blackness it floats in is so immense, it seems almost miraculously not to have swallowed it up long since.

Seeing it like that for the first time, you think of Jesus seeing Jerusalem for the last time. The ass he's riding comes clip-clopping around a bend in the road, and without warning there it is. His eyes fill with tears, as Luke describes it. "Would that even today you knew the things that make for peace," he says. "For the days shall come . . ." (Luke 19:41, 43). The holy city.

The holy earth. We must take such care of it. It must take such care of us. This side of paradise, we are each of us so nearly all the other has. There is darkness beyond our wildest imagining all around us. Among us there is just about enough light to get by.

EASTER

DAY 84

CHRISTMAS has a large and colorful cast of characters including not only the three principals themselves, but the angel Gabriel, the innkeeper, the shepherds, the heavenly host, the three Wise Men, Herod, the star of Bethlehem, and even the animals kneeling in the straw. In one form or another we have seen them represented so often that we would recognize them anywhere. We know about the birth in all its detail as well as we know about the births of ourselves or our children, maybe more so. The manger is as familiar as home. We have made a major production of it, and as minor attractions we have added the carols, the tree, the presents, the cards. Santa Claus, Ebenezer Scrooge, and so on. With Easter it is entirely different.

The Gospels are far from clear as to just what happened. It began in the dark. The stone had been rolled aside. Matthew alone speaks of an earthquake. In the tomb there were two white-clad figures or possibly just one. Mary Magdalen seems to have gotten there before anybody else. There was a man she thought at first was the gardener. Perhaps Mary the mother of James was with her and another woman named Joanna. One account says Peter came too with one of the other disciples. Elsewhere the suggestion is that there were only the women and that the disciples, who were somewhere else, didn't believe the women's story when they heard it. There was the sound of people running, of voices. Matthew speaks of "fear and great joy." Confusion was everywhere. There is no agreement even as to the role of Jesus himself. Did he appear at the tomb or only later? Where? To whom did he appear? What did he say? What did he do?

It is not a major production at all, and the minor attractions we have created around it—the bunnies and baskets and bonnets, the dyed eggs—have so little to do with what it's all about that they neither add much nor subtract much. It's not really even much of a story when you come right down to it, and that is of course the power of it. It doesn't have the ring of great drama. It has the ring of truth. If the Gospel writers had wanted to tell it in a way to convince the world that Jesus indeed rose from the dead, they would presumably have done it with all the skill and fanfare they could muster. Here there is no skill, no fanfare. They seem to be telling it simply the way it was. The narrative is as fragmented, shadowy, incomplete as life itself. When it comes to just what happened, there can be no certainty. That something unimaginable happened, there can be no doubt.

The symbol of Easter is the empty tomb. You can't depict or domesticate emptiness. You can't make it into pageants and string it with lights. It doesn't move people to give presents to each other or sing old songs. It ebbs and flows all around us, the Eastertide. Even the great choruses of Handel's *Messiah* sound a little like a handful of crickets chirping under the moon.

He rose. A few saw him briefly and talked to him. If it is true, there is nothing left to say. If it is not true, there is nothing left to say. For believers and unbelievers both, life has never been the same again. For some, neither has death. What is left now is the emptiness. There are those who, like Magdalen, will never stop searching it till they find his face.

ELIJAH

DAY 85

I N THE CONTEST BETWEEN ELIJAH and the prophets of Baal to see whose God was the real article, Elijah won the first round hands down. Starting out early in the morning on Mt. Carmel, the prophets of Baal pulled out all the stops to get their candidate to set fire to the sacrificial offering. They danced around the altar till their feet were sore. They made themselves hoarse shouting instructions and encouragement at the sky. They jabbed at themselves with knives thinking that the sight of blood would start things moving if anything would, but they might as well have saved themselves the trouble.

Although it was like beating a dead horse, Elijah couldn't resist getting in a few digs. "Maybe Baal's flown to Bermuda for the weekend," he said. "Maybe he's taking a nap." The prophets whipped themselves into greater and greater frenzies under his goading, but by mid-afternoon the sacrificial offering had begun to smell a little high, and there was still no sign of fire from above. Then it was Elijah's turn to show what Yahweh could do.

He was like a magician getting ready to pull a rabbit out of a hat. First he had a trench dug around the altar and filled with water.

Then he got a bucket brigade going to give the offering a good dousing too. Then as soon as they'd finished, he got them to do it again for good measure. By the time they'd finished a third go-round, the whole place was awash, and Elijah looked as if he'd just finished swimming the Channel. He then gave Yahweh the word to show his stuff and jumped back just in time.

Lightning flashed. The water in the trench fizzed like fat on a hot griddle. Nothing was left of the offering but a pile of ashes and a smell like the Fourth of July. The onlookers were beside themselves with enthusiasm and, at a signal from Elijah, demolished the losing team down to the last prophet. Nobody could say whose victory had been greater, Yahweh's or Elijah's.

But the sequel to the event seems to have made this clear. Queen Jezebel was determined to get even with Elijah for what he had done to her spiritual advisers, and to save his skin he went and hid out on Mt. Horeb. Again he gave Yahweh the word, not because he wanted anything set on fire this time, but just to keep his hand in.

Again the lightning flashed, and after that a wind came up that almost blew Elijah off his feet, and after that the earth gave such a shake that it almost knocked him silly. But there wasn't so much as a peep out of Yahweh, and Elijah stood there like a ringmaster when the lion won't jump through the hoop.

Only when the fireworks were finished and a terrible hush fell over the mountain did Elijah hear something, and what he heard was so much like silence that it was only through the ear of faith that he knew it was Yahweh. Nonetheless, the message came through loud and clear: that there was no longer any question who had been the star at Mt. Carmel and that not even Elijah could make the Lord God of Hosts jump through a hoop like a lion or pop out like a rabbit from a hat. *1 Kings 18–19*

See also Ahab.

ELISHA

DAY 86   IT WAS A HOT DAY as the prophet Elisha made his way up to Bethel where he had business to attend to. Pausing near a camping ground for a bit of shade, he was mopping his bald scalp with a corner of his prayer shawl when a Boy Scout troop broke ranks and surrounded him. They threw bottle caps at him, and they made rude gestures. They pulled their mouths out as wide as they could with their thumbs and at the same time pulled their lower lids down with their index fingers till you could see the wet, pink membrane inside. It was an unnerving spectacle.

"Skinhead" and "Chrome-dome" and "Curly" they called at him, till finally the old man had enough. He made a few passes at them, muttered a few words, and within seconds a couple of she-bears lumbered out from the trees behind the picnic tables and mauled some of the slower members of the troop rather badly.

It is not the most edifying story in the Old Testament, but there are perhaps some lessons to be learned from it even so. The Lord does not call everyone to be Mister Rogers, for instance, and there is no need to try making a fool out of a prophet, because sooner or later he will probably make one out of himself. It is not the most edifying story about Elisha either, but it is perhaps one of the more endearing.   *2 Kings 2:23–25*

See also Naaman.

ENEMY

DAY 87   CAIN HATED ABEL for standing higher in God's esteem than he felt he himself did, so he killed him. King Saul hated David for stealing the hearts of the people with his winning ways and tried to kill him every chance he got. Saul of Tarsus hated the followers of Jesus because he thought they were blasphemers and heretics and made a career of rounding them up so they could be stoned to death like Stephen. By and large most of us don't have enemies like that anymore, and in a way it's a pity.

It would be pleasant to think it's because we're more civilized nowadays, but maybe it's only because we're less honest, open, brave. We tend to avoid fiery outbursts for fear of what they may touch off both in ourselves and the ones we burst out at. We smolder instead. If people hurt us or cheat us or stand for things we abominate, we're less apt to bear arms against them than to bear grudges. We stay out of their way. When we declare war, it is mostly submarine warfare, and since our attacks are beneath the surface, it may be years before we know fully the damage we have either given or sustained.

Jesus says we are to love our enemies and pray for them, meaning love not in an emotional sense but in the sense of willing their good, which is the sense in which we love ourselves. It is a tall order even so. African Americans love white supremacists? The longtime employee who is laid off just before he qualifies for retirement with a pension love the people who call him in to break the news? The mother of the molested child love the molester? But when you see as clearly as that who your enemies are, at least you see your enemies clearly too.

You see the lines in their faces and the way they walk when they're tired. You see who their husbands and wives are, maybe. You see where they're vulnerable. You see where they're scared. Seeing what is hateful about them, you may catch a glimpse also of where the hatefulness comes from. Seeing the hurt they cause you, you may see also the hurt they cause themselves. You're still light-years away from loving them, to be sure, but at least you see how they are human even as you are human, and that is at least a step in the right direction. It's possible that you may even get to where you can pray for them a little, if only that God forgive them because you yourself can't, but any prayer for them at all is a major breakthrough.

In the long run, it may be easier to love the ones we look in the eye and hate, the enemies, than the ones whom—because we're as afraid of ourselves as we are of them—we choose not to look at, at all.

ENVIRONMENT

DAY 88 IT'S TOO BAD that such a poor word has come to refer to something so rich. The forests, the rivers, the mountains, the oceans, the deserts, the beaches, the fields, the flowers, the rain, the sky, the air. To speak of them collectively as the *environment* is to suggest that they are somehow lifeless and abstract. It makes it almost possible to forget that what we are in danger of ruining through our rapacity and folly is the mother who bore us and the green grave that awaits us. Is our hearts' delight. Is home.

ENVY

DAY 89 ENVY IS THE CONSUMING DESIRE to have everybody else be as unsuccessful as you are.

ESAU

DAY 90 ESAU WAS SO HUNGRY he could hardly see straight when his younger twin, Jacob, bought his birthright for a bowl of chili. He was off hunting rabbits when Jacob conned their old father,

Isaac, into giving him the blessing that should have been Esau's by right of primogeniture. Eventually it dawned on Esau what his brother was up to, and he went slogging after him with a blunt instrument; but the slowness of his wits was compensated for by the generosity of his disposition, and in time the two were reconciled.

Jacob stole Esau blind, in other words, got away with it, and went on to become the father of the twelve tribes of Israel. It was not all gravy, however. He knew famine and loss. He grieved for years over the supposed death of his favorite child. He was as hoodwinked by his own sons in this as both his father and Esau had been hoodwinked by him, and he died with the clamor of their squabbling shrill in his ears.

Esau, on the other hand, though he'd lost his shirt, settled down in the hill country, raised a large if comparatively undistinguished family, and died in peace. Thus it seems hard to know which of the two brothers came out ahead in the end.

It seems plain enough, however, that the reason God bypassed Esau and made Jacob heir to the great promise is that it is easier to make a silk purse out of a sow's ear than out of a dim bulb.

Genesis 25–27; 33

ESCAPISM

RELIGION HAS OFTEN BEEN DENOUNCED as escapism, and it often is. To deny the prevalence of pain in the world and the perennial popularity of evil. To abdicate responsibility for them by assuming that God will take care of them very nicely on his own. To accept them as divine judgment upon the sins especially of other people. To dismiss them or to encourage others to dismiss them by stressing the promise of pie in the sky. To pretend like a Forest

DAY 91

Lawn cosmetologist that there's no such thing as death. To maintain your faith by refusing to face any nasty fact that threatens it. These are all ways of escaping reality through religion and should be denounced right along with such other modes of escape as liquor, drugs, TV, or any simplistic optimism such as jingoism, right-wing evangelicalism, moralism, idealism, and so on, which assume that if everybody would only see it our way, evil would vanish and all would be sweetness and light.

But the desire to escape is not always something to be denounced, as any prisoner or slave could tell you. Jesus said, "If you continue in my word, you are truly my disciples, and you will know the truth, and the truth will make you free" (John 8:31–32). Free from sin, he explained when they pressed him. Free from imprisonment within the narrow walls of your own not all that enlightened self-interest. Free from enslavement to your own shabbiest instincts, deceits, and self-deceptions. Freedom not *from* responsibility, but *for* it. Escape not from reality, but into it.

The best moments we any of us have as human beings are those moments when for a little while it is possible to escape the squirrel cage of being *me* into the landscape of being *us.*

ETERNAL LIFE

DAY 92

WHEN YOU ARE WITH SOMEBODY you love, you have little if any sense of the passage of time, and you also have, in the fullest sense of the phrase, a *good* time.

When you are with God, you have something like the same experience. The biblical term for the experience is eternal life. Another is heaven.

What does it mean to be "with God"? It doesn't mean you have to be thinking about being with God, or feeling religious, or sitting in church, or saying your prayers, though it might mean any or all of these. It doesn't even mean you have to believe in God.

To say that a person is "with it" is slang for saying that whether he's playing an electric guitar or just watching the clouds roll by, he's so caught up in what he's doing and so totally himself while he's doing it that there's none of him left over to be doing anything else with in the back of his head or out of the corner of his eye. It's slang for saying that the temperature where she is is about forty degrees hotter than the temperature where she is not, and that whatever it is everybody's looking for, she's found it, and that if she were a flag and they ran her up the mast, we'd all have to salute whether we liked it or not. And the chances are we'd like it.

Being "with it" may not be the same as being with God, but it comes close.

We think of eternal life, if we think of it at all, as what happens when life ends. We would do better to think of it as what happens when life begins.

Saint Paul uses the phrase *eternal life* to describe the end and goal of the process of salvation. Elsewhere he writes the same thing in a remarkable sentence in which he says that the whole purpose of God's slogging around through the muck of history and of our own individual histories is somehow to prod us, jolly us, worry us, cajole us, and, if need be, bludgeon us into reaching "maturity . . . the measure of the full stature of Christ" (Ephesians 4:13).

In other words, to live eternal life in the full and final sense is to be with God as Christ is with him, and with each other as Christ is with us.

See also salvation.

ETERNITY

DAY 93 ETERNITY IS NOT ENDLESS TIME or the opposite of time. It is the essence of time.

If you spin a pinwheel fast enough, all its colors blend into a single color—white—which is the essence of all the colors of the spectrum combined.

If you spin time fast enough, time-past, time-present, and time-to-come all blend into a single timelessness or eternity, which is the essence of all times combined.

As human beings we know time as a passing of unrepeatable events in the course of which everything passes away—including ourselves. As human beings, we also know occasions when we stand outside the passing of events and glimpse their meaning. Sometimes an event occurs in our lives (a birth, a death, a marriage—some event of unusual beauty, pain, joy) through which we catch a glimpse of what our lives are all about and maybe even what life itself is all about, and this glimpse of what "it's all about" involves not just the present, but the past and future too.

Inhabitants of time that we are, we stand on such occasions with one foot in eternity. God, as Isaiah says (57:15), "inhabiteth eternity," but stands with one foot in time. The part of time where he stands most particularly is Christ, and thus in Christ we catch a glimpse of what eternity is all about, what God is all about, and what we ourselves are all about too.

ETHIOPIAN EUNUCH

DAY 94   THE NAME OF THE ETHIOPIAN EUNUCH isn't given, but he was Secretary of the Treasury under Queen Candace of Ethiopia, and he had been to Jerusalem on a religious pilgrimage. It was on his way home that the high point of the trip occurred.

He was cruising along in his chariot reading out loud to himself from the book of Isaiah when the apostle Philip happened to overhear him and asked if he understood what the words were all about. The eunuch said he could use some help on one passage in particular, and this was the passage:

> As a sheep led to the slaughter
> or a lamb before its shearers is dumb
> so he opens not his mouth.
> In his humiliation justice was denied him.
> Who can describe his generation?
> For his life is taken up from the earth.

(Acts 8:32–33; compare Isaiah 53:7–8)

Who in the world was Isaiah talking about? the eunuch wanted to know, and Philip said it was Jesus. Jesus was the one who was gentle as a sheep and innocent as a lamb. He was the one who had been unjustly humiliated and slaughtered and hadn't let out so much as a peep to save himself. As for describing his generation, his time, all you could say was that he belonged to all time and every generation because his life wasn't bound to the earth anymore. His life was everywhere, and any of us could live it for ourselves or let it live itself in us as easily as a fish circulates around in the water and the water circulates around in a fish.

The way things happened, a pond turned up by the side of the road as they traveled along, and the eunuch asked why he shouldn't give the thing a try right then and there and let Philip baptize him in it. So Philip baptized him, and when that black and mutilated potentate bobbed back to the surface, he was so carried away he couldn't even speak. The sounds of his joy were like the sounds of a brook rattling over pebbles, and Philip never saw him again and never had to.

Acts 8:26–39

EUTYCHUS

DAY 95 "SERMONETTES MAKE CHRISTIANETTES," the saying goes, so Saint Paul kept talking till midnight to make sure they all got the word. Then he thought of a few things he'd left out and went on a while longer. He was so caught up in his own eloquence that he didn't hear the bumblebee sounds that were emerging from a young man with his eyes more or less closed and his mouth more or less open who sat slumped over in the third-story window. It was only a woman's scream that alerted him to the fact that the boy had fallen asleep, and out, more or less simultaneously. When Paul asked his name, they told him it was Eutychus.

Everybody thought Eutychus was dead, but Paul said he'd see about that. Then he went back upstairs where, after a snack, he ran over his major points once more just to make sure. When he finally left on the early bus, they found Eutychus sitting up in bed asking for two over light and a toasted English.

This miraculous recovery, plus the fact that by then the saint was already well on his way to the next county, made them decide to throw a double celebration. Presumably somebody had the sense to suggest that this time they use the ground floor.

Acts 20:9–12

EVE

DAY 96 LIKE ADAM, Eve spent the rest of her days convincing herself that it had all worked out for the best. Their new life didn't turn out to be as bad as had been predicted, and somehow their marriage weathered the change. If they had moments of terrible bitterness over what had happened, they had other moments when it became more of a bridge than an abyss between them and when the question of which of them was to blame got lost in the question of how both of them were to survive. One son died an ugly, senseless death, and another went through life as disfigured by remorse as by a cleft palate. But all in all things didn't go too badly. When the last child left home, it wasn't the easiest thing in the world to be alone again with a man who, after his third martini, might still lash out at her as a snake in the grass and a bad apple, but at least they still had their independence and their principles, which as nearly as she could remember were what they'd given everything up for. They stood, however grimly at times, on their own feet.

It was only once in a while at night, just as she was going off to sleep with all her usual defenses down, that her mind drifted back to the days when, because there was nothing especially important to do, everything was especially important; when *too good not to be true* hadn't yet turned into *too good to be true;* when being alone was never the same as being lonely. Then sad and beautiful dreams overtook her, which she would wake up from homesick for a home she could no longer even name, to make something not quite love with a man whose face she could not quite see in the darkness at her side.   *Genesis 3:1–4:16*

See also Adam, Cain.

EVIL

DAY 97

- God is all-powerful.
- God is all-good.
- Terrible things happen.

You can reconcile any two of these propositions with each other, but you can't reconcile all three. The problem of evil is perhaps the greatest single problem for religious faith.

There have been numerous theological and philosophical attempts to solve it, but when it comes down to the reality of evil itself, they are none of them worth much. When a child is raped and murdered, the parents are not apt to take much comfort from the explanation (better than most) that since God wants us to love him, we must be free to love or not to love and thus free to rape and murder a child if we take a notion to.

Christian Science solves the problem of evil by saying that it does not exist except as an illusion of mortal mind. Buddhism solves it in terms of reincarnation and an inexorable law of cause and effect whereby the raped child is merely reaping the consequences of evil deeds she committed in another life.

Christianity, on the other hand, ultimately offers no theoretical solution at all. It merely points to the cross and says that, practically speaking, there is no evil so dark and so obscene—not even this—but that God can turn it to good.

See also atheist, Job.

EZEKIEL

DAY 98

A POPULAR VIEW has it that what Ezekiel really saw were flying saucers.

There were these gleaming wheels with spokes and rims and things that looked like eyes built into the rims, he said, and one minute they were resting on the ground, and the next minute they were shooting up into the sky. There were also these creatures who flew around with the wheels and made a noise like thunder or a sonic boom, he said. Above them was this one creature in particular who looked humanoid, but was clearly not human and seemed to be wearing something like bronze or a space suit from the loins up and something like fire from the loins down.

Then all of a sudden from way up in the air his voice came down, and all the other craft stopped shooting around and just hovered, and, to make a long story from outer space short, what the voice said was that if Israel didn't whip itself into some kind of shape, it would be curtains.

Ezekiel didn't think he'd seen flying saucers, of course. He thought he'd seen the glory of God. And the close encounter he thought he'd had wasn't of the third kind, but of a different kind altogether. It wasn't a thirty-foot praying mantis he thought had given him the word, but the Almighty himself. So you pay your money and take your choice.

In making that choice, however, you ought to take into consideration at least one other thing Ezekiel thought he saw. It was a boneyard. There were shinbones and arm bones and wishbones and collarbones and skulls enough to keep paleontologists busy indefinitely. What the voice said this time was for Ezekiel to speak the word of the Lord to this boneyard and then stand back. So he spoke it.

The first thing that happened was a sound of rattling and clicking like the tide going out over a million pebble beaches as the bones started snapping back together again. The next thing that happened was a million reassembled skeletons pulling on skin like long winter underwear. The last thing that happened was the color coming back to a million pairs of cheeks and the spark to a million pairs of eyes and the breath of life to a million pairs of lungs.

Then the voice asked Ezekiel to tell the Israelites that—with God in the wings—even though it would be curtains for sure the way they were heading, the curtain that goes down when you bomb in New Haven is also the curtain that goes up on the marvelous new rewrite that hits Broadway like a ton of bricks.

As far as is known, nobody's ever stepped out of a UFO and made a statement like that.

Ezekiel 1–2:7; 37:1–14

FACES

FACES, LIKE EVERYTHING ELSE, can be looked at and not seen. Walking down a sidewalk at rush hour or attending the World Series, you're surrounded by thousands of them, but they might as well be balloons at a political rally for all you notice them individually. Here and there one of them may catch your eye for a moment, but in another moment you've forgotten it. They are without personalities, without histories. There is nothing to remember them by. They are anonymous strangers. As far as you are concerned, they simply don't matter. They are too much to take in.

But the odds are that for at least one other person somewhere in the world, each of them—even the unlikeliest—matters enormously, or mattered enormously once, or someday, with any luck, will come to matter. The pimply boy with the beginnings of a mustache, the fat girl eating popcorn, the man with no upper teeth, the suntanned blonde with the disagreeable mouth—if you set your mind to it, there's hardly a one of them you can't imagine somebody *loving* even, conceivably even yourself. If the fat girl were your

DAY 99

kid sister, for instance. Or the pimply boy to grow up to be your father. Or the toothless man to have been your first great love. Each face you see has, or used to have, or may have yet, the power—out of all the other faces in creation—to make at least some one other person's heart skip a beat just by turning up in an old photograph album, maybe, or appearing unexpectedly at the front door.

Needless to say, it's easier to imagine it with some than with others. For all her good looks it's harder with the suntanned blonde than with the sweaty truck driver shooting a squirt of cut plug, but even with her you can probably manage it in the end. There's hardly a face coming at you down the supermarket aisle or up the subway escalator that you can't manage it with, given the right set of circumstances, the right pair of eyes. You can see even the bitter faces in terms of what probably made them that way. You can see even the hostile, ugly faces in terms of what they must have been once before the world got to them, what they might have become if they'd gotten the breaks.

Every now and again, however, you come across faces that are too much for you. There are people it's impossible to imagine loving if only because they look so much as though they wouldn't let you even if you could. If there are faces of the blessed to be seen in this world, there are also faces of the damned. Maybe you can love them for precisely that reason then. Maybe you're the one who has to love them because nobody else ever has.

In any case, the next time you find yourself in a crowd with nothing better to do, it's a game worth playing.

FAITH

DAY 100

WHEN GOD TOLD ABRAHAM, who was a hundred at the time, that at the age of ninety his wife, Sarah, was finally going to have a baby, Abraham came close to knocking himself out—"fell on his face and laughed," as Genesis puts it (17:17). In another version of the story (18:8ff.), Sarah is hiding behind the door eavesdropping, and here it's Sarah herself who nearly splits a gut—although when God asks her about it afterward, she denies it. "No, but you did laugh," God says, thus having the last word as well as the first. God doesn't seem to hold their outbursts against them, however. On the contrary, God tells them the baby's going to be a boy and they are to name him Isaac. Isaac in Hebrew means "laughter."

Why did the two old crocks laugh? They laughed because they knew only a fool would believe that a woman with one foot in the grave was soon going to have her other foot in the maternity ward. They laughed because God expected them to believe it anyway. They laughed because God seemed to believe it. They laughed because they half believed it themselves. They laughed because laughing felt better than crying. They laughed because if by some crazy chance it just happened to come true, they would really have something to laugh about, and in the meanwhile it helped keep them going.

Faith is "the assurance of things hoped for, the conviction of things not seen," says the Letter to the Hebrews (11:1). Faith is laughter at the promise of a child called Laughter.

Faith is better understood as a verb than as a noun, as a process than as a possession. It is on-again-off-again rather than once-and-for-all. Faith is not being sure where you're going, but going anyway. A journey without maps. Paul Tillich said that doubt isn't the opposite of faith; it is an element of faith.

I have faith that my friend is my friend. It is possible that all his motives are ulterior. It is possible that what he is secretly drawn to is not me, but my wife or my money. But there's something about the way I feel when he's around, about the way he looks me in the eye, about the way we can talk to each other without pretense and be silent together without embarrassment, that makes me willing to put my life in his hands, as I do each time I call him friend.

I can't prove the friendship of my friend. When I experience it, I don't need to prove it. When I don't experience it, no proof will do. If I tried to put his friendship to the test somehow, the test itself would queer the friendship I was testing. So it is with the Godness of God.

The five so-called proofs for the existence of God will never prove to unfaith that God exists. They are merely five ways of describing the existence of the God you have faith in already.

Almost nothing that makes any real difference can be proved. I can prove the law of gravity by dropping a shoe out the window. I can prove that the world is round if I'm clever at that sort of thing—that the radio works, that light travels faster than sound. I cannot prove that life is better than death or love better than hate. I cannot prove the greatness of the great or the beauty of the beautiful. I cannot even prove my own free will; maybe my most heroic act, my truest love, my deepest thought are all just subtler versions of what happens when the doctor taps my knee with his little rubber hammer and my foot jumps.

Faith can't prove a damned thing. Or a blessed thing either.

See also God.

FAMILY

DAY 101   THE HUMAN FAMILY. It's a good phrase, reminding us not only that we come from the same beginning and are headed toward the same conclusion, but that in the meantime our lives are elaborately and inescapably linked. A famine in one part of the world affects people in all parts of the world. An assassination in Dallas or Sarajevo affects everybody. No one is an island. It is well worth remembering.

But families have a way of being islands notwithstanding—the Flanagans as distinct from the Schwartzes and the Schwartzes never to be confused with the Cherbonneaus or the Riondas. You think of a row of houses on a street. The same drama is going on in all of them—the human drama—but in each of them a unique drama is also going on. Though the wood walls are so thin you can hear a baby's cry through them, they are solid enough to keep out the world. If in the Schwartzes' house the baby dies—or grows up and gets married by the rambler roses in the backyard—all the other families on the street rally round and do what they can. But it is in the Schwartzes' house alone that what happens happens fully. With the best will in the world, nobody on the outside can know the richness and mystery of it, the foreshadowings of it deep in the past, the reverberations of it far in the future. With the best will in the world, nobody on the inside can make it known.

It is not so much that things happen in a family as it is that the family is the things that happen in it. The family is continually becoming what becomes of it. It is every christening and every commencement, every falling in love, every fight, every departure and return. It is the moment at breakfast when for no apparent reason somebody gets up and leaves the table. It is the sound of the phone ringing in the middle of the night or the lying awake hours waiting for it to ring. It is the waves pounding the boardwalk to pieces and the undercurrents so deep beneath the surface that you're hardly aware of them.

A family is a web so delicately woven that it takes almost nothing to set the whole thing shuddering or even to tear it to pieces. Yet the thread it's woven of is as strong as anything on earth. Sixty years after his father's death, the old man can't bring himself to remember it, or to stop remembering. Even when the twenty-year-old daughter runs out and never comes back, she can hear the raised voices from downstairs as she's going to sleep a thousand miles away, and every year when the old birthdays or death days come by, she marks each of them as surely as she marks that the sun has gone under a cloud or the moon risen.

It is within the fragile yet formidable walls of your own family that you learn, or do not learn, what the phrase *human family* means.

FATHER

DAY 102

WHEN A CHILD IS BORN, a father is born. A mother is born too, of course, but at least for her it's a gradual process. Body and soul, she has nine months to get used to what's happening. She becomes what's happening. But for even the best-prepared father, it happens all at once. On the other side of the plate-glass window, a nurse is holding up something roughly the size of a loaf of bread for him to see for the first time. Even if he should decide to abandon it forever ten minutes later, the memory will nag him to the grave. He has seen the creation of the world. It has his mark upon it. He has its mark upon him. Both marks are, for better or worse, indelible.

All sons, like all daughters, are prodigals if they're smart. Assuming the old man doesn't run out on them first, they will run out on him if they are to survive, and if he's smart he won't put up too much of a fuss. A wise father sees all this coming, and maybe that's why he keeps his distance from the start. He must survive too. Whether they ever find their way home again, none can say for sure, but it's the risk he must take if they're ever to find their way at all. In the meantime, the world tends to have a soft spot in its heart for lost children. Lost fathers have to fend for themselves.

Even as the father lays down the law, he knows that someday his children will break it as they need to break it if ever they're to find something better than law to replace it. Until and unless that happens, there's no telling the scrapes they will get into trying to lose him and find themselves. Terrible blunders will be made—disappointments and failures, hurts and losses of every kind. And they'll keep making them even after they've found themselves too, of course, because growing up is a process that goes on and on. And every hard knock they ever get knocks the father even harder still, if that's possible, and if and when they finally come through more or less in one piece at the end, there's maybe no rejoicing greater than his in all creation.

It has become so commonplace to speak of God as "our Father" that we forget what an extraordinary metaphor it once was.

FEET

"Ｈow BEAUTIFUL upon the mountains are the feet of him who brings good tidings," says Isaiah (52:7). Not how beautiful are the herald's *lips,* which proclaim the good tidings, or his *eyes* as he proclaims them, or even the good tidings themselves, but how beautiful are the *feet*—the feet without which he could never have made it up into the mountains, without which the good tidings would never have been proclaimed at all. DAY 103

Who knows in what inspired way the heart, mind, or spirit of the herald came to receive the good tidings of peace and salvation in the first place, but as to the question whether he would actually do something about them—put his money where his mouth was, his shoe leather where his inspiration was—his feet were the ones that finally had to decide. Maybe it is always so.

When the disciples first came upon the risen Christ that Sunday morning of their confusion and terror, it wasn't his healing hands they touched or his teaching lips or his holy heart. Instead, it was those same ruined, tired dogs that had carried him to them three years earlier, when they were at their accounts and their nets, that had dragged him all the way from Galilee to Jerusalem, that had stumbled up the hill where what was to happen happened. "They took hold of his *feet* and worshiped him," Matthew says (28:9; italics mine).

Generally speaking, if you want to know who you really are, as distinct from who you like to think you are, keep an eye on where your feet take you.

FELIX

DAY 104   FELIX WAS THE ROMAN GOVERNOR of Cilicia. When Paul got into a knock-down drag-out with the Jerusalem Jews, Felix was the one that the Roman brass took him to in hopes of getting the matter settled once and for all. Paul's Roman passport entitled him to a Roman hearing, and Felix gave it to him. He seems to have listened sympathetically enough and to have had a fairly good understanding of both sides of the issue, since, on the one hand, he already knew about the Christian movement and, on the other, he had a Jewish wife. Under the pretext of awaiting further evidence, he then placed Paul in custody, but went out of the way to see to it that he was well taken care of. He could do what he wanted within reason, and his friends were allowed to supplement his rations from a kosher delicatessen.

The trouble came during a second interview a couple of days later. Felix had summoned him to find out how much his release was worth to him in hard cash, but with his usual tact Paul insisted on discussing justice, self-control, and future judgment instead. "Don't call me. I'll call you," Felix said and sent him back to the pokey. He dropped in on him there from time to time to pursue his original line of inquiry, but Paul never seemed to zero in on what he was after.

With three squares a day, a roof over his head, and plenty of time to write letters, Paul had no major complaints apparently, and as long as Felix didn't spring him, the Jews had no major complaints either. As for Felix himself, after two years he retired on a handsome government pension, leaving the problem of what to do with Paul for his successor to worry about. Felix, of course, means "the happy one" in Latin, and if happiness consists of having your cake and eating it too, he was well named.   *Acts 23:26–24:27*

FEMALE

GOD CREATED HUMANKIND in God's own image, in the image of God he created them; male and female he created them" (Genesis 1:27). In other words, the female as much as the male is a reflection of the Creator. They are created at the same time, and they are created equals. God blesses them and charges them together and gives the female, along with the male, dominion over the earth. In the next chapter, however, a different story is told. There God creates Adam first and only afterward, realizing that "it is not good that the man should be alone," decides to make a helper

DAY 105

for him, fashioning Eve out of one of Adam's ribs and calling her "Woman, because she was taken out of Man" (2:18–22).

These two conflicting views of the female's role in the order of things scarcely need to be spelled out further, nor is it necessary to point out that, generally speaking, it is the second of them that has prevailed down through the centuries.

Little by little women have turned things pretty much around. They vote. They get elected heads of state. They excel in arts and professions that were once for men only. Some of the stuffiest men's clubs accept them, as do virtually all of the most venerable men's colleges. They are increasingly successful in getting equal pay for equal jobs. Major denominations ordain them. It has been a long, slow exodus, but finally it seems to be paying off.

Feminism can become another form of sexism. Knee-jerk feminists can match their macho counterparts in pig-headedness, aggressiveness, humorlessness, and bigotry. Their shrill voices can make the head ache. When they refuse to read *King Lear* because it's full of sexist language and bar males from their lectures and demonstrations because they're males, their efforts are apt to be counterproductive. But no matter.

Prophets have always been strident and a little crazy. They've needed to be. The prophet Deborah wouldn't have beaten the tar out of the Canaanites by issuing directives from her living room any more than Moses would have gotten his people out of Egypt by writing letters to the *New York Times*.

FIRE

DAY 106   FIRE HAS NO SHAPE OR SUBSTANCE. You can't taste it or smell it or hear it. You can't touch it except at great risk. You can't weigh it or measure it or examine it with instruments. You can never grasp it in its fullness because it never stands still. Yet there is no mistaking its extraordinary power.

The fire that sweeps through miles of forest like a terrible wind and the flickering candle that lights the old woman's way to bed. The burning logs on the subzero night that save the pipes from freezing and give summer dreams to the tabby dozing on the hearth. Even from millions of miles away, the conflagration of the sun that can turn green earth into desert and strike blind any who fail to lower their gaze before it. The power of fire to devastate and consume utterly. The power of fire to purify by leaving nothing in its wake but a scattering of ash that the wind blows away like mist.

A pillar of fire was what led the children of Israel through the wilderness, and it was from a burning bush that God first spoke to Moses. There were tongues of fire leaping up from the disciples on the day of Pentecost. In John's apocalypse it is a lake of fire that the damned are cast into, and Faithful and True himself, he says, has eyes of fire as he sits astride his white horse.

In the pages of Scripture, fire is holiness, and perhaps never more hauntingly than in the little charcoal fire that Jesus of Nazareth, newly risen from the dead, kindles for cooking his friends' breakfast on the beach at daybreak.

FOOL

WORLDLY WISDOM is what more or less all of us have been living by since the Stone Age. It is best exemplified by such homely utterances as "You've got your own life to lead," "Business is business," "Charity begins at home," "Don't get involved," "God helps those who help themselves," "Safety first," and so forth.

DAY 107

Although this wisdom can lead on occasion to ruthlessness and indifference, it is by no means incompatible with niceness, as the life of anyone apt to read (or write) a book like this bears witness. We can be basically interested in nothing so much as old number one and still give generously to the American Cancer Society, be on the Board of Deacons, run for town office, and have a soft spot in our hearts for children and animals.

It is in contrast to all this that what Saint Paul calls "the foolishness of God" looks so foolish. Inspection stickers used to have printed on the back "Drive carefully—the life you save may be your own." That is worldly wisdom in a nutshell.

What God says, on the other hand, is "The life you save is the life you lose." In other words, the life you clutch, hoard, guard, and play safe with is in the end a life worth little to anybody, including yourself, and only a life given away for love's sake is a life worth living. To bring his point home, God shows us a man who gave his life away to the extent of dying a national disgrace without a penny in the bank or a friend to his name. In terms of human wisdom, he was a perfect fool. And if you think you can follow him without making something like the same kind of a fool of yourself, you are laboring under not a cross, but a delusion.

There are two kinds of fools in the world: damned fools and what Saint Paul calls "fools for Christ's sake" (1 Corinthians 4:10).

FORGIVENESS

DAY 108   To FORGIVE SOMEBODY is to say one way or another, "You have done something unspeakable, and by all rights I should call it quits between us. Both my pride and my principles demand no less. However, although I make no guarantees that I will be able to forget what you've done, and though we may both carry the scars for life, I refuse to let it stand between us. I still want you for my friend."

To accept forgiveness means to admit that you've done something unspeakable that needs to be forgiven, and thus both parties must swallow the same thing: their pride.

This seems to explain what Jesus means when he says to God, "Forgive us our trespasses as we forgive those who trespass against us." Jesus is *not* saying that God's forgiveness is conditional upon our forgiving others. In the first place, forgiveness that's conditional isn't really forgiveness at all, just fair warning; and in the second place, our unforgivingness is among those things about us that we need to have God forgive us most. What Jesus apparently *is* saying is that the pride that keeps us from forgiving is the same pride that keeps us from accepting forgiveness, and will God please help us do something about it.

When somebody you've wronged forgives you, you're spared the dull and self-diminishing throb of a guilty conscience.

When you forgive somebody who has wronged you, you're spared the dismal corrosion of bitterness and wounded pride.

For both parties, forgiveness means the freedom again to be at peace inside their own skins and to be glad in each other's presence.

See also principles.

FREEDOM

WE HAVE FREEDOM to the degree that the master whom we obey grants it to us in return for our obedience. We do well to choose a master in terms of how much freedom we get for how much obedience.

DAY 109

To obey the law of the land leaves us our constitutional freedom, but not the freedom to follow our own consciences wherever they lead.

To obey the dictates of our own consciences leaves us freedom from the sense of moral guilt, but not the freedom to gratify our own strongest appetites.

To obey our strongest appetites for drink, sex, power, revenge, or whatever leaves us the freedom of an animal to take what we want when we want it, but not the freedom of a human being to be human.

The old prayer speaks of God "in whose service is perfect freedom." The paradox is not as opaque as it sounds. It means that to obey Love itself, which above all else wishes us well, leaves us the freedom to be the best and gladdest that we have it in us to become. The only freedom Love denies us is the freedom to destroy ourselves ultimately.

See also hell.

FRIENDS

DAY 110

FRIENDS ARE PEOPLE you make part of your life just because you feel like it. There are lots of other ways people get to be part of each other's lives, like being related to each other, living near each other, sharing some special passion with each other like P. G. Wodehouse or jogging or lepidopterology, and so on, but though all or any of those may be involved in a friendship, they are secondary to it.

Basically your friends are not your friends for any particular reason. They are your friends for no particular reason. The job you do, the family you have, the way you vote, the major achievements and blunders of your life, your religious convictions or lack of them are all somehow set off to one side when the two of you get together. If you are old friends, you know all those things about each other and a lot more besides, but they are beside the point. Even if you talk about them, they are beside the point. Stripped, humanly speaking, to the bare essentials, you are yourselves the point. The usual distinctions of older-younger, richer-poorer, smarter-dumber, male-female even, cease to matter. You meet with a clean slate every time, and you meet on equal terms. Anything may come of it or nothing may. That doesn't matter either. Only the meeting matters.

"The Lord used to speak to Moses face to face, as a man speaks to a friend," the book of Exodus says (33:11), and in the book of Isaiah it is God himself who says the same thing of Abraham. "Abraham, my friend," he calls him (41:8). It is a staggering thought.

The love of God. The mercy of God. The judgment of God. You take the shoes off your feet and stand as you would before a mountain or at the edge of the sea. But the *friendship* of God?

It is not something God does. It is something Abraham and God or Moses and God do together. Not even God can be a friend all by himself apparently. You see Abraham, say, not standing at all, but sitting down, loosening his prayer shawl, trimming the end off his cigar. He is not being creature for the moment, and God is not being Creator. There is no agenda. They are simply being together, the two of them, and being themselves.

Is it a privilege only for patriarchs? Not as far as Jesus is concerned at least. "You are my friends," he says, "if you do what I command you." The command, of course, is "to love one another," as he puts it. To be his friends, that is to say, we have to be each other's friends, conceivably even lay down our lives for each other. You never know (John 15:12–15). It is a high price to pay, and Jesus does not pretend otherwise, but the implication is that it's worth every cent.

FUNERAL

IN ARAMAIC *talitha cumi* means "Little girl, get up." It's the language Jesus and his friends probably used when they spoke to each other, so these may well be his actual words, among the very few that have come down to us verbatim. He spoke them at a child's funeral, the twelve-year-old daughter of a man named Jairus (Mark 5:35–43).

The occasion took place at the man's house. There was plenty of the kind of sorrow you expect when anybody that young dies. And that's one of the great uses of funerals surely, to be cited when people protest that they're barbaric holdovers from the past, that you should celebrate the life rather than mourn the death, and so on. Celebrate the life by all means, but face up to the death of that life. Weep all the tears you have in you to weep, because whatever may happen next, if anything does, this has happened. Something precious and irreplaceable has come to an end and something in you has come to an end with it. Funerals put a period after the sentence's last word. They close a door. They let you get on with your life.

The child was dead, but Jesus, when he got there, said she was only asleep. He said the same thing when his friend Lazarus died. Death is not any more permanent than sleep is permanent is what he meant apparently. That isn't to say he took death lightly. When he heard about Lazarus, he wept, and it's hard to imagine him doing any differently here. But if death is the closing of one door, he seems to say, it is the opening of another one. *Talitha cumi.* He took the little girl's hand, and he told her to get up, and she did. The mother and father were there, Mark says. The neighbors, the friends. It is a scene to conjure with.

Old woman, get up. Young man. The one you don't know how you'll ever manage to live without. The one you don't know how you ever managed to live with. Little girl. "Get up," he says.

The other use of funerals is to remind us of those two words. When the last hymn has been sung, the benediction given, and the immediate family escorted out a side door, they may be the best we have to make it possible to *get up* ourselves.

GABRIEL

DAY 112 **S**HE STRUCK THE ANGEL GABRIEL as hardly old enough to have a child at all, let alone this child, but he'd been entrusted with a message to give her, and he gave it.

He told her what the child was to be named, and who he was to be, and something about the mystery that was to come upon her. "You mustn't be afraid, Mary," he said.

As he said it, he only hoped she wouldn't notice that beneath the great, golden wings he himself was trembling with fear to think that the whole future of creation hung now on the answer of a girl.

Luke 1:26–35

GAME

DAY 113 **G**AMES ARE SUPPOSED TO BUILD CHARACTER. The Battle of Waterloo was won on the playing fields of Eton and all that. Healthy competition is supposed to be good for you.

Is competition ever healthy—the desire to do better, be better, look better than somebody else? Do you write better poetry or play better tennis or do better in business or stand in higher esteem generally, even in self-esteem, if your chief motivation is to be head of the pack? Even if you win the rat race, as somebody has said, are you any less a rat?

Who wants to win if somebody else has to lose? Who dares to lose if it's crucial to win?

"Ah, but it's not winning that counts. It's how you play the game," they say. Maybe neither of them counts. Maybe it's not competition but cooperation and comradeship that build the only character worth building. If it's by playing games together that we learn to win battles, maybe it's by playing, say, music together that we learn to avoid them.

There are moments when Saint Paul sounds like a competitor with a vengeance, but there are happily other moments as well. "Let us run with perseverance the race that is set before us," he says (Hebrews 12:1), where the object is not to get there first, but just to get there. And "Fight the good fight," he says (1 Timothy 6:12), where it's not the fight to overcome the best of the competition that he's talking about, but the fight to overcome the worst in ourselves.

GAY

THE WORD *gay* in the sense of homosexual seems to have come into use somewhere in the 1930s or 1940s for reasons that are obscure. It was an improvement over the various terms that preceded it, but the choice was not a happy one.

In the first place *gay* in the original sense of lighthearted and debonair seems no more applicable to homosexuals than to anybody

DAY 114

else, and in the second place people rarely use it in that sense anymore for fear of being misunderstood or snickered at.

The result is that we have virtually replaced a lovely old adjective with a peculiarly misleading one and incidentally ruined some of the best lines W. B. Yeats ever wrote, in which he said of two old Chinamen that "Their eyes mid many wrinkles, their eyes, / Their ancient, glittering eyes, are gay."

It is nice to have more or less gotten rid of the likes of *faggot* and *queer,* but one can only hope that eventually, along with everybody else, homosexuals will be referred to simply as human beings.

See also homosexuality.

GENTLEMAN/GENTLEWOMAN

DAY 115

BY ONE DEFINITION gentlemen and gentlewomen are people who have gone to the schools and colleges everybody's heard of, don't talk with their mouths full, avoid using *like* as a conjunction, don't make scenes in public, and so on. They are apt to turn up in such places as country clubs, the society pages, and restaurants in which proper dress is required. They may commit murder from time to time, but they rarely end up in the electric chair. If a child of yours marries one of them, you figure he or she has done all right. If they're usually no better than other people, they are usually no worse either. Or if they are, it at least doesn't show so much.

But there are gentlewomen and gentlemen in another sense who may be none of the above. They may speak atrocious English and get their clothes at rummage sales. They may leave their spoons in their coffee cups and douse their french fries with ketchup. There are some of them who, if they turned up at a country club, would be directed to the service entrance. Some are educated, and some barely made it through grade school. Some are captains of industry, and some pump gas for a living. But whatever the differences between them, the common denominator is even more striking.

Gentle is the key word, of course. Their table manners may be appalling, but their courtesy is instinctive. They let you take the seat by the window or have first go at the morning paper not because it's in *Emily Post,* but because it's in their nature. They seem to be born knowing when to come around and when to stay away. If you have them over for supper, they know when it's time to go home. Their wit may be sharp, but it never cuts. Even in private they don't make scenes if they can possibly help it.

They have their hang-ups and abysses and blind spots like everybody else, but when Jesus said, "Blessed are the meek," if it wasn't exactly them he was talking about, the chances are it was people very much like them.

See also Beatitudes.

GHOST

WHAT KEEPS GHOSTS GOING seems to be usually some ancient tragedy they can't cut loose from or some dramatic event they are perpetually reenacting or some unfinished business they never seem able to resolve. They are so shadowy that it's hard to believe they exist. Some of the more spectacular hauntings—cups and saucers flying through the air, midnight wailings, a haggard face at the window—suggest they may have grave doubts on the subject themselves. It seems to be that if they can only make somebody's hair stand on end, possibly their own even, it helps

DAY 116

convince them they aren't just figments of their own imagination. They prefer deserted places because they feel deserted. They disappear at cockcrow because the idea of seeing themselves, or being seen, for what they truly are scares the daylights out of them.

If you want to see one, take a look in the mirror someday when you yourself are feeling particularly haggard and shadowy.

GIDEON

DAY 117

THE BEST THING THE JUDGE GIDEON ever did and the worst mistake he ever made came within moments of each other.

The best was when the Israelites asked him to be their king, and he turned down the invitation. Like the prophet Samuel years later, he knew that the only true king the Israelites would ever have was Yahweh, and he told them so. If he had any secret hankerings for personal power, he managed to squelch them. It was a noble move, and when you consider all the trouble Israel had with kings when it finally got them, it showed amazing wisdom and foresight.

And then the mistake. All the boys were wearing gold earrings that season, and when Gideon asked them to contribute them to the cause, they cheerfully agreed. Somebody laid a coat on the ground, and as soon as the earrings were all tossed in, Gideon added some more golden gewgaws he'd taken from the enemy, things like crescents and pendants and collars for prize camels. By the time he was through, he had a great glittering pile out of which he made an ephod. Nobody's quite sure what an ephod was in this case, but it was apparently some sort of religious *objet d'art* that Gideon thought would remind everybody who their true king really was. Only that's not the way things worked out.

Gideon's mistake was to forget that the second of the Ten Commandments is "Thou shalt not make unto thee any graven image" (Exodus 20:4) and that it's not by accident that it stands that high on the list. As soon as you've got a golden god you can shine up and deck out and push around like a doll in a baby carriage, you start thinking God himself is somebody you can push around too. The next step, of course, is that you think the graven image is God, and by that time it has about as much genuine religious significance as a rabbit's foot or a charm against the evil eye.

Instead of looking at the ephod and thinking about Yahweh, the Israelites started kowtowing to the ephod and hardly giving Yahweh the time of day. After Gideon died, they started kowtowing to the kinds of things you win tossing hoops at a carnival, and Yahweh was all but forgotten.

Poor Gideon. He might almost have done better to let them make him king when they wanted to. At least he would have been able to keep them on the right track that way, and they would have been able to keep their earrings, and Yahweh would have been able to keep in closer touch with his people than for their many long, sad years of god sampling was possible again. *Judges 8:22–28*

See also Samuel.

GLORY

Glory is to God what style is to an artist. A painting by Vermeer, a sonnet by Donne, a Mozart aria—each is so rich with the style of the one who made it that to the connoisseur it couldn't have been made by anybody else, and the effect is staggering. The style of artists brings you as close to the sound of their voices and the light in their eyes as it is possible to get this side of actually shaking hands with them.

DAY 118

In the words of Psalm 19:1, "The heavens are telling the glory of God." It is the same thing. To the connoisseur, not just sunsets and starry nights, but dust storms, rain forests, garter snakes, and the human face are all unmistakably the work of a single hand. Glory is the outward manifestation of that hand in its handiwork just as holiness is the inward. To behold God's glory, to sense God's style, is the closest you can get to God this side of paradise, just as to read *King Lear* is the closest you can get to Shakespeare.

Glory is what God looks like when for the time being all you have to look at him with is a pair of eyes.

See also holiness.

GLUTTONY

DAY 119   A GLUTTON IS ONE WHO RAIDS THE ICEBOX for a cure for spiritual malnutrition.

GOD

DAY 120   THERE MUST BE A GOD because (a) since the beginning of history, the most variegated majority of people have intermittently believed there was; (b) it is hard to consider the vast and complex structure of the universe in general and of the human mind in particular without considering the possibility that they issued from some ultimate source, itself vast, complex, and somehow mindful; (c) built into the very being of even the most primitive human there seems to be a profound psychophysical need or hunger for something like truth, goodness, love, and—under one alias or another—for God; and (d) every age and culture has produced mystics who have experienced a Reality beyond reality and have come back using different words and images but obviously and without collusion describing with awed adoration the same Indescribability.

Statements of this sort and others like them have been advanced for several thousand years as proofs of the existence of God. A twelve-year-old child can see that no one of them is watertight. And even all of them taken together won't convince any of us unless our predisposition to be convinced outweighs our predisposition not to be.

It is as impossible to prove or disprove that God exists beyond the various and conflicting ideas people have dreamed up about God as it is to prove or disprove that goodness exists beyond the various and conflicting ideas people have dreamed up about what is good.

It is as impossible for us to demonstrate the existence of God as it would be for even Sherlock Holmes to demonstrate the existence of Arthur Conan Doyle.

All-wise. All-powerful. All-loving. All-knowing. We bore to death both God and ourselves with our chatter. God cannot be expressed, only experienced.

See also religion, Yahweh.

GOLIATH

GOLIATH STOOD 10 FEET TALL in his stocking feet, wore a size 20 collar, a 9½-inch hat, and a 52-inch belt. When he put his full armor on, he looked like a Sherman tank. Even stripped to the bare essentials, he had plenty to carry around, and flesh and bones were the least of it. There was the burdensome business of having to defend his title against all comers. There were the mangled remains of the runners-up. When he tried to think something out,

DAY 121

it was like struggling through a hip-deep bog. When he tried to explain something, it was like pushing a truck uphill. His dark moods were leaden and his light moods elephantine. He considered underarm deodorants a sign of effeminacy.

The stone from David's slingshot caught him between the eyes, and when he hit the dirt, windows rattled in their frames as far away as Ashkelon. The ringing in his ears drowned out the catcalls of the onlooking armies, and his vision was all but shot, but he could still see enough to make out the naked figure of a boy running toward him through the scrub. His hair streamed out behind him like copper, and he was as swift and light-footed as a deer.

As he straddled Goliath with Goliath's sword in his hand, the giant believed that what he was seeing was his own soul stripped of the unwieldy flesh at last for its journey to paradise, and when David presented the severed head to Saul later, there was an unmistakable smile on its great lips.   *1 Samuel 17:4–55*

GOMER

DAY 122   GOMER WAS ALWAYS GOOD COMPANY—a little heavy with the lipstick maybe, a little less than choosy about men and booze, a little loud, but great at a party and always good for a laugh. Then the prophet Hosea came along wearing a sandwich board that read "The End Is at Hand" on one side and "Watch Out" on the other.

The first time he asked her to marry him, she thought he was kidding. The second time she knew he was serious, but thought he was crazy. The third time she said yes. He wasn't exactly a swinger, but he had a kind face, and he was generous, and he wasn't all that crazier than everybody else. Besides, any fool could see he loved her.

Give or take a little, she even loved him back for a while, and they had three children, whom Hosea named with queer names like Not-pitied-for-God-will-no-longer-pity-Israel-now-that-it's-gone-to-the-dogs so that every time the roll was called at school, Hosea would be scoring a prophetic bull's-eye in absentia. But everybody could see the marriage wasn't going to last, and it didn't.

While Hosea was off hitting the sawdust trail, Gomer took to hitting as many night spots as she could squeeze into a night, and any resemblance between her next batch of children and Hosea was purely coincidental. It almost killed him, of course. Every time he raised a hand to her, he burst into tears. Every time she raised one to him, he was the one who ended up apologizing.

He tried locking her out of the house a few times when she wasn't in by five in the morning, but he always opened the door when she finally showed up and helped get her to bed if she couldn't see straight enough to get there herself. Then one day she didn't show up at all.

He swore that this time he was through with her for keeps, but of course he wasn't. When he finally found her, she was lying passed out in a highly specialized establishment located above an adult bookstore, and he had to pay the management plenty to let her out of her contract. She'd lost her front teeth and picked up some scars you had to see to believe, but Hosea had her back again and that seemed to be all that mattered.

He changed his sandwich board to read "God Is Love" on one side and "There's No End to It" on the other, and when he stood on the street corner belting out

How can I give you up, O Ephraim!
How can I hand you over, O Israel!
For I am God and no mortal,
The Holy One in your midst.

(Hosea 11:8–9)

nobody can say how many converts he made, but one thing that's for sure is that, including Gomer's, there was seldom a dry eye in the house.

(Hosea 1–3; 11)

GOOD-BYE

DAY 123

A WOMAN WITH A SCARF over her head hoists her six-year-old up onto the first step of the school bus. "Good-bye," she says.

A father on the phone with his freshman son has just finished bawling him out for his poor grades. There is mostly silence at the other end of the line. "Well, good-bye," the father says.

When the girl at the airport hears the announcement that her plane is starting to board, she turns to the boy who is seeing her off. "I guess this is good-bye," she says.

The noise of the traffic almost drowns out the sound of the word, but the shape of it lingers on the old man's lips. He tries to look vigorous and resourceful as he holds out his hand to the other old man. "Good-bye." This time they say it so nearly in unison that it makes them both smile.

It was a long while ago that the words *God be with you* disappeared into the word *good-bye*, but every now and again some trace of them still glimmers through.

GOOD FRIDAY

DAY 124

A CCORDING TO JOHN, the last words Jesus spoke from the cross were, "It is finished." Whether he meant "finished" as

brought to an end, in the sense of finality, or "finished" as brought
to completion, in the sense of fulfillment, nobody knows. Maybe
he meant both.

What was brought to an end was of course nothing less than his
life. The Gospels make no bones about that. He died as dead as any
man. All the days of his life led him to this day, and beyond this day
there would be no other days, and he knew it. It was finished now,
he said. He was finished. He had come to the last of all his moments, and because he was conscious still—alive to his death—
maybe, as they say the dying do, he caught one final glimpse of the
life he had all but finished living.

Who knows what he glimpsed as that life passed before him.
Maybe here and there a fragment preserved for no good reason like
old snapshots in a desk drawer: the play of sunlight on a wall, a
half-remembered face, something somebody said. A growing sense
perhaps of destiny: the holy man in the river, a gift for prayer, a gift
for moving simple hearts. One hopes he remembered good times,
although the Gospels record few—how he once fell asleep in a boat
as a storm was coming up, and how he went to a wedding where
water was the least of what was turned into wine. Then the failures
of the last days, when only a handful gathered to watch him enter
the city on the foal of an ass—and those very likely for the wrong
reasons. The terror that he himself had known for a few moments
in the garden, and that finally drove even the handful away. *Shalom*
then, the God in him moving his swollen lips to forgive them all, to
forgive maybe even God. Finished.

What was brought to completion by such a life and such a death
only he can know now, wherever he is, if he is anywhere. The *Christ*
of it is beyond our imagining. All we can know is the flesh and
blood of it, the *Jesus* of it. In that sense, what was completed was at
the very least a hope to live by, a mystery to hide our faces before, a

shame to haunt us, a dream of holiness to help make bearable our night.

GOSPEL

DAY 125 AS EVERYBODY KNOWS BY NOW, *gospel* means "good news." Ironically, it is some of the gospel's most ardent fans who try to turn it into bad news. For instance:

- "It all boils down to the Golden Rule. Just love thy neighbor, and that's all you have to worry about." What makes this bad news is that loving our neighbor is exactly what none of us is very good at. Most of the time, we have a hard time loving even our family and friends very effectively.
- "Jesus was a great teacher and the best example we have of how we ought to live." As a teacher, Jesus is at least matched by, for instance, Siddhartha Gautama. As an example, we can only look at Jesus and despair.
- "The resurrection is a poetic way of saying that the spirit of Jesus lives on as a constant inspiration to us all." If all the resurrection means is that Jesus' spirit lives on like Abraham Lincoln's or Adolf Hitler's but that otherwise he is just as dead as anybody else who cashed in two thousand years ago, then, as Saint Paul puts it, "our preaching is in vain and your faith is in vain" (1 Corinthians 15:14). If the enemies of Jesus succeeded for all practical purposes in killing him permanently around A.D. 30, then like Socrates, Thomas More, Dietrich Bonhoeffer, Martin Luther King, Jr., and so on, he is simply another saintly victim of the wickedness and folly of humankind, and the cross is a symbol of ultimate defeat.

What is both good and new about the good news is the wild claim that Jesus did not simply tell us that God loves us even in our wickedness and folly and wants us to love each other the same way and to love God too, but that if we will allow it to happen, God will actually bring about this unprecedented transformation of our hearts himself.

What is both good and new about the good news is the mad insistence that Jesus lives on among us not just as another haunting memory but as the outlandish, holy, and invisible power of God working not just through the sacraments, but in countless hidden ways to make even slobs like us loving and whole beyond anything we could conceivably pull off by ourselves.

Thus the gospel is not only good and new but, if you take it seriously, a holy terror. Jesus never claimed that the process of being changed from a slob into a human being was going to be a Sunday school picnic. On the contrary. Childbirth may occasionally be painless, but rebirth, never. Part of what it means to be a slob is to hang on for dear life to our slobbery.

See also sacrament.

GOVERNMENT

IT SEEMS SAFE TO SAY that if you were to take a confidential poll of the private citizens of the nations of the world, all but a handful of firebrands and crazies would come out in favor of peace at pretty much any price. They have their conflicting political systems, ideologies, and holy causes to be sure, but by and large they give the strong impression of asking little more than a chance to raise their children as best they can, keep the wolf from the door,

DAY 126

have some fun when they're through working at the end of the day, find some sort of security against old age, and all such as that.

Their leaders, on the other hand, are continually delivering ultimatums to each other, plotting to confound each other any way they can manage it, spying on each other, vilifying each other, impugning each other's motives, spending billions on weapons to destroy each other, and all such as that.

If at this most basic level, governments don't reflect the dreams of the people they govern or serve their wills, you wonder what on earth governments are. Reading the papers, you get the sense of them as small, irascible groups within each capital—far more of them men than women—who behave in ways that under normal circumstances would land them in the slammer in no time flat. They seem to have a life and purpose of their own quite apart from the lives and purposes of anybody else. They are perpetually locked in desperate struggles with each other that have little if anything to do with the general human struggle to live and let live with as little fuss as possible. It's we ourselves who have given them the power to pull the whole world down on all our heads, and yet we seem virtually powerless to stop them.

We need governments to collect taxes, keep the roads in repair, maintain order in the streets and justice in the courts, and so on, but we certainly don't need this. They don't pay us—we pay them—yet they're the ones who call the shots while the rest of us stand by with our knees knocking. Gulliver in all his travels never came across anything to equal it.

GRACE

DAY 127   AFTER CENTURIES of handling and mishandling, most religious words have become so shopworn nobody's much interested anymore. Not so with *grace,* for some reason. Mysteriously, even derivatives like *gracious* and *graceful* still have some of the bloom left.

Grace is something you can never get but can only be given. There's no way to earn it or deserve it or bring it about any more than you can deserve the taste of raspberries and cream or earn good looks or bring about your own birth.

A good sleep is grace and so are good dreams. Most tears are grace. The smell of rain is grace. Somebody loving you is grace. Loving somebody is grace. Have you ever *tried* to love somebody?

A crucial eccentricity of the Christian faith is the assertion that people are saved by grace. There's nothing *you* have to do. There's nothing you *have* to do. There's nothing you have to *do.*

The grace of God means something like: "Here is your life. You might never have been, but you *are,* because the party wouldn't have been complete without you. Here is the world. Beautiful and terrible things will happen. Don't be afraid. I am with you. Nothing can ever separate us. It's for you I created the universe. I love you."

There's only one catch. Like any other gift, the gift of grace can be yours only if you'll reach out and take it.

Maybe being able to reach out and take it is a gift too.

See also justification.

GRANDCHILDREN

T O HAVE GRANDCHILDREN is not only to be given something but to be given something back.

DAY 128

You are given back something of your children's childhood all those years ago. You are given back something of what it was like to be a young parent. You are given back something of your own childhood even, as on creaking knees you get down on the floor to play tiddlywinks, or sing about Old MacDonald and his farm, or watch Saturday morning cartoons till you're cross-eyed.

It is not only your own genes that are part of your grandchildren but the genes of all sorts of people they never knew but who, through them, will play some part in times and places they never dreamed of. And of course along with your genes, they will also carry their memories of you into those times and places too—the afternoon you lay in the hammock with them watching the breezes blow, the face you made when one of them stuck out a tongue dyed Popsicle blue at you, the time you got a splinter out for one of them with the tweezers of your Swiss army knife. On some distant day they will hold grandchildren of their own with the same hands you once held them by as you searched the beach at low tide for Spanish gold.

In the meantime, they are the freshest and fairest you have. After you're gone, it is mainly because of them that the earth will not be as if you never walked on it.

GUILT

DAY 129

GUILT IS THE RESPONSIBILITY for wrongdoing. Apart from the wrong we are each of us responsible for personally, in a sense no wrong is done anywhere that we are not all of us responsible for collectively. With or without knowing it, either through what we have done or what we have failed to do, we have all helped create the kind of world mess that makes wrongdoing inevitable.

The danger of our guilt, both personal and collective, is less that we won't take it to heart than that we'll take it to heart overmuch and let it fester there in ways that we ourselves often fail to recognize. We condemn in others the wrong we don't want to face in ourselves. We grow vindictive against the right for showing up our wrong as wrong. The sense of our own inner brokenness estranges us from the very ones who could help patch us together again. We steer clear of setting things right with the people we have wronged since their mere presence is a thorn in our flesh. Our desire to be clobbered for our guilt and thus rid of it tempts us to do things we will be clobbered for. The dismal variations are endless. More often than not, guilt is not merely the consequence of wrongdoing, but the extension of it.

It is about as hard to absolve yourself of your own guilt as it is to sit in your own lap. Wrongdoing sparks guilt sparks wrongdoing ad nauseum, and we all try to disguise the grim process from both ourselves and everybody else. In order to break the circuit we need friends before whom we can put aside the disguise, trusting that when they see us for what we fully are, they won't run away screaming with, if nothing worse, laughter. Our trust in them leads us to trust their trust in us. In their presence the fact of our guilt no longer makes us feel and act out our guiltiness. For a moment at least the vicious circle stops circling and we can step down onto the firm ground of their acceptance, where maybe we'll be able to walk a straight line again. "Your sins are forgiven," Jesus said to the paralytic, then "Rise," whereupon the man picked up his bed and went home (Matthew 9:2–7).

HAGAR

DAY 130

SARAH COULDN'T HAVE CHILDREN, so she persuaded her husband, Abraham, to have a child with her lady's maid Hagar instead. Abraham and Hagar both proved willing, and soon a child
was on the way.

As you'd think one of them might have foreseen, however, there
are certain problems inherent in a *ménage à trois* that are not
solved by the prospect of its becoming a *ménage à quatre. Au con-
traire.*

As Sarah saw it, Hagar no longer walked around the house, she
flounced, and whenever she had a craving for things like bagels and
lox, naturally Abraham went out and got them for her. In no time
at all Sarah was livid with jealousy. Eager for peace at any price,
Abraham said to go ahead and fire Hagar then if that would make
things better, and within a short time Hagar was out on the street
with all her belongings piled around her, including a layette.

It wasn't long, however, before an angel found her there and
persuaded her to go back in and try to patch things up with her

mistress. Not having anything better in mind, Hagar agreed. Then the angel told her that the Lord had taken pity on her and wanted her to know that she was to name her baby Ishmael when he came. He also wanted her to know that though Ishmael was never going to win any popularity contests, he would nonetheless be the first of a multitude of descendants. It was a promise. Much cheered by this, Hagar returned to the house through the servants' entrance, ate humble pie, and was eventually given back her old job. A few months later, Ishmael was born, just as the Lord had said.

But her troubles weren't over. To the stupefaction of her gynecologists, it wasn't long before Sarah herself gave birth to a son named Isaac, who God promised would be the father of a great nation. This was so far beyond her wildest expectations, not to mention everybody else's, that for a while she was as happy as she'd ever been; but then one day she found Isaac and Ishmael playing together in the nursery, and once again the fat was in the fire.

She was convinced that her upstairs son would have to split his inheritance with Hagar's downstairs brat, so for the second time she nagged Abraham into driving them both out of the house permanently. When they got as far as Beersheba, they ran out of water. Hagar gave up her son for dead and sat down and wept.

It all ended happily, however. This time the Lord took care of her personally. First he produced a well and then he told her to dry her eyes because not only would her son live, but he gave her his word that the boy would grow up to be the father of a great nation just like his half brother, Isaac, back home. And so it came to pass.

The story of Hagar is the story of the terrible jealousy of Sarah and the singular ineffectuality of Abraham and the way Hagar, who knew how to roll with the punches, managed to survive them both. Above and beyond that, however, it is the story of how in the midst of the whole unseemly affair the Lord, half tipsy with compassion, went around making marvelous promises and loving everybody and creating great nations like the last of the big-time spenders handing out hundred-dollar bills.

Genesis 16; 21

HAM

DAY 131

H AM WAS THE YOUNGEST of Noah's three sons and by tradition the progenitor of the black race.

After the Flood was over and the family had settled down into the wine business, Noah did a little too much sampling one hot afternoon and passed out buck naked in his tent. Ham happened to stick his head in at just the wrong moment and then, instead of keeping his mouth shut, went out and treated his brothers to a lurid account of what he'd seen.

When Noah sobered up and found out about it, he blew his top. Among some other unpleasant things he had to say was a curse to the effect that from that day forward Ham was to be his brothers' slave.

For generations certain preachers have pointed to this text as biblical sanction for whatever form of white supremacy happened to be going on at the time, all the way from literal slavery to separate but equal schools, segregated toilet facilities, and restricted housing.

"The Devil can cite Scripture for his purpose," says Shakespeare, and you can just see him standing up there with his paunch and his black robe citing it. As somebody once said, comparing the church to Noah's ark, if it weren't for the storm without, you could never stand the stench within.

Genesis 9:18–27

HATE

HATE IS AS ALL-ABSORBING AS LOVE, as irrational, and in its own way as satisfying. As lovers thrive on the presence of the beloved, haters revel in encounters with the ones they hate. They confirm them in all their darkest suspicions. They add fuel to all their most burning animosities. The anticipation of them makes the hating heart pound. The memory of them can be as sweet as young love.

The major difference between hating and loving is perhaps that, whereas to love somebody is to be fulfilled and enriched by the experience, to hate somebody is to be diminished and drained by it. Lovers, by losing themselves in their loving, find themselves, become themselves. Haters simply lose themselves. Theirs is the ultimately *consuming* passion.

DAY 132

HEALING

THE GOSPELS DEPICT JESUS as having spent a surprising amount of time healing people. Although, like the author of Job before him, he specifically rejected the theory that sickness was God's way of getting even with sinners (John 9:1–3), he nonetheless seems to have suggested a connection between sickness and sin, almost to have seen sin as a kind of sickness. "Those who are well have no need of a physician, but those who are sick," he said. "I came not to call the righteous but sinners" (Mark 2:17).

This is entirely compatible, of course, with the Hebrew view of the human being as a psychosomatic unity, an indivisible amalgam

DAY 133

of body and soul in which if either goes wrong, the other is affected. It is significant also that the Greek verb *sōzō* was used in Jesus' day to mean both "to save" and "to heal," and *sōtēr* could signify either "savior" or "physician."

Ever since the time of Jesus, healing has been part of the Christian tradition. Nowadays, it has usually been associated with religious quackery or the lunatic fringe; but as the psychosomatic dimension of disease has come to be taken more and more seriously by medical science, it has regained some of its former respectability. How nice for God to have this support at last.

Jesus is reported to have made the blind see and the lame walk, and over the centuries countless miraculous healings have been claimed in his name. For those who prefer not to believe in them, a number of approaches are possible, among them:

1. The idea of miracles is an offense both to our reason and to our dignity. Thus, a priori, miracles don't happen.

2. Unless there is objective medical evidence to substantiate the claim that a miraculous healing has happened, you can assume it hasn't.

3. If the medical authorities agree that a healing is inexplicable in terms of present scientific knowledge, you can simply ascribe this to the deficiencies of present scientific knowledge.

4. If otherwise intelligent and honest human beings are convinced, despite all arguments to the contrary, that it is God who has healed them, you can assume that their sickness, like its cure, was purely psychological. Whatever that means.

5. The crutches piled high at Lourdes and elsewhere are a monument to human humbug and credulity.

If your approach to this kind of healing is less ideological and more empirical, you can always give it a try. Pray for it. If it's somebody else's healing you're praying for, you can try at the same time laying your hands on her as Jesus sometimes did. If her sickness involves her body as well as her soul, then God may be able to use your inept hands as well as your inept faith to heal her.

If you feel like a fool as you are doing this, don't let it throw you. You are a fool, of course, only not a damned fool for a change.

If your prayer isn't answered, this may tell you more about you and your prayer than it does about God. Don't try too hard to feel religious, to generate some healing power of your own. Think of yourself instead (if you have to think of yourself at all) as a rather small-gauge clogged-up pipe that a little of God's power may be able to filter through if you can just stay loose enough. Tell the one you're praying for to stay loose too.

If God doesn't seem to be giving you what you ask, maybe he's giving you something else.

See also prayer.

HEARING

I F I CAN'T SEE YOU FOR SOME REASON but can only hear you, you don't exist for me in space, which is where seeing happens, but in time, which is where hearing happens. Your words follow one after the other the way tock follows tick. When I have only the sound of you to go by, I don't experience you as an object the way I would if you stood before me—something that I can walk around, inspect from all angles, more or less define. I experience you more the way I experience the beating of my own heart or the flow of my

DAY 134

own thoughts. A deaf man coming upon me listening to you would think that nothing of importance was going on. But something of extraordinary importance is going on. I am taking you more fully into myself than I can any other way. Hearing you speak brings me by the most direct of all routes something of the innermost secret of who you are.

It is no surprise that the Bible uses hearing, not seeing, as the predominant image for the way human beings know God. They can't walk around God and take God in like a cathedral or an artichoke. They can only listen to time for the sound of God—to the good times and bad times of their own lives for the words God is addressing to, of all people, them.

HEAVEN

DAY 135

A ND I SAW THE HOLY CITY, new Jerusalem, coming down out of heaven from God, prepared as a bride adorned for her husband; and I heard a great voice from the throne saying . . . 'Behold, I make all things new'" (Revelation 21:2–5).

Everything is gone that ever made Jerusalem, like all cities, torn apart, dangerous, heartbreaking, seamy. You walk the streets in peace now. Small children play unattended in the parks. No stranger goes by whom you can't imagine a fast friend. The city has become what those who loved it always dreamed and what in their dreams it always was. The *new* Jerusalem. That seems to be the secret of heaven. The new Chicago, Leningrad, Hiroshima, Baghdad. The new bus driver, hot-dog man, seamstress, hairdresser. The new you, me, everybody.

It was always buried there like treasure in all of us—the best we had it in us to become—and there were times you could almost see it. Even the least likely face, asleep, bore traces of it. Even the bombed-out city after nightfall with the public squares in a shambles and moonlight silvering the broken pavement. To speak of heavenly music or a heavenly day isn't always to gush but sometimes to catch a glimpse of something. "Death shall be no more, neither shall there be mourning nor crying nor pain any more," the book of Revelation says (21:4). You can catch a glimpse of that too in almost anybody's eyes if you choose the right moment to look, even in animals' eyes.

If the new is to be born, though, the old has to die. It is the law of the place. For the best to happen, the worst must stop happening— the worst we are, the worst we do. But maybe it isn't as difficult as it sounds. It was a hardened criminal within minutes of death, after all, who said only, "Jesus, remember me," and that turned out to be enough. "This day you will be with me in paradise" was the answer he just managed to hear.

See also eternal life.

HELL

PEOPLE ARE FREE IN THIS WORLD to live for themselves alone if they want to and let the rest go hang, and they are free to live out the dismal consequences as long as they can stand it. The doctrine of hell proclaims that they retain this same freedom in whatever world comes next. Thus the possibility of making damned fools of ourselves would appear to be limitless.

Or maybe hell is the limit. Since the damned are said to suffer as dismally in the next world as they do in this one, they must still have enough life left in them to suffer with, which means that in their flight from Love, God apparently stops them just this side of

DAY 136

extinguishing themselves utterly. Thus the bottomless pit is not really bottomless. Hell is the bottom beyond which the terrible mercy of God will not let them go.

Dante saw written over the gates of hell the words "Abandon all hope ye who enter here," but he must have seen wrong. If there is suffering life in hell, there must also be hope in hell, because where there is life there is the Lord and giver of life; and where there is suffering he is there too, because the suffering of the ones he loves is also his suffering.

"He descended into hell," the Apostles' Creed says, and "If I make my bed in Sheol, thou art there," says the Psalmist (139:8). It seems there is no depth to which he will not sink. Maybe not even Old Scratch will be able to hold out against him forever.

HELP

DAY 137   As they're used psychologically, words like *repression, denial, sublimation,* and *defense* all refer to one form or another of the way human beings erect walls to hide behind, both from each other and from themselves. You repress the memory that is too painful to deal with, say. You deny your weight problem. You sublimate some of your sexual energy by channeling it into other forms of activity more socially acceptable. You conceal your sense of inadequacy behind a defensive bravado. And so on and so forth. The inner state you end up with is a castlelike affair of keep, inner wall, outer wall, and moat, which you erect originally to be a fortress to keep the enemy out, but which turns into a prison where you become the jailer and thus your own enemy. It is a wretched and lonely place. You can't be what you want to be there or do what you want to do. People can't see through all that masonry to who you truly are, and half the time you're not sure you can see who you truly are yourself, you've been walled up so long.

Fortunately there are two words that offer a way out, and they're simply these: "Help me." It's not always easy to say them—you have your pride after all, and you're not sure there's anybody you trust enough to say them to—but they're always worth saying. To another human being—a friend, a stranger? To God? Maybe it comes to the same thing.

Help me. They open a door through the walls, that's all. At least hope is possible again. At least you're no longer alone.

HERETICS

Heretics are people who hold opinions at variance with established religious beliefs. In the old days, they were burned at the stake. Their books were banned. Wars were fought against them. They were an endangered species. As time passed, they grew to be so much in the majority that the tables have turned, and now what's in danger are established religious beliefs.

It's not that the opinions of heretics on matters like the Trinity, the sacraments, and the divinity of Jesus are at variance with orthodoxy, but that they have few if any opinions on such matters at all because such matters strike them as utterly irrelevant to the human condition. They're no longer out to bring the church around to their way of thinking, because by and large they're about as interested in what the church thinks as they are in how many angels could dance on the head of a pin if there were such things as angels.

Modern-day heretics are less opposed to religion than they are simply left cold by it, and when you consider how the church more

DAY 138

often than not proclaims the gospel—either passionlessly and un-convincingly or flamboyantly and phonily—it is no great wonder.

HEROD ANTIPAS

DAY 139

HEROD ANTIPAS, the tetrarch of Galilee and the son of Herod the Great, seems to have spent much of his life running scared.

When John the Baptist started criticizing his private life in pub-lic, Herod had him locked up for fear that otherwise he might be-come a fad, but he didn't dare have him executed for fear that John's fans might get themselves a new tetrarch if he did.

On his birthday he told Salome that he'd give her anything she asked for if she'd do her act with the seven veils for him, and when what she asked for was John the Baptist's head on a platter, he shook in his boots but gave it to her because he was afraid of what might happen if word got around that he was turning chicken.

He turned pale when he heard that a new prophet named Jesus was stirring up trouble because he was sure that it must be John come back from the grave to get even, and he decided to have him taken care of a second time. This threat doesn't seem to have espe-cially bothered Jesus, because when news of it reached him, he re-ferred to Herod as a fox and sent word back that he had bigger things on his mind to worry about. (His use of the word *fox* is in-teresting because, although then as now it could be used to suggest slyness, its more common use apparently was a term of contempt. *Pussycat* might be a better rendering. The fact that the Greek word is in the feminine gender may or may not be an allusion to some of Herod's more exotic proclivities.)

They finally came face-to-face, of course, Jesus of Nazareth and the tetrarch of Galilee. It was the night of Jesus' arrest, and when Pilate found out he was a Galilean and thus under that jurisdiction, he had him bundled off to Herod's headquarters immediately. He'd never been able to stand Herod's guts, Luke tells us, and was probably tickled pink to find this way of needling him.

Ironically enough, it appears that Herod was tickled pink too, because he'd apparently given up the idea that the man was John the Baptist's ghost and, again according to Luke, had been looking forward for a long time to seeing him perform some of his more spectacular tricks. He thought that if he was who they claimed he was, it should be quite a show. Unfortunately, Jesus refused to accommodate him or even to answer his questions, and, taking this to be a sign of weakness, Herod decided to have a little fun with him.

He had his soldiers rough him up for a while and then let them do some other things to him that struck them as appropriate to do to a man who'd been the cause of their having been woken up in the middle of the night. When all of this was finished, Herod had them doll him up in one of his fanciest tetrarch uniforms with a few hilarious additions and deletions and in that state sent him back to Pilate.

As luck would have it, Pilate turned out to have the same sense of humor, and Luke tells us that he and Herod became great friends from then on. It is nice to think that at least one good thing thus came out of that dark and harrowing night, and it is interesting also to note that on this one occasion when Herod might justifiably have been scared out of his wits, you would have thought he was watching a Punch and Judy show the way he threw back his head and howled. *Luke 13:31–35; 23:1–12; Matthew 14:1–12*

HEROD THE GREAT

DAY 140   THE FOOLISHNESS OF THE WISE is perhaps nowhere better illustrated than by the way the three Magi went to Herod the Great, king of the Jews, to find out the whereabouts of the holy child who had just been born king of the Jews to supplant him. It did not even strike them as suspicious when Herod asked them to be sure to let him know when they found him so he could hurry on down to pay his respects.

Luckily for the holy child, after the three Magi had followed their star to the manger and left him their presents, they were tipped off in a dream to avoid Herod like the plague on their way home.

Herod was fit to be tied when he realized he'd been had and ordered the murder of every male child two years old and under in the district. For all his enormous power, he knew there was somebody in diapers more powerful still. The wisdom of the foolish is perhaps nowhere better illustrated.   *Matthew 2*

HIRAM

DAY 141   HIRAM, KING OF TYRE, was in the lumber business, and when Solomon, king of Israel, decided he wanted to build the Temple in Jerusalem, Hiram let him have all the cedar and cypress he needed. He also charged such a cutthroat price for it that in order to pay up, Solomon had to tax his people blind and increase tolls on all the major highways.

Twenty years later, however, when the job was done and Hiram submitted his final bill, Solomon got a little of his own back by paying it in the form not of cash but of twelve Galilean cities whose turn-in value is suggested by the fact that when Hiram saw them, he called them Cabul, which means "No Place." According to the historian Josephus, Solomon followed this up by proposing a riddle contest, which Hiram lost hands down. As a result he had to give Solomon an enormous prize.

Josephus reports that Hiram bided his time for a while but then got hold of a friend named Abdemon, who made hash of Solomon's riddles in about twenty-five minutes, and at the end of that round it was Solomon who had to cough up an enormous prize for Hiram.

Unfortunately neither Josephus nor the book of Kings reports what new heights the friendship rose to after that.   *1 Kings 5; 9*

HISTORY

UNLIKE BUDDHISM OR HINDUISM, biblical faith takes his-   DAY 142
tory very seriously because God takes it very seriously. God took it seriously enough to begin it and to enter it and to promise that one day it will be brought to a serious close. The biblical view is that history is not an absurdity to be endured or an illusion to be dispelled or an endlessly repeating cycle to be escaped. Instead, it is for each of us a series of crucial, precious, and unrepeatable moments that are seeking to lead us somewhere.

The true history of humankind and the true history of each individual has less to do than we tend to think with the kind of information that gets into most histories, biographies, and autobiographies. True history has to do with the saving and losing of souls, and both of these are apt to take place when most people—including the one whose soul is at stake—are looking the other way. The real turning point in our lives is less likely to be the day we win the election or get married than the morning we decide not to mail the letter or the afternoon we watch the woods fill up with snow. The real turning point in human history is less apt to be the day the wheel is invented or Rome falls than the day a child is born in a stable.

HOLINESS

DAY 143

ONLY GOD IS HOLY, just as only people are human. God's holiness is God's Godness. To speak of anything else as holy is to say that it has something of God's mark upon it. Times, places, things, and people can all be holy, and when they are, they are usually not hard to recognize.

One holy place I know is a workshop attached to a barn. There is a wood-burning stove in it made out of an oil drum. There is a workbench, dark and dented, with shallow, crammed drawers behind one of which a cat lives. There is a girlie calendar on the wall, plus various lengths of chain and rope, shovels and rakes of different sizes and shapes, some worn-out jackets and caps on pegs, an electric clock that doesn't keep time. On the workbench are two small plug-in radios, both of which have serious things wrong with them. There are several metal boxes full of wrenches and a bench saw. There are a couple of chairs with rungs missing. There is an old yellow bulldozer with its tracks caked with mud parked against one wall. The place smells mainly of engine oil and smoke—both wood smoke and pipe smoke. The windows are small, and even on bright days what light there is comes through mainly in window-sized patches on the floor.

I have no idea why this place is holy, but you can tell it is the moment you set foot in it if you have an eye for that kind of thing. For reasons known only to God, it is one of the places God uses for sending God's love to the world through.

HOLOCAUST

I T IS IMPOSSIBLE to think about the Holocaust. It is impossible not to think about it. Nothing in history equals the horror of it. There is no way to imagine it. There is no way to speak of it without diminishing it. Thousands upon thousands were taken away in Nazi Germany during World War II. They were gassed. Their corpses were burned. Many were old men. Many were small children. Many were women. They were charged with nothing except being Jews. In the end there were apparently something like six million of them who died, six thousand thousands.

Anyone who claims to believe in an all-powerful, all-loving God without taking into account this devastating evidence either that God is indifferent or powerless, or that there is no God at all, is playing games.

Anyone who claims to believe in the inevitable perfectibility of the human race without taking this into account is either a fool or a lunatic.

That many of the people who took part in the killings were professing Christians, not to mention many more who knew about the killings but did nothing to interfere, is a scandal the church of Christ perhaps does not deserve to survive.

For people who don't believe in God, suffering can be understood simply as part of the way the world works. The Holocaust is

DAY 144

no more than an extreme example of the barbarities that human beings have been perpetrating on each other since the start. For people who do believe in God, it must remain always a dark and awful mystery.

If Love itself is really at the heart of all, how can such things happen? What do such things mean? The Old Testament speaks of the elusive figure of the Suffering Servant, who though "despised and rejected of men" and brutally misused, has nonetheless willingly "borne our griefs and carried our sorrows" and thereby won an extraordinary victory in which we all somehow share (Isaiah 52:13–53:12). The New Testament speaks of the cross, part of whose meaning is that even out of the worst the world can do, God is still able to bring about the best.

But all such explanations sound pale and inadequate before the gas chambers of Buchenwald and Ravensbrück, the ovens of Treblinka.

HOMELESSNESS

DAY 145   WE LIE IN OUR BEDS IN THE DARK. There is a picture of the children on the bureau. A patch of moonlight catches our clothes thrown over the back of a chair. We can hear the faint rumble of the furnace in the cellar. We are surrounded by the reassurance of the familiar. When the weather is bad, we have shelter. When things are bad in our lives, we have a place where we can retreat to lick our wounds while tens of thousands of people, many of them children, wander the dark streets in search of some corner to lie down in out of the wind.

Yet we are homeless even so in the sense of having homes but not being really at home in them. To be really at home is to be really at peace, and there can be no real peace for any of us until there is some measure of real peace for all of us. When we close our eyes to the deep needs of other people, whether they live on the streets or under our own roof—and when we close our eyes to our own deep need to reach out to them—we can never be fully at home anywhere.

HOMOSEXUALITY

ONE OF THE MANY WAYS that we are attracted to each other is sexually. We want to touch and be touched. We want to give and receive pleasure with our bodies. We want to know each other in our full nakedness, which is to say in our full humanness, and in the moment of passion to become one with each other. Whether it is our own gender or the other that we are chiefly attracted to seems a secondary matter. There is a female element in every male just as there is a male element in every female, and most people, if they're honest, will acknowledge having been at one time or another attracted to both.

DAY 146

To say that morally, spiritually, humanly, homosexuality is always bad seems as absurd as to say that in the same terms heterosexuality is always good, or the other way round. It is not the object of our sexuality that determines its value but the inner nature of our sexuality. If (a) it is as raw as the coupling of animals, at its worst it demeans us and at its best still leaves our deepest hunger for each other unsatisfied. If (b) it involves some measure of kindness, understanding, and affection as well as desire, it can become an expression of human love in its fullness and can thus help to complete us as humans. Whatever our sexual preference happens to be, both of these possibilities are always there. It's not whom you go to bed with or what you do when you get there that matters so much. It's what besides sex you are asking to receive, and what besides sex you are offering to give.

Here and there the Bible condemns homosexuality in the sense of (a), just as under the headings of adultery and fornication it also condemns heterosexuality in the sense of (a). On the subject of homosexuality in the sense of (b), it is as silent as it is on the subject of sexuality generally in the sense of (b). The great commandment is that we are to love one another—responsibly, faithfully, joyfully—and presumably the biblical view is implied in that.

Beyond that, "Love is strong as death," sings Solomon in his song. "Many waters cannot quench love, neither can floods drown it" (Song of Solomon 8:6–7). Whoever you are and whoever it is you desire, the passion of those lines is something you are quick to recognize.

HOPE

DAY 147

For CHRISTIANS, hope is ultimately hope in Christ. The hope that he really is what for centuries we have been claiming he is. The hope that despite the fact that sin and death still rule the world, he somehow conquered them. The hope that in him and through him all of us stand a chance of somehow conquering them too. The hope that at some unforeseeable time and in some unimaginable way he will return with healing in his wings.

No one in the New Testament calls a spade a spade as unflinchingly as Saint Paul. "If Christ has not been raised, your faith is futile," he wrote to the Corinthians. "If for this life only we have hoped in Christ, we are of all people most to be pitied" (1 Corinthians 15:17, 19). That is the possibility in spite of which Saint Paul and the rest of us go on hoping even so. That is the possibility that led Dostoyevski to write to a friend, "If anyone proved to me that Christ was outside the truth, and it really was so that the truth was outside Christ, then I would prefer to remain with Christ than with the truth."

See also cross, wishful thinking.

HUMANKIND

HUMANS ARE SO THE UNIVERSE will have something to talk through, so God will have something to talk with, and so the rest of us will have something to talk about.

DAY 148

The biblical view of the history of humankind and of each individual man or woman is contained in the first three chapters of Genesis. We are created to serve God by loving God and each other in freedom and joy, but we invariably choose bondage and woe instead as prices not too high to pay for independence. To say that God drove Adam and Eve out of Eden is apparently a euphemism for saying that Adam and Eve, like the rest of us, made a break for it as soon as God happened to look the other way. If God really wanted to get rid of us, the chances are God wouldn't have kept hounding us every step of the way ever since.

See also history, justification.

HUMILITY

HUMILITY IS OFTEN CONFUSED with saying you're not much of a bridge player when you know perfectly well you are.

DAY 149

Conscious or otherwise, this kind of humility is a form of gamesmanship.

If you really *aren't* much of a bridge player, you're apt to be rather proud of yourself for admitting it so humbly. This kind of humility is a form of low comedy.

True humility doesn't consist of thinking ill of yourself but of not thinking of yourself much differently from the way you'd be apt to think of anybody else. It is the capacity for being no more and no less pleased when you play your own hand well than when your opponents do.

See also pride.

HUMOR

DAY 150

A GOOD JOKE is one that catches you by surprise—like God's, for instance. Who would have guessed that Israel of all nations would be the one God picked or Sarah would have Isaac at the age of ninety or the Messiah would turn up in a manger? Who could possibly see the duck-billed platypus coming or Saint Simeon Stylites or the character currently occupying the pulpit at First Presbyterian? The laugh in each case results from astonished delight at the sheer unexpectedness of the thing.

Satan's jokes, on the other hand, you can usually spot a mile off. As soon as the serpent came slithering up to Adam and Eve, almost anybody could tell that the laugh was going to be on them. That a person as blameless, upright, and well-heeled as Job was bound to have the rug pulled out from under him before he was through. That Faust, being Faust, was sure to be conned out of his soul. And so on.

In the last analysis, the only one who gets much of a kick out of Satan's jokes is Satan himself. With God's, however, even the most hardened cynics and bitterest pessimists have a hard time repressing an occasional smile. When God really gets going, even the morning stars burst into singing and all the sons of God shout for joy.

IDOLATRY

IDOLATRY IS THE PRACTICE of ascribing absolute value to things of relative worth. Under certain circumstances, money, patriotism, sexual freedom, moral principles, family loyalty, physical beauty, social or intellectual preeminence, and so on are fine things to have around; but to make them the standard by which all other values are measured, to make them your masters, to look to them to justify your life and save your soul is sheerest folly. They just aren't up to it.

Idolatry is always popular among religious people, but idols made out of things like the denomination, the Bible, the liturgy, the holy images are apt to seem so limited in real power even to their idolaters that there is always the hope that in time they will overthrow themselves.

It is among the unreligious that idolatry is a particular menace. Having ushered God out once and for all through the front door, the unbeliever is under constant temptation to replace God with something spirited in through the service entrance. From the moment the eighteenth-century French revolutionaries set up the goddess of Reason on the high altar of Notre Dame, there wasn't a head in all Paris that was safe.

IMAGINATION

EVEN A THOUSAND MILES inland you can smell the sea and hear the mewing of gulls if you give thought to it. You can see in your mind's eye the living faces of people long dead or hear in the mind's ear the United States Marine Band playing "The Stars and Stripes Forever." If you work at it, you can smell the smell of autumn leaves burning or taste a chocolate malted. You don't have to be asleep to dream dreams either. There are those who can come up with dramas laid twenty thousand leagues under the sea or take a little girl through a looking glass. Imagining is perhaps as close as humans get to creating something out of nothing the way God is said to. It is a power that to one degree or another everybody has or can develop, like whistling. Like muscles, it can be strengthened through practice and exercise. Keep at it until you can actually hear your grandfather's voice, for instance, or feel the rush of hot air when you open the 450-degree oven.

DAY 152

If imagination plays a major role in the creation of literature, it plays a major one also in the appreciation of it. It is essential to read imaginatively as well as to write imaginatively if you want to know what's really going on. A good novelist helps us do this by stimulating our imaginations—sensory detail is especially useful in this regard, such as the way characters look and dress, the sounds and smells of the places they live and so on—but then we have to do our part. It is especially important to do it in reading the Bible. *Be* the man who trips over a suitcase of hundred-dollar bills buried in the field he's plowing if you want to know what the Kingdom of Heaven is all about (Matthew 13:44). Listen to Jesus saying, "Come unto me, all ye that labor and are heavy laden, and I will give you rest" (Matthew 11:28) until you can *hear* him, if you want to know what faith is all about.

If you want to know what loving your neighbors is all about, look at them with more than just your eyes. The bag lady settling down for the night on the hot-air grating. The two children chirping like birds in the branches of a tree. The bride as she walks down the aisle on her father's arm. The old man staring into space in the nursing-home TV room. Try to know them for who they are inside their skins. Hear not just the words they speak, but the words they do not speak. Feel what it's like to be who they are—chirping like a bird because for the moment you are a bird, trying not to wobble as you move slowly into the future with all eyes upon you.

When Jesus said, "All ye that labor and are heavy laden," he was seeing the rich as well as the poor, the lucky as well as the unlucky, the idle as well as the industrious. He was seeing the bride on her wedding day. He was seeing the old man in front of the TV. He was seeing all of us. The highest work of the imagination is to have eyes like that.

IMMORTALITY

DAY 153   IMMORTAL MEANS DEATH-PROOF. To believe in the immortality of the soul is to believe that though John Brown's body lies a-moldering in the grave, his soul goes marching on simply because marching on is the nature of souls just the way producing butterflies is the nature of caterpillars. Bodies die, but souls don't.

True or false, this is not the biblical view, although many who ought to know better assume it is. The biblical view differs in several significant ways:

1. As someone has put it, the biblical understanding of human beings is not that they *have* bodies, but that they *are* bodies. God made Adam by slapping some mud together to make a body and then breathing some breath into it to make a living soul. Thus the body and soul that make up human beings are as inextricably part and parcel of each other as the leaves and flames that make up a bonfire. When you kick the bucket, you kick it 100 percent. All of you. There is nothing left to go marching on with.

2. The idea that the body dies and the soul doesn't is an idea that implies that the body is something rather gross and embarrassing, like a case of hemorrhoids. The Greeks spoke of it as the prison house of the soul. The suggestion was that to escape it altogether was something less than a disaster.

    The Bible, on the other hand, sees the body in particular and the material world in general as a good and glorious invention. How could it be otherwise when it was invented by a good and glorious God?

    The Old Testament rings loud with the praise of trees and birds and rain and mountains, of wine that gladdens our hearts and oil that makes our faces shine and bread that strengthens us. Read Psalm 104, for instance. Or try the Song of Solomon for as abandoned and unabashed a celebration of the physical as you're apt to find anywhere.

As for the New Testament, Jesus himself, far from being a world-denying ascetic, was accused of being a wino and a chowhound (Matthew 11:19). When he heard that his friend Lazarus was dead, he didn't mouth any pious clichés about what a merciful release it was. He wept.

The whole idea of incarnation, of the word becoming flesh, affirms the physical and fleshly in yet another way, by declaring that it was a uniform even God wasn't ashamed to wear.

Saint Paul undoubtedly had his hang-ups, but when he compares flesh unfavorably to spirit, he is not talking about body versus soul, but about the old person without Christ versus the new person with him.

3. Those who believe in the immortality of the soul believe that life after death is as natural a human function as waking after sleep.

The Bible, instead, speaks of resurrection. It is entirely unnatural. We do not go on living beyond the grave because that's how we are made. Rather, we go to our graves as dead as a doornail and are given our lives back again by God (i.e., resurrected), just as we were given them by God in the first place, because that is the way God is made.

4. All the major Christian creeds affirm belief in resurrection *of the body.* In other words, they affirm the belief that what God in spite of everything prizes enough to bring back to life is not just some disembodied echo of human beings but a new and revised version of all the things that made them the particular human beings they were and that they need something like a body to express: their personality, the way

they looked, the sound of their voices, their peculiar capacity for creating and loving, in some sense their *faces*.

5. The idea of the immortality of the soul is based on the experience of humanity's indomitable spirit. The idea of the resurrection of the body is based on the experience of God's unspeakable love.

See also incarnation.

INCARNATION

"THE WORD BECAME FLESH," wrote John, "and dwelt among us, full of grace and truth" (John 1:14). That is what incarnation means. It is untheological. It is unsophisticated. It is undignified. But according to Christianity, it is the way things are. DAY 154

All religions and philosophies that deny the reality or the significance of the material, the fleshly, the earthbound, are themselves denied. Moses at the burning bush was told to take off his shoes because the ground on which he stood was holy ground (Exodus 3:5), and incarnation means that all ground is holy ground because God not only made it but walked on it, ate and slept and worked and died on it. If we are saved anywhere, we are saved here. And what is saved is not some diaphanous distillation of our bodies and our earth, but our bodies and our earth themselves. Jerusalem becomes the New Jerusalem coming down out of heaven like a bride adorned for her husband (Revelation 21:2). Our bodies are sown perishable and raised imperishable (1 Corinthians 15:42).

One of the blunders religious people are particularly fond of making is the attempt to be more spiritual than God.

INNOCENCE

DAY 155   "BE WISE AS SERPENTS and innocent as doves," Jesus told the disciples when he sent them off to spread the good news (Matthew 10:16). In other words, you can be both. Innocence doesn't mean being Little Red Riding Hood. You can know which side is up. You can have been around. Certainly the disciples had—fishermen, husbands and fathers, a tax collector—and Jesus thought them capable of being innocent even so. But they were to be sharp-eyed, not wide-eyed. He was sending them out "as sheep in the midst of wolves," he said, and they would need their wits about them. They were to be smart sheep.

Innocent people may be up to their necks in muck with the rest of us, but the mark of their innocence is that it never seems to stick to them. Things may be rotten all around them, but they preserve a curious freshness. Even when, like the disciple Peter, they are guilty of tragic flaws and failures, you feel that some inner purity remains untouched. Everybody knew, for instance, that the woman who washed Jesus' feet in Simon the Pharisee's house was no better than she ought to be, but as she dried them with her hair and kissed them, apart from Simon there was no one there, least of all Jesus, who would have dreamed of holding it against her (Luke 7:36–49).

INSECTS

DAY 156   THE FLY IN THE SOUP. The ant at the picnic. The silverfish in the shirt drawer. The mosquito at three o'clock in the morning. *Pests* is what we have come to call them, as if that were their proper name, and it is not hard to see why. Even the most tenderhearted among us exterminates them without a qualm, and my guess is that St. Francis himself would understand and forgive.

It takes a microscope to see them in all their indescribable intricacy, but even the naked eye can see enough to know that no less than ourselves, they are part of the great web of life and that even the tiniest and most tiresome among them, as also among us, is precious beyond telling.

ISAAC

WITH ONE POSSIBLE EXCEPTION, there has perhaps never DAY 157 been a birth more longed for and rejoiced in than Isaac's. Sarah was in her nineties when an angel told her that after years of barrenness she and her centenarian husband, Abraham, were finally going to have the child God had promised them, and their wild and incredulous mirth at this news prompted them to name him Isaac, which in Hebrew means "laughter." He is a shadowy figure compared to his father, Abraham, and his son Jacob, but at certain moments in his life the shadows recede, and he stands on the stage in a flood of light.

He was just a boy when, to see what Abraham was made of, God said that he was to take Isaac up into the hills and make a burnt offering of him. Abraham didn't have the heart to tell him what was going to happen, and if Isaac guessed, he didn't have the heart to admit that he did as they trudged side by side up the steep track. A mule was loaded down with the things they needed for making the fire, but the sacrificial animal was conspicuously absent, and when Isaac asked about it, Abraham choked out an evasive answer as best he could. By the time the wood was all laid out and ready to be lit, Isaac no longer had any doubts as to what lay in store for him, and maybe the reason he didn't fight for his life was that suddenly it didn't seem to him all that much worth fighting for. He let himself be tied up and laid out on top of the wood like an unblemished lamb, and, shaking like a leaf, the old man got as far as raising the knife over his head when God spoke up at last and said he'd seen all he needed to see and Abraham could use it on a ram instead. The lights switch off there, and the stage is returned mercifully to darkness.

Isaac was getting pretty long in the tooth himself when Abraham finally died, and he and his half brother, Ishmael, buried him in the same cave that years before Abraham had bought to bury Sarah in. If either of them said anything while they were at it, their words were not recorded, and maybe the scene was played out in silence— the two old men leaning on their shovels, out of breath, with the old man who had nearly been the end of both of them in his day lying six feet deep beneath their aching feet.

Isaac was on the verge of second childhood and almost blind when his son Jacob conned him into thinking he was his other son, Esau, so he could get the old man's blessing and the lion's share of the estate when that time came. Isaac had a hunch there was something fishy going on and called the young man over to be sure. The young man said he was Esau, but it was in Jacob's voice that he said it. Isaac couldn't trust his hearing all that much better than his eyesight, however, so he told him to let him touch him with his hands. Esau's hands were hairy, and he knew he'd know them anywhere. But Jacob had seen that coming, and Isaac wasn't sure whether what he felt were Esau's hairy hands or a pair of bearskin gloves. In fact, there was so little he could be sure of anymore, he thought, and he felt so old and hopeless and dumb, that he almost didn't care by then which son it was if he'd only stop badgering him.

He sent out for a drink and a sandwich, which revived him a little, and then with a sudden rush of emotion, his all but useless eyes welling with tears, he reached out, pulled the young man to him, and kissed him. Clover and timothy, black earth, horse manure, rain—his ears and his eyes were all shot, he thought, and he couldn't even tell what he was touching half the time, what with his bad circulation, but at least he still had a nose that worked, and by now the lump in his throat was so big he could hardly get the words out of his mouth.

"See, the smell of my son is as the smell of a field which the Lord has blessed," he said (Genesis 27:27), and then, not caring whether it was Esau or Jacob or Napoleon Bonaparte who was there on his knees before him, he gave out with a blessing that made all the other blessings he'd ever given sound like two cents.

Jacob had to get out of town in a hurry when Esau found out, and he was gone off and on for twenty years, but he came back again finally just in time to see Isaac once more before he died, although it's doubtful that Isaac was in any condition by then to know much about it. Then Jacob and Esau together, the guller and the gulled, buried him as by then they had also buried the hatchet, and thus the shadowy old man disappeared permanently into the shadows at last.   *Genesis 18:1–15; 21:1–22:19; 25:7–11; 35:27–29*

See also Esau, Hagar, Jacob, Rebekah.

ISAIAH

THERE WERE BANKS OF CANDLES flickering in the distance and clouds of incense thickening the air with holiness and stinging his eyes, and high above him, as if it had always been there   DAY 158 but was only now seen for what it was (like a face in the leaves of a tree or a bear among the stars), there was the Mystery Itself, whose gown was the incense and the candles a dusting of gold at the hem. There were winged creatures shouting back and forth the way excited children shout to each other when dusk calls them home, and the whole vast, reeking place started to shake beneath his feet like a wagon going over cobbles, and he cried out, "O God, I am done for! I am foul of mouth and the member of a foul-mouthed race. With my own two eyes I have seen him. I'm a goner and sunk." Then one of the winged things touched his mouth with fire and said, "There, it will be all right now," and the Mystery Itself said, "Who will it be?" and with charred lips he said, "Me," and Mystery said *"Go."*

Mystery said, "Go give the deaf hell till you're blue in the face and go show the blind heaven till you drop in your tracks, because they'd sooner eat ground glass than swallow the bitter pill that puts roses in the cheeks and a gleam in the eye. Go do it."

Isaiah said, "Do it till when?"

Mystery said, "Till hell freezes over."

Mystery said, "Do it till the cows come home."

And that is what a prophet does for a living and, starting from the year that King Uzziah died, when he saw and heard all these things, Isaiah went and did it.   *Isaiah 6*

ISRAEL

DAY 159   ONCE HAVING DECIDED to take a hand in history, God had to start somewhere. What God elected to start with was Israel. This election has been a constant source of dismay, delight, and embarrassment to them both ever since. The account of the first few millennia of their stormy affair is contained in the Old Testament.

When the Israelites asked the question why God elected them, of all people, they arrived at two main answers. One answer was that God elected them for special privilege, but the tragic course of their own history soon disabused them of that. The other answer was that God elected them for terrible responsibility.

When they asked the question what the responsibility was that God had saddled them with, they arrived at two main answers. One answer was that their responsibility was to impose upon the world the knowledge of the One True God—but they were never very successful in doing that. The other answer was that their responsibility was to suffer and die for the world.

None of them wanted to suffer and die very much, including Jesus, but Jesus did it anyway. It was only afterward that people began to understand why this was necessary, although nobody has ever explained it very well and Jesus himself never seems to have tried. When Jesus died, something happened in the lives of certain people that made explanations as unnecessary as they were inevitable, and it has gone on happening ever since.

JACOB

DAY 160 THE BOOK OF GENESIS makes no attempt to conceal the fact that Jacob was, among other things, a crook. What's more, you get the feeling that whoever wrote up his seamy adventures got a real kick out of them.

Twice he cheated his lame-brained brother, Esau, out of what was coming to him. At least once he took advantage of the blindness of his old father, Isaac, and played him for a sucker. He outdid his double-crossing father-in-law, Laban, by conning him out of most of his livestock and, later on, when Laban was looking the other way, by sneaking off with not only both the man's daughters, but just about everything else that wasn't nailed down including his household gods. Jacob was never satisfied. He wanted the moon, and if he'd ever managed to bilk heaven out of that, he would have been back the next morning for the stars to go with it. But then one day he learned a marvelous lesson in a marvelous and unexpected way.

It happened just after he'd ripped Esau off for the second time and was making his getaway into the hill country to the north. When sunset came and nobody seemed to be after him, he decided that it was safe to camp out for the night and, having left in too much of a hurry to take his bedroll with him, tucked a stone under his head for a pillow and prepared to go to sleep. You might think that what happened next was that he lay there all night bug-eyed as a result of his guilty conscience or, if he did finally manage to drop off, that he was tormented by conscience-stricken dreams, but neither of these was the case. Instead, he dropped off like a baby in a cradle and dreamed the kind of dreams you would have thought were reserved for the high saints.

He dreamed that there was a ladder reaching up to heaven and that there were angels moving up and down it with golden sandals and rainbow-colored wings and that standing somewhere above it was God himself. And the words God spoke in the dream were not the chewing-out you might have expected, but something altogether different. God told Jacob that the land he was lying on was to belong to him and his descendants and that someday his descendants would become a great nation and a great blessing to all the other nations on earth. And as if that wasn't enough, God then added a personal P.S. by saying, "Behold, I am with you and will keep you wherever you go."

It wasn't holy hell that God gave him, in other words, but holy heaven, not to mention the marvelous lesson thrown in for good measure. The lesson was, needless to say, that even for a dyed-in-the-wool, double-barreled con artist like Jacob there are a few things in this world you can't get but can only be given, and one of these things is love in general, and another is the love of God in particular.

Jacob didn't have to climb his ladder to bilk heaven of the moon and the stars, even if that had been possible, because the moon and the stars looked like peanuts compared to what God and the angels were using the ladder to hand down to him for free.

Another part of the lesson was that, luckily for Jacob, God doesn't love people because of who they are, but because of who God is. "It's on the house" is one way of saying it and "It's by grace" is another, just as it was by grace that it was Jacob of all people who became not only the father of the twelve tribes of Israel, but the many-times great-grandfather of Jesus of Nazareth, and just as it was by grace that Jesus of Nazareth was born into this world at all.

Genesis 25:24–28:17

See also Dinah, Esau, Isaac, Laban, Rachel, Rebekah.

JAEL

DAY 161

A CANAANITE WARLORD NAMED SISERA had recently been trounced by an Israelite strongman named Barak and was heading for the border to save his skin. On the way, he was invited to hide out with a Kenite woman named Jael, who belonged to a tribe that had not been involved in the skirmish at all. This was his second bad break that day.

Jael was all smiles as she issued her invitation and gave him the red-carpet treatment. She fixed him a drink and suggested he stretch out for a while on the couch. While he was asleep, she crept in and disposed of him by the ingenious if cumbersome technique of hammering a tent peg in one temple and out the other.

The female judge Deborah wrote a song in her honor in which she referred to her as "most blessed among women" for the job she had done, and Jael has been remembered as a great hero and patriot ever since.

In view of the fact that her victim (a) was her guest and (b) was asleep and (c) had never harmed a hair of either her head or her people's, it would seem that to call her deed heroic is to stretch the term to the breaking point. As for calling it patriotic, if she had done it for love of country—maybe. But (a) her country had no quarrel with Sisera and (b) if she killed him for anything but kicks, it was out of love for nothing more exalted than the idea of maybe getting a payoff from the Israelites the next time they hit town. It is not the only instance, of course, of how people in wartime get medals for doing what in peacetime would get them the chair.

Judges 4–5

See also Deborah.

JEREMIAH

THE WORD *jeremiad* means a doleful and thunderous denunciation, and its derivation is no mystery. There was nothing in need of denunciation that Jeremiah didn't denounce. He denounced the king and the clergy. He denounced recreational sex and extramarital jamborees. He denounced the rich for exploiting the poor, and he denounced the poor for deserving no better. He denounced the way every new god that came sniffing around had them all after him like so many bitches in heat; and right at the very gates of the Temple he told them that if they thought God was impressed by all the mumbo-jumbo that went on in there, they ought to have their heads examined.

When some of them took to indulging in a little human sacrifice on the side, he appeared with a clay pot, which he smashed into

DAY 162

smithereens to show them what God planned to do to them as soon as he got around to it. He even denounced God for saddling him with the job of trying to reform such a pack of hyenas, degenerates, ninnies. "You have deceived me," he said, shaking his fist. You are "like a deceitful brook, like waters that fail" (Jeremiah 15:18), and God took it.

But the people didn't. When he told them that the Babylonians were going to come in and rip them to shreds as they richly deserved, they worked him over and threw him in jail. When the Babylonians did come in and not only ripped them to shreds but tore down their precious Temple and ran off with all the expensive hardware, he told them that since it was God's judgment upon them, they better submit to it or else; whereupon they threw him into an open cistern that happened to be handy. Luckily the cistern had no water in it, but Jeremiah sank into the muck up to his armpits and stayed there till an Ethiopian eunuch pulled him out with a rope.

He told them that if they were so crazy about circumcision, then they ought to get their minds above their navels for once and try circumcising "the foreskins of their hearts" (Jeremiah 4:4); and the only hope he saw for them was that someday God would put the law in their hearts too instead of in the books, but that was a long way off.

At his lowest ebb he cursed the day he was born, like Job, and you can hardly blame him. He had spent his life telling the people to shape up, with the result that they were in just about as miserable shape as they'd have been if he'd never bothered, and urging them to submit to Babylon as the judgment of God when all their patriotic instincts made that sound like the worst kind of defeatism and treachery.

He also told them that, Babylonian occupation or no Babylonian occupation, they should stick around so that someday they could rise up and be a new nation again; and then the first chance they got, a bunch of them beat it over the border into Egypt. What's even worse, they dragged old Jeremiah, kicking and screaming, along with them, which seems the final irony: that he, who had fought so long and hard against all forms of idolatry—the nation as idol, the Temple as idol, the king as idol—should at last have been tucked into their baggage like a kind of rabbit's foot or charm against the evil eye or idol himself.

What became of him in Egypt afterward is not known, but the tradition is that his own people finally got so exasperated with him there that they stoned him to death. If that is true, nothing could be less surprising.   *The Book of Jeremiah*

JESUS

MAYBE ANY ONE DAY OF A LIFE, even the most humdrum,   DAY 163
has in it something of the mystery of that life as a whole.

People had been flocking up to Jesus the way they always seemed to when word got around that he was in the neighborhood. A Roman officer came up to ask if he would do something for a paralyzed servant back home, and Jesus said he'd go have a look at him. When the officer said he hated to take that much of his time and asked if he couldn't just do something from right there where they were standing, Jesus was so impressed by the way the man trusted him that he told him he'd see to it that what he trusted would happen would happen indeed, and when the officer got home, he found his servant up and around again. Later on, when

Jesus dropped in at Peter's house, he found Peter's mother-in-law in bed with a fever, and all he did that time was touch the old lady's hand, but that turned out to be all it took.

A scribe showed up and in a burst of enthusiasm said he was all set to follow him any place he went, to which Jesus answered, "Foxes have holes, and birds have nests, but if you stick with me, you'll find yourself out in the cold" (Matthew 8:20). One of the disciples asked for a few days off to attend his father's funeral, and Jesus said, "Look, you've got to follow me. When life's at stake, burying the dead is for deadbeats" (Matthew 8:22). When he saw a big crowd approaching, he figured he didn't have enough steam left to do much for them that day, so he went and climbed into a boat for a few hours' peace, only to find that the disciples were hot on his heels and wanted to go along too. So he took them. Then he lay down in the stern of the boat with a pillow under his head, Mark says (4:34), and went to sleep.

Matthew leaves out the details about the stern and the pillow presumably because he thought they weren't important, which of course they're not, and yet the account would be greatly impoverished without them. There's so little about Jesus in the Gospels you can actually *see*.

He didn't doze off in the bow where the spray would get him and the whitecaps slapped harder. He climbed back into the stern instead. There was a pillow under his head. Maybe somebody put it there for him. Maybe they didn't think to put it there till after he'd gone to sleep, and then somebody lifted his head a little off the hard deck and slipped it under.

He must have gone out like a light because Mark says the storm didn't wake him, not even when the waves got so high they started washing in over the sides. They let him sleep on until finally they were so scared they couldn't stand it any longer and woke him up.

They addressed him respectfully enough as Teacher, but what they said was reproachful, petulant almost. "Don't you see that we're all *drowning?*" (Mark 4:38).

It was the wind rather than the disciples that Jesus seems to have spoken to first, as soon as he'd gotten his eyes open. "He rebuked it," Mark says (4:38). *"Cut that out!"*—you can almost picture him staring it down with the hair lashing his face as he holds on to the gunwales to keep from being blown overboard. He was gentler with the sea. "Take it easy," he said. "Quiet down." When it came the disciples' turn, he said, "Why did you panic?" and then "What kind of faith do you call that?" but they were so impressed to find that the wind had stopped blowing and the sea had flattened out again that they didn't get around to answering him (4:39–41).

On the far shore was a cemetery where a crazy man lived covered with scars from where he was always smashing at himself with stones and from the chains they tried to tie him down with when he got even more violent than usual. As soon as the boat landed, he came gibbering out from behind the graves and went tearing down to the beach, but as soon as he saw Jesus, he stopped in his tracks and quieted down. They talked together a little, and then Jesus healed him.

The Roman officer, the sick old lady, the overenthusiastic scribe, the terrified disciples, the lunatic—something of who he was and what he was like and what it was like to be with him filters through each meeting as it comes along, but for some reason it's the moment in the boat that says most. The way he lay down, bone tired, and fell asleep with the sound of the lapping waves in his ears. The way, when they woke him, he opened his eyes to the howling storm and to all the other howling things that he must have known were in the cards for him and that his nap had been a few moments of vacation from. The helplessness of the disciples and the way he spoke to them. The things he said to the wind and to the sea.

Lamb of God, Rose of Sharon, Prince of Peace—none of the things people have found to call him has ever managed to say it quite right. You can see why when he told people to follow him, they often did, even if they backed out later when they started to catch on to what lay ahead. If you're religiously inclined, you can see why they went even so far as to call him Messiah, the Lord's Anointed, the Son of God, and call him these things still, some of them. And even if you're not religiously inclined, you can see why it is you might give your immortal soul, if you thought you had one to give, to have been the one to raise that head a little from the hard deck and slip a pillow under it.   *Matthew 8:5–34; compare Mark 4:35–41*

See also Barabbas, Caesar Augustus, Caiaphas, David, Ethiopian eunuch, Gabriel, Good Friday, Herod the Great, Herod Antipas, Jacob, John the Baptist, John the Evangelist, Joseph of Arimathea, Joseph the husband of Mary, Judas, Lazarus, Luke, Mark, Mary, Mary Magdalene, Matthew, Nathaniel, Nicodemus, Paul, Peter, Pilate, Quirinius, Rahab, Simeon, Thomas, Wise Men, Yahweh, Zaccheus.

JEWELS

DAY 164   "Y OU WERE IN EDEN, the garden of God; every precious stone was your covering," the Lord said to the king of Tyre, "carnelian, topaz, and jasper, chrysolite, beryl, and onyx; sapphire, carbuncle, and emerald." But then, as the Lord goes on to explain, because the king fell from innocence into sin, "I cast you as a profane thing from the mountain of God, and the guardian cherub drove you out from the midst of the stones of fire" (Ezekiel 28:13, 16).

One way or another, we have all fallen like the king. Yet we all also carry within us a memory of Eden. It is perhaps why jewels fascinate us so and why we value them above almost all things. In their starry depths we see glimmers of where we have come from and also of where, according to ancient prophecy, we are going: the city whose "walls are . . . chrysoprase . . . jacinth . . . amethyst . . . and the twelve gates . . . twelve pearls . . . and the street . . . gold" (Revelation 21:19–21).

JOB

JOB WAS THE RICHEST MAN AROUND, but in a single day he was wiped out. The Sabeans ran off with his asses and oxen and slaughtered the hired hands. Lightning struck his sheep barn and burned up the whole flock, not to mention the shepherds. The Chaldeans rustled his camels and made short work of the camel drivers. And a hurricane hit with such devastating effect the house where his seven sons and three daughters were having a party that there wasn't enough of them left in the wreckage to identify.

DAY 165

What happened next was that Job came down with leprosy. And what happened after that was that he cursed the day that he was born. He said that if he had his way, it would be stricken off the calendar entirely and never so much as mentioned again. He prayed to die, but his heart went on beating. He prayed for the sun to go out like a match, but it kept on shining. His wife advised him to curse God and then go hang himself, but he stopped just short of that because he was a very good man and a very religious man and there were some lengths to which, even though he was almost out of his head with the horror of it all, he couldn't quite bring himself to go. And that was the crux of his problem—the fact that he was a very good and a very religious man and knew it. Why had God let such things happen to him?

He had four well-meaning but insufferable friends who came over to cheer him up and try to explain it. They said that anybody with enough sense to come in out of the rain knew that God was just. They said that anybody old enough to spell his own name knew that since God was just, he made bad things happen to bad people and good things happen to good people. They said that, such being the case, you didn't need a Harvard diploma to figure out that, since bad things had happened to Job, then ipso facto he must have done something bad himself. But Job hadn't, and he said so, and that's not all he said either. "Worthless physicians are you all," he said. "Oh that you would keep silent, and it would be your wisdom" (Job 13:4–5). They were a bunch of theological quacks, in other words, and the smartest thing they could do was shut up. But they were too busy explaining things to listen.

Eliphaz the Temanite proceeded to make a few helpful suggestions about some of the bad things that Job must have done and then let slip his mind. He must have robbed a few beggars of the rags on their backs, he said. He must have refused food to some poor soul who was starving to death. There must have been several widows and orphans he'd ground his heel in the faces of without stopping to think what he was doing. But Job didn't even dignify these charges by refuting them. He talked about God instead.

There had been a time when God and he had been *like that*, he said, holding up side by side what the leprosy had left of two fingers. There was a time "when his lamp shone upon my head," he said, "and by his light I walked through darkness. When the Almighty was with me, and when my children were about me" (29:3, 5), and then he had to stop for a few minutes and blow what was left of his nose before going on.

The question, he said once he'd had time to pull himself back together, was where was God now? He had looked for him in front, and he had looked for him in back; he had looked for him to the right, and he had looked for him to the left; but he wasn't anywhere to be found. If he only knew where God might be keeping himself, he'd go tell him his troubles and get an explanation at least, but God had made himself scarce as hen's teeth, and looking for him was like looking for a needle in a haystack.

"God has cast me into the mire, and I have become like dust and ashes," he said, too miserable to worry about mixing his metaphors. "I cry to thee, and thou dost not answer me," he said, "and with the might of thy hand thou dost persecute me" (30:19–21). It was the closest he had come yet to taking his wife's advice and calling him a sonofabitch. "My skin turns black and falls from me," he said (30:30) and then took advantage of a long speech by a friend named Elihu to change a few of his dressings.

Elihu went over many of the same points his colleagues had already ticked off and then added the idea that the destruction of all Job's property, the death of all his children, and his leprosy were probably just God's way of helping him to improve his character and sharpen his sensitivities. "He delivers the afflicted by their afflictions," he explained, "and opens their ears by adversity" (36:15), but Job had no chance to respond to this new and comforting insight because at that point another speaker made himself heard, and this time the speaker was God.

Just the way God cleared his throat almost blasted Job off his feet, and that was only for starters. It is the most gorgeous speech that God makes in the whole Old Testament, and it is composed almost entirely of the most gorgeous and preposterous questions that have ever been asked by God or anybody else.

"Have you entered into the springs of the sea, or walked in the recesses of the deep?" he asked. "Where is the dwelling of light? Have you entered the storehouses of the snow, or has the rain a father? Can you bind the chain of the Pleiades? Who has put wisdom in the clouds or given understanding to the mists?" (Job 38 passim). And by this time he was just starting to get wound up.

"Is the wild ox willing to serve you?" he asked. "Will he spend the night at your crib? The wings of the ostrich wave proudly, but are they the pinions and plumage of love? Have you given the horse strength? Have you clothed his neck with thunder, who says among the trumpets 'Ha, ha!' and smells the battle afar off? Does the hawk fly by your wisdom and stretch her wings toward the south?" (Job 39 passim).

There was obviously only one thing for Job to say, and he said it. "Behold, I am of small account. What shall I answer thee?" he said, coming out with that one frail question of his own. "I will proceed no further" (40:3–5). But God wasn't through yet.

You can think of God as a great cosmic bully here if you want, but you can think of him also as a great cosmic artist, a singer, say, of such power and magnificence and so caught up in the incandescence of his own art that he never notices that he has long since ruptured the eardrums of his listeners and reduced them to quivering pulp. "Have you an arm like God, and can you thunder with a voice like his?" he asked (40:9), and then he launched off into a devastating aria about Behemoth, the hippopotamus he had made, and Leviathan, the crocodile he had made, challenging Job or anybody else, if they thought they could, to take them for walks on leashes or pierce their armored hides with cold steel.

You feel that God had only paused to catch his breath when Job saw his chance to break in again at last. "I have uttered what I did not understand, things too wonderful for me, which I did not know," he said (42:3). And then he said something else.

All his life he had heard about God, about his glory and his holiness, about his terrible wrath and his great mercy, about the way he had created the earth and all its creatures and set the sun, moon, and stars in the sky so there would always be light to see by and beauty to gladden the heart. He had sometimes thrilled and sometimes trembled at the sound of these descriptions, and they had made such an impression on him over the years that not even the terrible things that had happened to him or the terrible question as to *why* they had happened or the miserable answers to that question proposed by his friends could quite make him curse God as had been suggested, although there were a few times when he came uncomfortably close to it. But now it was no longer a matter of hearing descriptions of God, because finally he had heard and seen him for himself.

He had seen the great glory so shot through with sheer, fierce light and life and gladness, had heard the great voice raised in song so full of terror and wildness and beauty, that from that moment on, nothing else mattered. All possible questions melted like mist, and all possible explanations withered like grass, and all the bad times of his life together with all the good times were so caught up into the fathomless life of this God, who had bent down to speak with him, though by comparison he was no more than a fleck of dust on the head of a pin in the lapel of a dancing flea, that all he could say was, "I had heard of thee by the hearing of the ear, but now my eye sees thee; therefore I despise myself and repent in dust and ashes" (42:5–6).

But God didn't let him despise himself for long. He turned to the garrulous friends and said, "You have not spoken of me what is right as my servant Job has" (42:7), with the clear implication that Job had been right in standing up to him, if only because it showed he was worth listening to, as his friends preeminently were not. And then he gave back to Job more riches than he had ever had before together with his health, and Job lived to have a whole new set of children and to see them through four generations before he died old and full of days.

As for the children he had lost when the house blew down, not to mention all his employees, he never got an explanation about them because he never asked for one, and the reason he never asked for one was that he knew that, even if God gave him one that made splendid sense out of all the pain and suffering that had ever been since the world began, it was no longer splendid sense that he needed, because with his own eyes he had beheld, and not as a stranger, the One who in the end clothed all things, no matter how small or confused or in pain, with his own splendor.

And that was more than sufficient.   *The Book of Job*

JOBS

DAY 166   JOBS ARE WHAT PEOPLE DO for a living, many of them for eight hours a day, five days a week, minus vacations, for most of their lives. It is tragic to think how few of them have their hearts in it. They work mainly for the purpose of making money enough to enjoy their moments of not working.

If not working is the chief pleasure they have, you wonder if they wouldn't do better just to devote themselves to that from the start. They would probably end up in breadlines or begging, but, even so, the chances are they would be happier than they would be pulling down a good salary as a bank teller or a dental technician or a supermarket bagger and hating every minute of it.

"What do people gain from all the toil at which they toil under the sun?" asks the Preacher (Ecclesiastes 1:3). If people are in it only for the money, the money is all they gain, and when they finally retire, they may well ask themselves if it was worth giving most of their lives for. If they're doing it for its own sake—if they enjoy doing it and the world needs it done—it may very possibly help to gain them their own souls.

JOGGING

JOGGING IS SUPPOSED TO BE GOOD for the heart, the lungs, DAY 167
the muscles, and physical well-being generally. It is also said to produce a kind of euphoria known as joggers' high.

The look of anguish and despair that contorts the faces of most of the people you see huffing and puffing away at it by the side of the road, however, is striking. If you didn't know directly from them that they are having the time of their lives, the chances are you wouldn't be likely to guess it.

JOHN THE BAPTIST

JOHN THE BAPTIST didn't fool around. He lived in the wilder- DAY 168
ness around the Dead Sea. He subsisted on a starvation diet, and so did his disciples. He wore clothes that even the rummage-sale people wouldn't have handled. When he preached, it was fire and brimstone every time.

The Kingdom was coming all right, he said, but if you thought it was going to be a pink tea, you'd better think again. If you didn't shape up, God would give you the ax like an elm with the blight or toss you into the incinerator like chaff. He said being a Jew wouldn't get you any more points than being a Hottentot, and one of his favorite ways of addressing his congregation was as a snake pit. Your only hope, he said, was to clean up your life as if your life depended on it, which it did, and get baptized in a hurry as a sign that you had. Some people thought he was Elijah come back from the grave, and some others thought he was the Messiah, but John would have none of either. "I'm the one yelling himself blue in the face in the wilderness," he said, quoting Isaiah. "I'm the one trying to knock some sense into your heads" (Matthew 3:3).

One day who should show up but Jesus. John knew who he was in a second. "You're the one who should be baptizing me," he said (Matthew 3:14), but Jesus insisted, and so they waded out into the Jordan together, and it was John who did the honors.

John apparently had second thoughts about him later on, however, and it's no great wonder. Where John preached grim justice and pictured God as a steely-eyed thresher of grain, Jesus preached forgiving love and pictured God as the host at a marvelous party or a father who can't bring himself to throw his children out even when they spit in his eye. Where John said people had better save their skins before it was too late, Jesus said it was God who saved their skins, and even if you blew your whole bankroll on liquor and sex like the Prodigal Son, it still wasn't too late. Where John ate locusts and honey in the wilderness with the church crowd, Jesus ate what he felt like in Jerusalem with as sleazy a bunch as you could expect to find. Where John crossed to the other side of the street if he saw any sinners heading his way, Jesus seems to have preferred their company to the WCTU, the Stewardship Committee, and the World Council of Churches rolled into one. Where John baptized, Jesus healed.

Finally John decided to settle the thing once and for all and sent a couple of his disciples to put it to Jesus straight. "John wants to know if you're the One we've been waiting for or whether we should cool our heels a while longer," they said (Luke 7:20), and Jesus said, "You go tell John what you've seen around here. Tell him there are people who have sold their seeing-eye dogs and taken up bird-watching. Tell him there are people who've traded in aluminum walkers for hiking boots. Tell him the down-and-out have turned into the up-and-coming and a lot of deadbeats are living it up for the first time in their lives. And three cheers for the one who can swallow all this without gagging" (Luke 7:22–23). When they asked Jesus what he thought about John, he said, "They don't come any better, but when the Big Party Up There really gets off the ground, even John will look like small potatoes by comparison" (Luke 7:28).

Nobody knows how John reacted when his disciples came back with Jesus' message, but maybe he remembered how he had felt that day when he'd first seen him heading toward him through the tall grass along the riverbank and how his heart had skipped a beat when he heard himself say, "Behold the Lamb of God who taketh away the sins of the world" (John 1:29), and maybe after he remembered all that and put it together with what they'd told him about the deadbeats and the aluminum walkers, he decided he must have been right the first time.

Luke 3:1–22; 7:18–35; Matthew 3:1–17; 9:14–17; John 1:1–34

See also Salome.

JOHN THE EVANGELIST

JOHN WAS A POET, and he knew about words. He knew that all men and all women are mysteries known only to themselves until they speak a word that opens up the mystery. He knew that the words people speak have their life in them just as surely as they have their breath in them. He knew that the words people speak have dynamite in them and that a word may be all it takes to set somebody's heart on fire or break it in two. He knew that words break silence and that the word that is spoken is the word that is

DAY 169

heard and may even be answered. And at the beginning of his Gospel he wrote a poem about the Word that God spoke.

When God speaks, things happen, because the words of God aren't just as good as God's deeds; they *are* God's deeds. When God speaks, John says, creation happens, and when God speaks to the creation, what comes out is not ancient Hebrew or the King James Version or a sentiment suitable for framing in the pastor's study. On the contrary. "The word became flesh," John says (1:14), and that means that when God wanted to say what God is all about and what humankind is all about and what life is all about, it wasn't a sound that emerged, but a man. Jesus was his name. He was dynamite. He was the word of God.

As this might lead you to expect, the Gospel of John is as different from the other three as night from day. Matthew quotes Scripture, Mark lists miracles, Luke reels off parables, and each has his own special ax to grind too, but the one thing they all did in common was to say something also about the thirty-odd years Jesus lived on this earth, the kinds of things he did and said, and what he got for his pains as well as what the world got for his pains too. John, on the other hand, clearly has something else in mind, and if you didn't happen to know, you'd hardly guess that his Jesus and the Jesus of the other three Gospels are the same man.

John says nothing about when or where or how he was born. He says nothing about how the Baptist baptized him. There's no account of the temptation in John, or the transfiguration, nothing about how he told people to eat bread and drink wine in his memory once in a while, or how he sweated blood in the garden the night they arrested him, or how he was tried before the Sanhedrin as well as before Pilate. There's nothing in John about the terrible moment when he cried out that God had forsaken him at the very time he needed him most. Jesus doesn't tell even a single parable in John. So what then, according to John, does Jesus do?

He speaks words. He speaks poems that sound much like John's poems, and the poems are about himself. Even when he works his miracles, you feel he's thinking less about the human needs of the people he's working them for than about something else he's got to say about who he is and what he's there to get done. When he feeds a big, hungry crowd on hardly enough to fill a grocery bag, for instance, he says, "I am the bread of life. Whoever comes to me will never be hungry, and whoever believes in me will never be thirsty" (6:35). When he raises his old friend Lazarus from the dead, he says, "I am the resurrection and the life. Those who believe in me, even though they die, will live, and everyone who lives and believes in me will never die" (11:25–26). "I am the gate," he says. "Whoever enters by me will be saved" (10:9). "I am the good shepherd" (10:14), "the light of the world" (8:12), "I am the way, and the truth, and the life," he says (14:6) and "The Father and I are one" (10:30).

You miss the Jesus of Matthew, Mark, and Luke, of course—the one who got mad and tired and took naps in boats. You miss the Jesus who healed people because he felt sorry for them and made jokes about camels squeezing through the eyes of needles and had a soft spot in his heart for easy-going ladies and children who didn't worry about heaven like the disciples because in a way they were already there. There's nothing he doesn't know in John, nothing he can't do, and when they take him in the end, you feel he could blow them right off the map if he felt like it. Majestic, mystical, aloof, the Jesus of the Fourth Gospel walks three feet off the ground, you feel, and you can't help wishing that once in a while he'd come down to earth.

But that's just the point, of course—John's point. It's not the Jesus people knew on earth that he's mainly talking about, and everybody agrees that the story about how he saved the adulteress's skin by saying, "Let him who is without sin cast the first stone" (8:7), must have been added by somebody else, it seems so out of place with all the rest.

Jesus, for John, is the Jesus he knew in his own heart and the one he believed everybody else could know too if they only kept their hearts open. He is Jesus as the Word that breaks the heart and sets the feet to dancing and stirs tigers in the blood. He is the Jesus John loved not just because he'd healed the sick and fed the hungry but because he'd saved the world. Jesus as the *mot juste* of God.

JOKE

DAY 170

MANY MINISTERS INCLUDE in their sermons a joke or two that may or may not be relevant to what the sermons are about but in any case are supposed to warm up the congregation and demonstrate that preachers are just plain folks like everybody else.

There are two dangers in this. One is that if the joke is a good one, the chances are it will be the only part of the sermon that anybody remembers on Monday morning. The other is that when preachers tell jokes, it is often an unconscious way of telling both their congregations and themselves that the gospel is all very well but in the last analysis not to be taken too seriously.

JONAH

DAY 171

WITHIN A FEW MINUTES of swallowing the prophet Jonah, the whale suffered a severe attack of acid indigestion, and it's not hard to see why. Jonah had a disposition that was enough to curdle milk.

When God ordered him to go to Nineveh and tell them there to shape up and get saved, the expression on Jonah's face was that of a man who has just gotten a whiff of septic-tank trouble. In the first place, the Ninevites were foreigners and thus off his beat. In the second place, far from wanting to see them get saved, nothing would have pleased him more than to see them get what he thought they had coming to them.

It was as the result of a desperate attempt to get himself out of the assignment that he got himself swallowed by the whale instead; but the whale couldn't stomach him for long, and in the end Jonah went ahead and, with a little more prodding from God, did what he'd been told. He hated every minute of it, however, and when the Ninevites succumbed to his eloquence and promised to shape up, he sat down under a leafy castor oil plant to shade him from the blistering sun and smoldered inwardly. It was an opening that God could not resist.

He caused the castor oil plant to shrivel up to the last leaf, and when Jonah got all upset at being back in the ghastly heat again, God pretended to misunderstand what was bugging him.

"Here you are, all upset out of pity for one small castor oil plant that has shriveled up," he said, "so what's wrong with having pity for this whole place that's headed for hell in a handcart if something's not done about it?" (Jonah 4:10–11).

It is one of the rare instances in the Old Testament of God's wry sense of humor, and it seems almost certain that Jonah didn't fail to appreciate it.   *The Book of Jonah*

See also whale.

JONATHAN

W HEN KING SAUL found his oldest son, Jonathan, siding   DAY 172
     with David, whom he considered his archenemy, he cursed
him out by saying that he had made David a friend "to your own

shame, and to the shame of your mother's nakedness" (1 Samuel 20:30). They are strong words, and some have interpreted them as meaning that Saul suspected a sexual relationship between the two young men.

This view can be further buttressed by such verses as "The soul of Jonathan was knit to the soul of David, and Jonathan loved him as his own soul" (1 Samuel 18:1) and the words David spoke when he learned of Jonathan's death, "Your love to me was wonderful, passing the love of women" (2 Samuel 1:26). When David and Jonathan said good-bye to each other for almost the last time, they "kissed one another and wept" (1 Samuel 20:41), we're told, and there are undoubtedly those who would point to that too as evidence.

There seem to be at least three things to say in response to all this.

The first is that both emotions and the language used to express them ran a good deal higher in the ancient Near East than they do in Little Rock, Arkansas, or Boston, Massachusetts, or even Los Angeles, California, and for that and other reasons the theory that such passages as have been cited necessarily indicate a homosexual relationship is almost certainly false.

The second is that it's sad, putting it rather mildly, that we live at a time when in many quarters two men can't embrace or weep together or speak of loving one another without arousing the suspicion that they must also go to bed together.

Third, in the event that there was a sexual dimension to the friendship between Jonathan and David, it is significant that the only one to see it as shameful was King Saul, who was a manic depressive with homicidal tendencies and an eventual suicide.

Everywhere else in the book of Samuel it seems to be assumed that what was important about the relationship was not what may or may not have gone on behind closed doors, but the affection, respect, and faithfulness that kept it alive through thick and thin until finally Jonathan was killed in battle and David rent his garments and wept over him. *1 Samuel 19–2 Samuel 1, passim*

See also Mephibosheth.

JOSEPH AND HIS BROTHERS

JOSEPH'S BROTHERS TRIED to murder him by throwing him into a pit, but if they had ever been brought to trial, they wouldn't have needed Clarence Darrow to get them an acquittal in any court in the land. Not only did Joseph have offensive dreams in which he was Mr. Big and they were all groveling at his feet, but he recounted them in sickening detail at the breakfast table the next morning. He was also his father's pet, and they seethed at the sight of the many-colored coat he flaunted while they were running around in T-shirts and dirty jeans.

DAY 173

After tossing him into the pit, the brothers decided to tell Jacob, their father, that his fair-haired boy had had a fatal tangle with bobcats, and in order to convince him they produced a shirt that they'd dipped in goat's blood. Jacob was convinced, and they didn't even have to worry too much about the lie they'd told him because by the time they got around to telling it, they figured that one way or another it, or something like it, must have come true.

Unknown to them, however, Joseph was rescued from the pit by some traveling salesmen who happened to be passing by and eventually wound up as a slave in Egypt, where he was bought by an army man named Potiphar. He got into trouble over an embarrassing misunderstanding with Potiphar's prehensile wife and did some time in jail for it as a result, but Pharaoh got wind of the fact that he was big on dream interpretations and had him sprung to see what he could do with a couple of wild ones he'd had himself. When Joseph passed with flying colors, Pharaoh promoted him to be head of the Department of Agriculture and eventually his right-hand man.

Years later, Joseph's brothers, who had long since succeeded in putting him out of their minds, turned up in Egypt too, looking for something to eat because they were having a famine back home. Joseph knew who they were right off the bat, but because he was wearing his fancy uniform and speaking Egyptian, they didn't recognize him.

Joseph couldn't resist getting a little of his own back for a while. He pretended he thought they were spies. He gave them some grain to take home, but made one of them stay behind as a hostage. He planted some silverware in their luggage and accused them of copping it. But though with part of himself he was presumably getting a kick out of all this, with another part he was so moved and pleased to be back in touch with his own flesh and blood after so long that every once in a while he had to get out of the room in a hurry so they wouldn't see how choked up he was and discover his true identity.

Finally he'd had enough. He told them who he was, and they all fell into each other's arms and wept. He then invited them to come live with him in Egypt and to bring old Jacob along with them too, who was so delighted to find Joseph alive after all these years that he didn't even seem too upset about the trick that had been played on him with the bloody shirt.

The real moment of truth came, however, when Jacob finally died. Generous and forgiving as Joseph had been, his brothers couldn't avoid the nasty suspicion that once the old man wasn't around anymore to put in a good word for them, Joseph might start thinking again about what it had felt like when they tossed him into that pit and decide to pay them back as they deserved. So they went to see him, fell down on their knees, and begged his pardon.

Joseph's answer rings out like a bell. "Don't be scared. Of course you're pardoned," he said. "Do you think I'm God to grovel before me like that?" In the old days, of course, God was just who he'd rather suspected he was and the dreams in which they groveled were his all-time favorites.

Almost as much as it is the story of how Israel was saved from famine and extinction, it is the story of how Joseph was saved as a human being. It would be interesting to know which of the two achievements cost God the greater effort and which was the one he was prouder of. *Genesis 37–50*

JOSEPH OF ARIMATHEA

A S A PROMINENT MEMBER of the Jewish establishment, Joseph of Arimathea needed guts to go to Pilate and ask for the dead body of Jesus so he could give it a decent burial. It is presumably no easier for a closet Christian to come out of the closet than it is for anybody else, and you can't help admiring him for it. In view of the events of Easter morning, however, you can't help noting that if he'd only waited a few days, he could have spared himself a thumping bill from the undertaker.

DAY 174

It is important to give Joseph of Arimathea his due for his mortuary solicitude, but at the same time it is hard not to see him as the first of many Christians who spend so much time stewing about the blood of the lamb that they lose sight of the fact that the lamb has long since gone on to greener pastures, where he's kicking up his heels in the sunshine and calling to others to come join the dance. *Luke 23:50–56*

JOSEPH THE HUSBAND OF MARY

DAY 175   YOU CAN HARDLY BLAME JOSEPH for considering divorce when he discovered that, through no fault of his, Mary was pregnant. Nevertheless, when it was explained to him, he took it like a man, and all was forgiven. As soon as he got word in a dream that King Herod was planning to massacre all male babies in the neighborhood in hopes that the newborn Messiah would be one of them, he took the child and Mary and beat it to Egypt, where he had the good sense to remain till he found Herod's name in the obituary column. Later on, when they lost Jesus in Jerusalem at the age of twelve, Joseph was as nervous a wreck over it as Mary and every bit as delighted once the boy was found.

When Matthew in his Gospel records Jesus' genealogy, he traces it back through his mother's line in deference to the doctrine that the one whose son Jesus was was God. When Luke records it, on the other hand, although he was no less a true believer, he makes no bones about listing Joseph as the father of Jesus and tracing the line back through him.

Since Jesus himself never seems to have worried much about theology, it is hard not to believe that, for auld lang syne, he would have preferred Luke's version.   *Matthew 1–2; Luke 2:41–51; 3:23–38*

JOSHUA

DAY 176   MOSES WAS A HARD ACT TO FOLLOW. After the tired old man breathed his last on the slopes of Mt. Pisgah overlooking the Promised Land, which he never quite made it to, the job of leading the Israelites on in fell to Joshua. Since the Promised Land was inhabited by a group of native Canaanite tribes who weren't about to give it up without an argument, the result was years of war at its cruelest and most savage. And in the eyes of Joshua and his people, it wasn't just any old war. It was a holy war. It was Yahweh they were fighting for, because the land they were out to get, come hell or high water, was the land that centuries before, in Abraham's time, Yahweh had promised them so they could settle down in it and become a great nation and a blessing to all nations. Prisoners weren't supposed to be taken, and spoils weren't supposed to be divided, because Yahweh was the one they all belonged to. Ai, Jericho, Gibeon—cities fell like clay pigeons at Joshua's feet, and everything that would burn was put to the torch, and everything that wouldn't, like men, women, and children, was put to the sword. Holy wars are the unholiest kind.

The battle at Gibeon was one of the worst parts of it. Five Amorite kings were drawn up against the Israelites, and Joshua launched his attack just before dawn. His men leapt out of the mists with a terrible light in their eyes. There was a wild storm with hailstones as big as hand grenades. The Amorites panicked. The slaughter was on. It was a long, bloody massacre, and in order to have enough daylight to finish it by, Joshua fixed the sun with his stern military gaze and gave it his orders.

"Sun, stand thou still at Gibeon!" he said (Joshua 10:12), and because he was in command of the operation and because Yahweh was in command through him, the sun snapped to attention and kept shining till the job was done. It was the longest day on record, and when it was finally over, the ground was strewn with the dead, and the mutilated bodies of the five kings were hanging from five trees like meat in a butcher shop.

With one exception, there was nothing that Joshua hadn't been able to see in the prolonged and relentless light the sun had supplied him with. The one exception was that the God he was fighting for was the God of the Amorites too, whether they realized it or not. But Yahweh saw it and brooded over it and more than a thousand years later, through the mouth of his Anointed, spoke about it.

"Blessed are those who mourn, for they shall be comforted," he said (Matthew 5:4), and then he also blessed the peacemakers, so that even without any extra sunshine everybody would be able to see that peace is better than even the holiest wars, especially the kind of peace that not even a holy terror like Joshua can either give or take away.   *Joshua 10*

See also Rahab.

JOY

DAY 177   IN THE GOSPEL OF JOHN, Jesus sums up pretty much everything by saying, "These things I have spoken to you, that my joy may be in you, and that your joy may be full" (John 15:11). He said it at the supper that he knew was the last one at which he'd have a mouth to eat with.

Happiness turns up more or less where you'd expect it to—a good marriage, a rewarding job, a pleasant vacation. Joy, on the other hand, is as notoriously unpredictable as the one who bequeaths it.

JUDAS

DAY 178   NOBODY CAN BE SURE, of course, why Judas sold Jesus out, although according to John's Gospel, he already had a reputation for dipping into the poor box from time to time, so the cash may have been part of it. If, like the other disciples, he was perennially worried about where he stood in the pecking order, he may also have been reacting to some imagined slight. Maybe he thought his job as treasurer to the outfit was beneath him. Another possibility is that he had gotten fed up with waiting for Jesus to take the world by storm and hoped that betraying him might force him to show his hand at last. Or maybe, because nothing human is ever uncomplicated, something of all of these was involved. Anyway, whatever his reasons were, the whole thing went sour for him soon enough.

Slipping out of the Last Supper before the party was over, he led the Romans to the garden that he knew his friends were planning to adjourn to afterward and said to lay low till he gave the signal. It was dark by the time the others showed up, and maybe for fear that he might scare them off if he used any other method, the way he showed the soldiers which was the one to jump was by kissing him. That was all he'd been paid to do, and as soon as he'd done it, there was no earthly reason why he couldn't have taken off with his laundered cash and found a place to spend it. But when the time came, he wasn't in the mood.

There are several versions of what he did instead, of which the most psychologically plausible seems to be that he tried to give the money back to the ones who'd given it to him and went out and hanged himself. This time there doesn't seem to be any ambiguity about the motive.

There is a tradition in the early church, however, that his suicide was based not on despair but on hope. If God was just, then he knew there was no question where he would be heading as soon as he'd breathed his last. Furthermore, if God was also merciful, he knew there was no question either that in a last-ditch effort to save the souls of the damned as God's son, Jesus would be down there too. Thus the way Judas figured it, hell might be the last chance he'd have of making it to heaven, so to get there as soon as possible, he tied the rope around his neck and kicked away the stool. Who knows?

In any case, it's a scene to conjure with. Once again they met in the shadows, the two old friends, both of them a little worse for wear after all that had happened, only this time it was Jesus who was the one to give the kiss, and this time it wasn't the kiss of death that was given.   *John 12:1–8; 13:21–30; 18:1–12; Matthew 27:3–10*

JUDGMENT

DAY 179

WE ARE ALL OF US JUDGED EVERY DAY. We are judged by the face that looks back at us from the bathroom mirror. We are judged by the faces of the people we love and by the faces and lives of our children and by our dreams. We are judged by the faces of the people we do not love. Each day finds us at the junction of many roads, and we are judged as much by the roads we have not taken as by the roads we have.

The New Testament proclaims that at some unforeseeable time in the future, God will ring down the final curtain on history, and there will come a Day on which all our days and all the judgments upon us and all our judgments upon each other will themselves be judged. The judge will be Christ. In other words, the one who judges us most finally will be the one who loves us most fully.

Romantic love is blind to everything except what is lovable and lovely, but Christ's love sees us with terrible clarity and sees us whole. Christ's love so wishes our joy that it is ruthless against everything in us that diminishes our joy. The worst sentence Love can pass is that we behold the suffering that Love has endured for our sake, and that is also our acquittal. The justice and mercy of the judge are ultimately one.

JUDITH

K ING NEBUCHADNEZZAR OF ASSYRIA had a nasty temper and a long memory, and after pulverizing his enemies the Medes, he sent a man named Holofernes with a hundred and thirty-two thousand men to straighten out all the peoples who hadn't coughed up military aid when he needed it. The ones who resisted were to be liquidated. The rest were to tear down their temples, throw out their gods, and see to it that from then on the only god they had any dealings with was Nebuchadnezzar himself.

DAY 180

The Jews were among the others on Nebuchadnezzar's black list, and the place where Holofernes attacked them was a town called Bethulia, to which he laid siege. In Bethulia there lived a very attractive, well-heeled young widow named Judith, and she decided to go to Holofernes and see what she could do.

First she prayed to Yahweh to prosper her cause and then, just to play it safe, made a few preparations of a more secular nature. She skinned out of the drab black clothes she'd been wearing in memory of her late husband and took a long, hot tub. Then she sprayed herself with some expensive eau de cologne, had her maid give her a permanent, and slipped into a dazzling little number left over from happier days. She polished things off by decorating herself with all the chains, bracelets, earrings, and assorted bric-a-brac she could put her hands on and set out with her maid for the enemy lines (Judith 10:1–5).

As a Jew, she had a little trouble getting to see Holofernes, but when she said she was going to show him how to take Bethulia without losing a single man, they let her in. "I will declare unto the Lord no lie this night," she told him as soon as they'd been introduced (Judith 11:6), and you can only hope she had her fingers crossed at the time.

The only circumstances under which Yahweh would think of letting his people be defeated, she said, was if they sinned. As it happened, she went on to say, right that minute they were sinning like crazy back in Bethulia by eating a lot of unkosher food because, thanks to the siege, that was all there was left. She knew for a fact that the Jews in Jerusalem were about to pull the same stunt, and as soon as they did, Holofernes would be able to take the lot of them with both hands tied behind his back, and Yahweh wouldn't lift a finger to interfere. All Holofernes had to do was wait till she gave him the word.

Holofernes was not only much encouraged by what she had to say, but he was also knocked right off his pins by her good looks and fancy clothes. For three days he tried to lure her into his tent for an intimate little supper, and for three days she played hard to get. On the fourth day she finally said she'd come and put on an even flashier number for the occasion than the one she'd started out in. They had a gourmet meal together, during which Holofernes had three glasses of wine for every one of Judith's, and when it was over, he sent his servants packing so that it was just the two of them at last.

Unfortunately, he'd gotten himself so tanked up by then that before anything much had a chance to happen, he passed out on his bed. His scimitar was lying nearby, and with two good whacks Judith cut off his head, put it in her picnic basket, and went back to Bethulia, where she had it prominently displayed on the battlements. When the Assyrians saw it there the next day, they ran like rabbits, and the Jews drew their first easy breath in months.

They rewarded Judith by giving her the entire contents of Holofernes' tent including the silver cups and the bed he'd passed out on, but Judith turned around and gave them all to Yahweh. For all she knew, she might have forgotten to keep her fingers crossed when she said all those things to Holofernes the first time they met and thought the present might help make it up to Yahweh for having stretched things a little. And apparently she gauged things right because, although she never married again, she lived a long, happy life as Bethulia's leading citizen, and died peacefully in her bed at the age of one hundred and five. *The Book of Judith*

See also Nebuchadnezzar.

JUSTICE

I F YOU BREAK A GOOD LAW, justice must be invoked not only for goodness' sake but for the good of your own soul. Justice may consist of paying a price for what you've done or simply of the painful knowledge that you deserve to pay a price, which is payment enough. Without one form of justice or the other, the result is ultimately disorder and grief for you and everybody. Thus justice is itself not unmerciful.

DAY 181

Justice also does not preclude mercy. It makes mercy possible. Justice is the pitch of the roof and the structure of the walls. Mercy is the patter of rain on the roof and the life sheltered by the walls. Justice is the grammar of things. Mercy is the poetry of things.

The cross says something like the same thing on a scale so cosmic and full of mystery that it is hard to grasp. As it represents what one way or another human beings are always doing to each other, the death of that innocent man convicts us as a race, and we deserve the grim world that over the centuries we have made for ourselves.

As it represents what one way or another we are always doing not so much to God above us somewhere as to God within us and among us everywhere, we deserve the very godlessness we have brought down on our own heads. That is the justice of things.

But the cross also represents the fact that goodness is present even in grimness and God even in godlessness. That is why it has become the symbol not of our darkest hopelessness, but of our brightest hope. That is the mercy of things. Granted who we are, perhaps we could have seen it no other way.

JUSTIFICATION

DAY 182   IN PRINTERS' LANGUAGE, to *justify* means to set type in such a way that all full lines are of equal length and flush both left and right; in other words, to put the printed lines in the right relationship with the page they're printed on and with each other. The religious sense of the word is very close to this. Being justified means being brought into right relation. Paul says simply that being justified means having peace with God (Romans 5:1). He uses the noun *justification* for the first step in the process of salvation.

During his Pharisee phase, or "blue period," Paul was on his way to Damascus to mop up some Christians, when suddenly he heard the voice of Jesus Christ, whose resurrection he had up till now considered only an ugly rumor. What he might have expected the Voice to say was, "Just you wait." What in effect it did say was, "I want you on my side." Paul never got over it.

As far as Paul was concerned, he was the last man in the world for God to have called this way, but God had, thereby revealing that God was willing to do business with him even if he was in the process of mopping up Christians at the time. Paul also discovered that all the brownie points he had been trying to rack up as a super-Pharisee had been pointless. God did business with you not because of who you were, but because of who God was.

All the Voice seemed to want Paul to do was believe that it meant what it said and do as it asked. Paul did both.

At a moment in his life when he had least reason to expect it, Paul was staggered by the idea that no matter who you are or what you've done, God wants you on God's side. There is nothing you have to do or be. It's on the house. It goes with the territory. God has *justified you,* lined you up. To feel this somehow in your bones is the first step on the way to being saved.

You don't have to hear a Voice on the road to Damascus to feel it in your bones either. Maybe just noticing that the sun shines every bit as bright and sweet on Jack the Ripper as it does on Little Orphan Annie will do the trick. Maybe just noticing the holy and hallowing givenness of your own life.

See also salvation.

K

KING

YOU THINK OF THE NEWLY anointed King David conquering unconquerable Jerusalem and crowning his triumph by bringing into it the ark of God as all the people made merry with lyres, harps, tambourines, castanets, and cymbals. You think of the pope himself proclaiming Charlemagne emperor and *augustus* on Christmas Day and all Rome going mad with enthusiasm. You think of Shakespeare's Henry V comforting his troops on the eve of Agincourt and of the *grands levers* of Louis XIV, which rivaled in splendor the rising of the sun. Muffled drums and vast crowds of mourners followed the deaths of kings, and the peal of bells and dancing in the streets their births. The person of the king was so sacred that affronts upon him were punished with the most horrible of torments, and his touch had the power to heal.

Passionate loyalty, adoration, terror, awe—no words are perhaps too strong to describe the feelings evoked in his subjects by the mere sight of him, and it's no wonder. He held the power of life and death over them. Their destiny was in his keeping. He defended the kingdom against all enemies both from within and from without. He *was* the kingdom. If he rejoiced, it rejoiced with him. If he was angry, the earth trembled and the crops might fail.

"Who is this King of glory? The Lord of hosts, he is the King of glory!" proclaims the Psalmist (24:10). This rich metaphor is used again and again in Scripture. Yahweh alone was King over Israel, the prophets thundered: to be feared, to be loved, above all else to be obeyed. When the people decided they wanted a king of flesh and blood like all the other nations, Samuel warned them that the consequences would be tragic (1 Samuel 8:4–18), and history proved him correct in every particular. In the long run Israel as king and kingdom vanished from history altogether.

When Jesus entered Jerusalem for the last time, it was as King and Son of David that his followers hailed him. If it was a king like David the conquering hero that they were looking for, they were of course bitterly disappointed. What they got was a king like David the father, who, when he heard of his treacherous son's death, went up to his chamber and wept. "Would I had died instead of thee, O Absalom, my son, my son!" he cried out. They were the most kingly words he ever uttered and an uncanny foreshadowing of his many-times great-grandson who some thousand years later put his money where David's mouth had been.

KINGDOM OF GOD

THE KINGDOM OF GOD is not a place, of course, but a condition. *Kingship* might be a better word. "Thy kingdom come, thy will be done," Jesus prayed. The two are in apposition.   DAY 184

Insofar as here and there, and now and then, God's kingly will is being done in various odd ways among us even at this moment, the Kingdom has come already.

Insofar as all the odd ways we do God's will at this moment are at best half-baked and halfhearted, the Kingdom is still a long way off—a hell of a long way off, to be more precise and theological.

As a poet, Jesus is maybe at his best in describing the feeling you get when you glimpse the Thing Itself—the kingship of the king official at last and all the world his coronation. It's like finding a million dollars in a field, he says, or a jewel worth a king's ransom. It's like finding something you hated to lose and thought you'd never find again—an old keepsake, a stray sheep, a missing child. When the Kingdom really comes, it's as if the thing you lost and thought you'd never find again is yourself.

See also eternal life.

KNOWLEDGE

DAY 185

K NOWING SOMETHING or somebody isn't the same as know-ing *about* them. More than just information is involved. When you are a knower, you don't simply add to your mental store and go your way otherwise unchanged. To know is to participate in, to be-come imbued with, for better or worse to be affected by. When you really *know* a person or a language or a job, the knowledge becomes part of who you are. It gets into the bloodstream. That is presum-ably why the Tree of the Knowledge of Good and Evil was the one tree Adam and Eve were warned to steer clear of.

When in their innocence they knew only good, they could be only good. As soon as they knew evil too, a whole new glittering vista opened up before them. Next to obedience appeared the pos-sibility of disobedience; next to faithfulness, faithlessness; next to love, lust; next to kindness, cruelty; and so on. Even when they chose the good way, their knowledge of the evil way remained as a conscious and by no means unattractive alternative, preventing them except on the rarest occasions from being good wholeheartedly. And when they chose the evil way, their knowledge of good tended to turn even the sweetness of forbidden fruit to ashes in their mouths. Thus they became the hapless hybrids their descendants have been ever since. It was the curse God had tried to spare them. The serpent did its work well.

According to Thomas Aquinas, God can know evil by pure intelligence without becoming tainted by it the way a doctor can know the nature of disease without becoming diseased. Humans, on the other hand, not being pure intelligences but creatures of flesh and blood inhabiting a world of space and time, can know only through the likes of experience, experiment, will, and imagination, and once they start knowing evil that way, the fat is in the fire.

KOHELETH

KOHELETH MEANS "PREACHER" and is the name by which the author of the book of Ecclesiastes is known. When the rabbis got together to decide which books to put into the Old Testament and which to throw out, it is reported that Koheleth's almost didn't make it. You can't help seeing why, but at the same time you can't help being grateful to them for letting it in under the wire even so. In that great chorus of voices that speak out of the Bible, it is good to have this one long-drawn sigh of disillusion, skepticism, and ennui, if only because the people who read the Bible sometimes feel that way themselves, not to mention also the ones who wouldn't be caught dead reading it.

People are born and people die, Koheleth says, and the sun goes up and the sun goes down, and first the wind blows from the north

DAY 186

and then it blows from the south, and if you think you're seeing something for the first time, just go ask your grandmother, and if you think you're seeing something for the last time, just hang around for a while, and the whole thing is as pointless and endless and dull as a drunk singing all six dozen verses of "Roaming in the Gloaming" and then starting in from the beginning again in case you missed anything. There is nothing new under the sun, Koheleth says, with the result that everything that there is under the sun both is old and, as you might expect in all that heat, stinks.

If you decide to knock yourself out getting rich and living it up, he points out, all you have to show for it in the end is the biggest income tax in town and a bad liver; and when you finally kick the bucket, the chances are that your dim-witted heirs will sink the whole thing in a phony Florida real-estate deal or lose it at the track in Saratoga. If you decide to break your back getting a decent education and end up a Columbia Ph.D. and an adviser to presidents, you'll be just as dead when the time comes as the high-school dropout who went into stuffing sausages, and you'll be forgotten just about as soon.

If you decide to be Mr. Nice Guy or Miss Goody Two-Shoes and never do the dirty on a pal, that may win you a gold star somewhere, but it won't keep you from getting it in the teeth like everybody else, because "there are righteous people who are treated according to the conduct of the wicked, and there are wicked people who are treated according to the conduct of the righteous," Koheleth says (Ecclesiastes 8:14), and we're all in the hands of God, all right, but "whether it is love or hate, one does not know" (9:1).

God has a plan for us, to be sure, but he leaves us in the dark as to what that plan is, and if God's plan happens to conflict with some plans of our own, guess whose way wins out? That is what the famous "A time to weep and a time to laugh" passage is all about

(3:1–9)—that is, if you feel like laughing at a time that God has already pegged as a time for weeping, start reaching for the Kleenex.

"The race is not to the swift," he says, "nor the battle to the strong, nor bread to the wise, nor riches to the intelligent, nor favor to the skillful" (9:11), and that about sums it up. The dead are luckier than the living, he says, but luckiest of all are the ones who had the good sense never to get born in the first place.

But the rabbis in their wi⸱'⸱m let Koheleth into the Good Book anyway, placing him not far ᵤfrom the Psalms of David on one side and the prophecies of Isaiah on the other. Maybe it was their hope that in that location a little of David and Isaiah might rub off on him, especially one of the insights they more or less shared, which was that often people are closest to God when they need him most and that sometimes they know him best by missing him.

The Book of Ecclesiastes

KORAH

AFTER YEARS OF KNOCKING AROUND the Promised Land with the children of Israel, Moses already had problems enough on his hands when some of his own people, led by a man named Korah, challenged his religious authority. "What makes you and your brother think you've got a corner on holiness?" Korah said and then added, "We're all holy, every last one of us." Moses was so undone by these remarks that, as the narrator reports, "he fell on his face" (Numbers 16:4).

He eventually picked himself up, however, and asked God to help him take care of these troublemakers. God obliged by causing the ground to open up beneath their feet. Korah and his crowd were swallowed up and taken down alive to Sheol, the abode of the

DAY 187

dead, and Moses was able to get on with the business of leading the way to the Promised Land.

You can't blame Moses for having overreacted the way he did. Leading the Israelites anywhere was no pushover, and he needed all the unchallenged authority he could get. On the other hand, you can't really blame Korah either, who, by insisting that nobody was any holier than anybody else, was simply anticipating by a few thousand years the doctrine of the priesthood of all believers.

As for God, there seems to be a strong possibility that the reason he caused the rebels to be swallowed down into Sheol *alive* was so that later on, when the whole thing had blown over, he could let them out again quietly through the back door.   *Numbers 16*

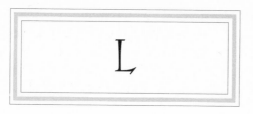

LABAN

Having promised his nephew Jacob the hand of his daughter Rachel in return for seven years' hard work, in the dark of the night Laban slipped his older, weak-eyed daughter, Leah, into the marriage bed in her place. When Jacob woke up to discover he'd been had, Laban not only convinced him that it was all a misunderstanding, but managed to get a second seven years out of him by declaring that only then would Rachel finally be his.

On another occasion he promised to pay Jacob all his speckled and spotted goats plus all his black lambs if he would go on working for him a while longer and then proceeded to spirit those very ones away so that only the unblemished white ones were left. But this time Jacob trumped his uncle's ace. By means of some arcane breeding techniques, he saw to it that the next time his flocks produced young, they were almost all of them speckled or spotted or black.

They are not the most admirable pair in the Old Testament, but it's hard to avoid a sneaking affection for them anyway—Jacob because in spite of everything he was renamed Israel and became father of the twelve tribes, and Laban because he was such an unabashed and genial crook. They parted friends in the end, swearing before God never to con each other again, and then celebrated with a feast that lasted till daybreak, whereupon Laban kissed his nephew's entire family good-bye and gave them all his blessing.

See also Jacob, Rachel.

LAW

DAY 189   THERE ARE BASICALLY TWO KINDS OF LAW: (1) law as the way things ought to be, and (2) law as the way things are. An example of the first is "No Trespassing." An example of the second is the law of gravity.

God's law has traditionally been spelled out in terms of category no. 1, a compendium of dos and don'ts. These dos and don'ts are the work of moralists and, when obeyed, serve the useful purpose of keeping us from each other's throats. They can't make us human, but they can help keep us honest.

God's law *in itself,* however, comes under category no. 2 and is the work of God. It has been stated in seven words: "Whoever does not love abides in death" (1 John 3:14). Like it or not, that's how it is. If you don't believe it, you can always put it to the test just the way if you don't believe the law of gravity, you can always step out a tenth-story window.

See also morality.

LAW OF LOVE

DAY 190   JESUS SAID THAT THE ONE SUPREME LAW is that we are to love God with all our hearts, minds, and souls, and our neighbors as ourselves. "On these two commandments depend all the law and the prophets" is the way he put it (Matthew 22:40), meaning that all lesser laws are to be judged on the basis of that supreme one. In any given situation, the lesser law is to be obeyed if it is consistent with the law of love and superseded if it isn't.

The law against working on the Sabbath is an example found in the Gospels. If it is a question of whether or not you should perform the work of healing people on the Sabbath, Jesus' answer is clear. *Of course* you should heal them is his answer. Obviously healing rather than preserving your own personal piety is what the law of love would have you do. Therefore you put the lesser law aside.

The Mosaic law against murder is an example of precisely the opposite kind. In this case, far from setting it aside as a lesser law, you radicalize it. That is to say, if we are above all else to love our neighbors, it is not enough simply not to kill them. We must also not lose our tempers at them, insult them, or call them fools, Jesus says (Matthew 5:21–22).

A legalistic religion like the Pharisees' is in some ways very appealing. All you have to do in any kind of ethical dilemma is look it up in the book and act accordingly. Jesus, on the other hand, says all you have to do is love God and your neighbors. That may seem more appealing still until, in dilemma after dilemma, you try to figure out just how to go about doing it.

The difficulty is increased when you realize that by loving God and your neighbors, Jesus doesn't mean loving as primarily a feeling. Instead, he seems to mean that whether or not any feeling is involved, loving God means honoring and obeying and staying in constant touch with God, and loving your neighbors means acting in their best interests no matter what, even if personally you can't stand them.

Nothing illustrates the difficulty of all this better than the situation of a man and woman who for one reason or another decide to divorce, but take their faith seriously enough to want to do what's right. Jesus himself comes out strongly against it. "What God has joined together, let no one separate" is the way he puts it (Mark 10:9). In one place he is quoted as acknowledging that unchastity on the woman's part may be considered justifiable grounds, but he is clearly not happy about it (Matthew 5:31–32; Mark 10:2–9). In other words, insofar as Jesus lays down the law on the subject, divorce is out.

But presumably his laws are to be judged by the same standards as the next person's.

Who knows what has gone amiss in the marriage? Who knows which partner, if either, is more at fault? Who knows what the long-term results either of splitting up or of staying together will be? If there are children, who can say which will be better for them, those small neighbors we are commanded to love along with the rest of them? Will it be living on with married parents whose constant battling, say, can do terrible things to children? Or will it be going off with one divorced parent or the other and falling victim thereby to all the feelings of rejection, guilt, and loss, which can do equally terrible things to children if not more so?

What would the law of love have you do in a situation so complex, precarious, fateful? How can you best serve, in love, the best interests of the husband or wife you are miserable with, your children, yourself, God? There is no book to look up the answer in. There is only your own heart and whatever by God's grace it has picked up in the way of insight, honesty, courage, humility, and, maybe above everything else, compassion.

LAZARUS

L AZARUS AND HIS TWO SISTERS lived in a town called Bethany
a couple of miles outside Jerusalem and according to the Gospel
of John were among the best friends Jesus had. He used to drop in
on them whenever he was in the neighborhood, and when he made
his entrance into Jerusalem on Palm Sunday, it was from Bethany
that he took off, and it was also to Bethany that he went back to
take it easy for a few days before his final arrest.

When Lazarus died, Jesus didn't arrive on the scene until several
days afterward, but he found the sisters still so broken up they hardly
knew what they were saying. With one breath they reproached him
for not having come in time to save their brother and with the next
they told him they knew he could save him still. Then, for the first
and only time such a thing is recorded of him in the New Testament, Jesus broke down himself. Then he went out to where his
friend's body lay and brought him back to life again.

Recent interviews with people who have been resuscitated after
being pronounced clinically dead reveal that, after the glimpse they
evidently all of them get of a figure of light waiting for them on the
other side, they are very reluctant to be brought back again to this
one. On the other hand, when Lazarus opened his eyes to see the
figure of Jesus standing there in the daylight beside him, he couldn't
for the life of him tell which side he was on. *John 11:1–44*

LENT

I N MANY CULTURES there is an ancient custom of giving a tenth
of each year's income to some holy use. For Christians, to observe the forty days of Lent is to do the same thing with roughly a

tenth of each year's days. After being baptized by John in the river Jordan, Jesus went off alone into the wilderness, where he spent forty days asking himself the question what it meant to be Jesus. During Lent, Christians are supposed to ask one way or another what it means to be themselves.

If you had to bet everything you have on whether there is a God or whether there isn't, which side would get your money and why?

When you look at your face in the mirror, what do you see in it that you most like and what do you see in it that you most deplore?

If you had only one last message to leave to the handful of people who are most important to you, what would it be in twenty-five words or less?

Of all the things you have done in your life, which is the one you would most like to undo? Which is the one that makes you happiest to remember?

Is there any person in the world or any cause that, if circumstances called for it, you would be willing to die for?

If this were the last day of your life, what would you do with it?

To hear yourself try to answer questions like these is to begin to hear something not only of who you are, but of both what you are becoming and what you are failing to become. It can be a pretty depressing business all in all, but if sackcloth and ashes are at the start of it, something like Easter may be at the end.

LIFE

DAY 193 LIFE—THE TEMPTATION is always to reduce it to size. A bowl of cherries. A rat race. Amino acids. Even to call it a mystery smacks of reductionism. It is *the* mystery.

As far as anybody seems to know, the vast majority of things in the universe do not have whatever life is. Sticks, stones, stars, space—they simply *are*. A few things *are* and are somehow alive to it. They have broken through into Something, or Something has broken through into them. Even a jellyfish, a butternut squash. They're in it with us. We're all in it together, or it in us. Life is *it*. Life is *with*.

After lecturing learnedly on miracles, a great theologian was asked to give a specific example of one. "There is only one miracle," he answered. "It is life."

Have you wept at anything during the past year?

Has your heart beat faster at the sight of young beauty?

Have you thought seriously about the fact that someday you are going to die?

More often than not, do you really *listen* when people are speaking to you instead of just waiting for your turn to speak?

Is there anybody you know in whose place, if one of you had to suffer great pain, you would volunteer yourself?

If your answer to all or most of these questions is no, the chances are that you're dead.

LIGHT

WE CAN'T SEE LIGHT ITSELF. We can see only what light lights up, like the little circle of night where the candle flickers—a sheen of mahogany, a wineglass, a face leaning toward us out of the shadows.

DAY 194

When Jesus says that he is the Light of the World (John 8:12), maybe something like that is part of what he is saying. He himself is beyond our seeing, but in the darkness where we stand, we see, thanks to him, something of the path that stretches out from the door, something of whatever it is that keeps us trying more or less to follow the path even when we can hardly believe that it goes anywhere worth going or that we have what it takes to go there, something of whoever it is that every once in a while seems to lean toward us out of the shadows.

LONELINESS

DAY 195

THAT YOU CAN BE LONELY in a crowd, maybe especially there, is readily observable. You can also be lonely with your oldest friends, or your family, even with the person you love most in the world. To be lonely is to be aware of an emptiness that takes more than people to fill. It is to sense that something is missing which you cannot name.

"By the waters of Babylon, there we sat down and wept, when we remembered Zion," sings the Psalmist (137:1). Maybe in the end it is Zion that we're lonely for, the place we know best by longing for it, where at last we become who we are, where finally we find home.

LORD'S PRAYER

DAY 196

IN THE EPISCOPAL ORDER OF WORSHIP, the priest sometimes introduces the Lord's Prayer with the words, "Now, as our Savior Christ hath taught us, we are bold to say . . ." The word *bold* is worth thinking about. We do well not to pray the prayer lightly. It takes guts to pray it at all. We can pray it in the unthinking and perfunctory way we usually do only by disregarding what we are saying.

"Thy will be done" is what we are saying. That is the climax of the first half of the prayer. We are asking God to be God. We are asking God to do not what we want, but what God wants. We are asking God to make manifest the holiness that is now mostly hidden, to set free in all its terrible splendor the devastating power that is now mostly under restraint. "Thy kingdom come . . . on earth" is what we are saying. And if that were suddenly to happen, what then? What would stand and what would fall? Who would be welcomed in and who would be thrown the hell out? Which if any of our most precious visions of what God is and of what human beings are would prove to be more or less on the mark and which would turn out to be phony as three-dollar bills? Boldness indeed. To speak those words is to invite the tiger out of the cage, to unleash a power that makes atomic power look like a warm breeze.

You need to be bold in another way to speak the second half. Give us. Forgive us. Don't test us. Deliver us. If it takes guts to face the omnipotence that is God's, it takes perhaps no less to face the impotence that is ours. We can do nothing without God. We can have nothing without God. Without God we are nothing.

It is only the words "Our Father" that make the prayer bearable. If God is indeed something like a father, then as something like children maybe we can risk approaching him anyway.

LORD'S SUPPER

THE LORD'S SUPPER is make-believe. You make believe that the one who breaks the bread and blesses the wine is not the plump parson who smells of Williams' Aqua Velva but Jesus of Nazareth. You make believe that the tasteless wafer and cheap port are his flesh and blood. You make believe that by swallowing them you are swallowing his life into your life and that there is nothing in earth or heaven more important for you to do than this.

It is a game you play because he said to play it. "Do this in remembrance of me." Do *this*.

DAY 197

Play that it makes a difference. Play that it makes sense. If it seems a childish thing to do, do it in remembrance that you are a child.

Remember Max Beerbohm's *Happy Hypocrite,* in which a wicked man wore the mask of a saint to woo and win the saintly girl he loved. Years later, when a castoff girlfriend discovered the ruse, she challenged him to take off the mask in front of his beloved and show his face for the sorry thing it was. He did what he was told, only to discover that underneath the saint's mask, his face had become the face of a saint.

This same reenactment of the Last Supper is sometimes called the Eucharist, from a Greek word meaning "thanksgiving," that is, at the Last Supper itself Christ gave thanks, and on their part Christians have nothing for which to be more thankful.

It is also called the Mass, from *missa,* the word of dismissal used at the end of the Latin service. It is the end. It is over. All those long prayers and aching knees. Now back into the fresh air. Back home. Sunday dinner. Now life can begin again. *Exactly.*

It is also called Holy Communion because, when feeding at this implausible table, Christians believe that they are communing with the Holy One himself, his spirit enlivening their spirits, heating the blood, and gladdening the heart just the way wine, as spirits, can.

They are also, of course, communing with each other. To eat any meal together is to meet at the level of our most basic need. It is hard to preserve your dignity with butter on your chin, or to keep your distance when asking for the tomato ketchup.

To eat this particular meal together is to meet at the level of our most basic humanness, which involves our need not just for food but for each other. I need you to help fill my emptiness just as you need me to help fill yours. As for the emptiness that's still left over, well, we're in it together, or it in us. Maybe it's most of what makes us human and makes us brothers and sisters.

The next time you walk down the street, take a good look at

every face you pass and in your mind say, "Christ died for thee." That girl. That slob. That phony. That crook. That saint. That damned fool. *Christ* died for thee. Take and eat this in remembrance that Christ died for *thee*.

See also bread, ritual, sacrament, wine.

LOT

WHEN GOD DECIDED to wipe the city of Sodom off the map for its sins, he sent a couple of angels down to make sure that Lot was safely out of it first. Therefore he must have had something going for him. On the other hand, it's hard to see just what.   DAY 198

There was the way he conducted himself the day the angels arrived at his house, for instance. The first thing to happen was that some local weirdos started pounding on the front door demanding that he send the angels out to them for purposes that, though never spelled out, Lot seems to have understood well enough since, to save his guests, he immediately suggested that maybe they'd just as soon have his two unmarried daughters instead. The angels evidently thought this was carrying the laws of hospitality too far since, before Lot had a chance to make good on his offer, they struck the door-pounders blind and sent them groping their way back to wherever they'd come from.

The next thing was that Lot went to the two young men who were engaged to his daughters, told them what the angels said was about to happen to Sodom, and advised them to pack their bags in a hurry. The two young men refused to take him seriously. "They thought he was jesting," Genesis says (19:14), and you can hardly blame them.

When the next morning arrived, Lot himself still hadn't gotten out of town, and the angels were in a snit. God had already started the countdown, and there wasn't a moment to lose. Lot refused to budge an inch, however, so finally in desperation the angels "seized him and his wife and his two daughters by the hand, the Lord being merciful to him, and they brought him forth and set him outside the city" (19:16). Then they told him to flee to the hills before it was too late.

Lot's response must be read to be believed. "Oh no, my lords," he said. "Behold, your servant has found favor in your sight, and you have shown me great kindness in saving my life; but I cannot flee to the hills lest the disaster overtake me and I die. Behold, yonder city is near enough to flee to, and it is a little one. Let me escape there— is it not a little one?—and my life will be saved" (19:18–20).

All of Lot is somehow in that speech. To begin with, not so much as a passing thought is given to the imminent liquidation of all his fellow citizens. Beyond that, he knows perfectly well that he'll be safe in the hills or the angels would never have told him to go there, but wilderness camping isn't for him. He had already made it clear that he would rather be blown sky-high than leave and have to do without indoor plumbing, the morning paper delivered to the door, the restaurants. But he had a hunch the angels mightn't think all that highly of cities after their recent experience in one, so he tried to wheedle them as tactfully and unobtrusively as he could. Wouldn't it be all right if he fled just as far as that little city over there—that tiny little bit of a one you'd hardly even notice if you weren't looking straight at it? Just to get him moving, the angels gave him the nod, and by the time they'd finished giving it, he was already halfway there.

His wife disobeyed the angels' instructions by looking back longingly at what they were leaving behind and was turned into a pillar of salt because of it. It was a dismal fate to be sure, but when you consider all the years of marriage to Lot that would probably have been in store for her otherwise, she may not have done all that badly at that.   *Genesis 19:1–29*

LOVE

THE FIRST STAGE IS TO BELIEVE that there is only one kind of   DAY 199
love. The middle stage is to believe that there are many kinds
of love and that the Greeks had a different word for each of them.
The last stage is to believe that there is only one kind of love.

The unabashed *eros* of lovers, the sympathetic *philia* of friends, *agape* giving itself away freely no less for the murderer than for the victim (the King James Version translates it as "charity")—these are all varied manifestations of a single reality. To lose yourself in another's arms, or in another's company, or in suffering for all who suffer, including the ones who inflict suffering upon you—to lose yourself in such ways is to find yourself. Is what it's all about. Is what love is.

Of all powers, love is the most powerful and the most powerless. It is the most powerful because it alone can conquer that final and most impregnable stronghold that is the human heart. It is the most powerless because it can do nothing except by consent.

To say that love is God is romantic idealism. To say that God is love is either the last straw or the ultimate truth.

In the Christian sense, love is not primarily an emotion, but an act of the will. When Jesus tells us to love our neighbors, he is not telling us to love them in the sense of responding to them with a cozy emotional feeling. You can as easily produce a cozy emotional feeling on demand as you can a yawn or a sneeze. On the contrary, he is telling us to love our neighbors in the sense of being willing to work for their well-being even if it means sacrificing our own well-being to that end, even if it means sometimes just leaving them alone. Thus in Jesus' terms, we can love our neighbors without necessarily liking them. In fact liking them may stand in the way of loving them by making us overprotective sentimentalists instead of reasonably honest friends.

When Jesus talked to the Pharisees, he didn't say, "There, there. Everything's going to be all right." He said, "You brood of vipers! how can you speak good, when you are evil!" (Matthew 12:34). And he said that to them because he loved them.

This does not mean that liking may not be a part of loving, only that it doesn't have to be. Sometimes liking follows on the heels of loving. It is hard to work for people's well-being very long without coming in the end to rather like them too.

LUCIFER

DAY 200

LUCIFER MEANS "LIGHT-GIVER" or "Morning star" or "Son of dawn" and, ever since the Middle Ages, has been one of the aliases the Devil goes by, along with Satan, Old Nick, Old Scratch, the Old Harry, and so forth. Thus the Bible's blackest villain is known by one of the Bible's loveliest names, and not by accident either.

"How art thou fallen from heaven, O Lucifer, son of the morning!" the prophet Isaiah says (14:12), the point being that it was while he was still at the height of his loveliness that the ugly episode took place.

Lucifer was a leading member of the heavenly chorus that sings Bach around the throne of grace and as such seemed so infinitely removed from all temptation that both to him and to his fellow angels the very possibility must have seemed ludicrous. Then one day he made the mistake of saying to himself, "Just see how far I have come," with the emphasis on the first-person singular, and from there to "Just see how far I can still go" was of course only a hop, skip, and a jump.

When you are one of God's right-hand angels, there is clearly only one step farther you can go, and with his usual uncanny combination of justice and mercy, God let him go there.

Lucifer was no longer called upon to love anybody except himself or to sing Bach anywhere but in the bathtub or to follow anything or anybody except his own instincts and inclinations. He was given an office with mottoes like "Nobody loves you like yourself" and "Nice guys finish last" on the walls and was named to the number-one job in charge of everybody else who both then and for all time felt the same way, and they have been having one hell of a time together ever since.

LUKE

O F THE FOUR EVANGELISTS, Luke wrote the best Greek and, unlike the other three, was almost certainly a Greek-speaking Gentile himself, who put his Gospel together for a Gentile audience, translating Jewish names and explaining Jewish customs when he thought they wouldn't be understood if he didn't. In his Letter to the Colossians, Paul refers to somebody as "Luke the beloved physician," and without stretching things too far, you could point to three blocks of material in Luke's Gospel, omitted from the others, that might suggest that he was the same man.

DAY 201

First of all, there's the parable of the Prodigal Son, the account of the whore who washed Jesus' feet and dried them with her hair, and the scrap of conversation Jesus had with one of the two crooks who was crucified with him.

Smelling of pig and cheap gin, the Prodigal comes home bleary-eyed and dead broke, but his father's so glad to see him anyway that he almost falls on his face. Jesus tells Simon the blue-nosed Pharisee that the whore's sins are forgiven her because, even painted up like a cigar-store Indian and smelling like the perfume counter at the five-and-dime, she's got more in her of what the gospel of love is all about than the whole Ladies' Missionary Society laid end to end. The thief Jesus talked to on the cross may have been a purse snatcher and second-story man from way back, but when he asked Jesus to remember him when he made it to where he was going, Jesus told him he'd make sure they got rooms on the same floor. Different as they all are in some ways, it's not hard to see that they all make the same general point, which is that, though he could give them hell when he felt like it, Jesus had such a soft spot in his heart for the scum of the earth that you would have almost thought he considered them the salt of the earth the way he sometimes treated them.

Second, Luke is the one who goes out of his way to make it clear how big Jesus was on praying. He prayed when he was baptized and after he healed the leper and the night before he called the twelve disciples, and Luke was the only one to mention these together with a few others like them and also was the only one to say that the last words Jesus ever spoke were the prayer, "Father, into thy hand I commend my spirit." It's also thanks to Luke that there's a record of the jokes Jesus told about the man who kept knocking at his friend's door till he finally got out of bed to open it and the widow who kept bugging the crooked judge till he finally heard her case just to get a little peace, the point of both of which seems to be that if you don't think God has heard you the first time, don't give up till you're hoarse. Luke wanted that to be remembered too.

Third and last, Luke makes sure that nobody misses the point that Jesus was always stewing about the terrible needs of poor people. He is the one who tells us that when Jesus preached at Nazareth, his text was "he has appointed me to preach good news to the poor" from Isaiah (Luke 4:18), and whereas Matthew says that the first Beatitude was "Blessed are the poor in spirit," according to Luke it was just plain "Blessed are the poor" period (Luke 6:20). He also recorded some parables, like the one about the rich man and the beggar, that come right out and say that if the haves don't do their share to help the have-nots, they better watch out, and he's the only one to quote the song Mary sang that includes the words "he has filled the hungry with good things, and the rich has sent empty away" (Luke 1:53).

To put it in a nutshell, by playing all these things up Luke shows he was a man who believed that you shouldn't let the fact that a person is jailbait keep you from treating that person like a human being, and that if you pray hard enough, there's no telling what may happen, and that if you think you've got heaven made but don't let it worry you that there are children across the tracks who are half starving to death, then you're kidding yourself. These characteristics may not prove that he was a doctor, like the Luke in Paul's Letter, but if he wasn't, it was a serious loss to the medical profession.

LUST

DAY 202 LUST IS THE CRAVING for salt of a person who is dying of thirst.

LYING

DAY 203 THERE IS PERHAPS NOTHING that so marks us as human as the gift of speech. Who knows to what degree and in what ways animals have the power to communicate with each other, but to all appearances it is only a shadow of ours. By speaking, we can reveal the hiddenness of thought, we can express the subtlest as well as the most devastating of emotions, we can heal, we can make poems, we can pray. All of which is to say we can speak truth—the truth of what it is to be ourselves, to be with each other, to be in the world— and such speaking as that is close to what being human is all about. What makes lying an evil is not only that the world is deceived by it, but that we are dehumanized by it.

MAGIC

M AGIC IS SAYING "ABRACADABRA" and pulling the rabbit out of the hat, is stepping on a crack to break your mother's back, is a dashboard Jesus to prevent smashups. Magic is going to church so you will get to heaven. Magic is using mouthwash so everybody will love you. Magic is the technique of controlling unseen powers and will always work if you do it by the book. Magic is manipulation and says, "My will be done." Religion is propitiation and says, "Thy will be done."

Religion is praying, and maybe the prayer will be answered and maybe it won't, at least not the way you want or when you want and maybe not at all. Even if you do it by the book, religion doesn't always work, as Jesus pointed out in one of his more somber utterances when he said, "Not everyone who says, 'Lord, Lord,' shall enter the kingdom of heaven" (Matthew 7:21), the corollary to which would appear to be, "Not everyone who wouldn't be caught dead saying, 'Lord, Lord,' shall be blackballed from the kingdom of heaven." He softened the blow somewhat then by adding that the way to enter the kingdom of heaven is to do the will of his Father in heaven; but when religion claims that it's always sure what that will is, it's only bluffing. Magic is always sure.

If security's what you're after, try magic. If adventure is what you're after, try religion. The line between them is notoriously fuzzy.

MALE

DAY 205   MALES ARE STRONG, daring, aggressive. Females are gentle, prudent, sensitive. That's the way it was always supposed to be. If a particular male didn't fit the picture by nature, he generally tended to let on that he did. He wasn't free to be himself that way, but at least it was better than drawing unfavorable attention and possible ridicule. Artists of various kinds—together with priests, ministers, and actors—were sometimes exceptions, but everybody knew they were a peculiar crowd anyhow.

When the old stereotypes began to break down in the middle of the twentieth century—a revolution crystallized in the musical *Hair*—it was of course a liberating experience for males just as for everybody else. Starting with the younger ones, they could put an earring in one ear and wear a ponytail without having their masculinity called into question. If they opposed war, violence, and nuclear power, they might get into trouble with the cops, but most people no longer considered them traitors to their gender. It was even acceptable for them to stay home and take care of the children while their wives went out to earn the family living.

Needless to say, males continue to be as much of a problem to themselves now that the sky's the limit as they ever were. Maybe more so. With females more or less liberated right alongside them, they're not quite as much in charge as they used to be, and that leaves them feeling a little vulnerable and disoriented. Free to be almost anything these days, now they've got a harder time figuring out what to be. With everything pretty much up for grabs, they're not sure what's most worth grabbing.

Father and husband, brother and son, lover and friend—all the old roles are still there for them to fill, but with the old scripts discarded, they're left to wing it as best they can.

MARK

NOBODY KNOWS FOR SURE who wrote the Gospel that bears Mark's name because the book itself doesn't say. Some people claim it was the John Mark who turns up in the book of Acts as a traveling companion of Paul's and the son of a woman named Mary, who owned a place where the group used to meet and pray back in the days when the church was young (Acts 12:12). And maybe this John Mark was the same person who appears in the scene of Jesus' arrest at Gethsemane as a boy who managed to escape from the soldiers' clutches but not without leaving his shirt behind, so that he ran off into the dark scared out of his wits and naked as the day he was born (Mark 14:51–52). Mark is the only one who reports the incident, and maybe he put it in as a kind of signature. An early historian says he was a friend of Peter's and got some of his information from him. Who knows? In the long run, the only things you can find out about him for certain are from the book he wrote. Whoever he was, Mark is as good a name to call him by as any other.

DAY 206

He was a man in a hurry, out of breath, with no time to lose because that's how the people were he was writing for too. The authorities were out for their blood, and they were on the run. At any moment of day or night a knock might come at the door, and from there to getting thrown to the lions or set fire to as living torches at one of Nero's evening entertainments took no time at all. So he leaves a lot out; it's amazing how much. There's no family tree for Jesus as there is in Matthew and Luke. There's nothing about how he was born, no angel explaining it ahead of time, no Wise Men, no Herod, no star. There's nothing about his childhood. There's precious little about his run-ins with the Pharisees, no Sermon on the Mount, only four parables. His teaching in general is brushed past hurriedly—except for one long speech, just a word here, a word there. "Immediately" is one of Mark's favorite words, and he uses it three times more than either Matthew or Luke, fifteen times more than John. "Immediately he called them" (1:20), "immediately on the sabbath he entered the synagogue" (1:21). Immediately the girl got up and walked (5:30), or the father cried (9:24), or the cock crowed (14:72). Jesus himself races by, scattering miracles like rice at a wedding. Mark is alive with miracles, especially healing ones, and Jesus rushes from one to another. He had no time to lose either.

Mark writes for people who already believe instead of the ones who need things explained, and therefore it's who Jesus was, rather than what he said, that Mark's book is bursting with—who he was and what he did with what little time he had. He was the "Son of God," that's who he was. Mark says it right out in the first sentence so nobody will miss it (1:1). And he came "not to be served but to serve, and to give his life as a ransom for many" (10:45). That's what he did, and he died doing it. The whole book is obsessed with the fact of his death. And with good reason.

If Jesus died as dead as anybody, what hope did the rest of them have who woke every morning to the taste of their own death in their mouths? Why did he die? He died because the Jews had it in for him, Mark says, because he is hard on the Jews, himself very likely a Gentile and writing for Gentiles. He died because that's the way he wanted it—that "ransom for many" again, a wonderful thing to be bought at a terrible price. He died because that's the way God wanted it. Marvelous things would come of his death, and the one long speech Mark gives has to do with those marvelous things. "The stars will be falling from heaven," Jesus says, "and the powers in the heavens will be shaken, and then they will see the Son of man coming in clouds with great power and glory" (13:25–26). Of course there was hope—hope that would set the stars reeling.

But even in the midst of his great haste, Mark stops and looks at Jesus, *sees* him better than any of the others do. When Jesus naps in a boat, it's in the *stern* he does it, with a *pillow* under his head (4:38). The others don't say that. And the grass was *green* when he fed the five thousand on hardly enough to feed five (6:39), not dry grass, crackling and brown. He got up "a great while before day" to go pray by himself (1:35), not at nine, not after a hot breakfast, and he was sitting down "opposite the treasury" when he saw the old lady drop her two cents in the collection box (12:41). Only Mark reports how the desperate father said, "I believe. Help thou my unbelief" (9:24), and how Jesus found it belief enough to heal his sick boy by. You can say they make no difference, such details as these, which the others skip, or you can say they make all the difference.

Then the end comes, and even Mark has to slow down there. Half his book has to do with the last days in Jerusalem and the way Jesus handled them and the way he was handled himself. And when he died, Mark is the one who reports what his last words were, even the language he spoke them in—*"Eloi, Eloi, lama sabachthani"*—which he translates, "My God, my God, why hast thou forsaken me?" (15:34). Only Matthew had the stomach to pick them up from Mark and report them too. Luke and John apparently couldn't bring themselves to.

Mark ends his book, as he begins it, almost in the middle of a sentence. There was no time to gather up all the loose ends. The world itself was the loose ends, and all history would hardly be enough to gather them up in. The women went to the tomb and found it empty. A young man in white was sitting there—"on the right," Mark says, not on the left. "He has risen," the young man said. "Go tell his disciples. And Peter," Mark adds, unlike Matthew and Luke again. Was it because he'd known Peter and the old man had wanted his name there? So the women ran out as if the place was on fire, which in a way of course it was, "for trembling and astonishment had come upon them, and they said nothing to anyone for they were afraid" (16:1–8). Later editors added a few extra verses to round things off, but that's where Mark ended it. In mid-air.

Mark's last word in his Gospel is *afraid,* and it makes you wonder if maybe the theory is true after all that he was the boy who streaked out of Gethsemane in such a panic. He knew how the women felt as they picked up their skirts and made a dash for it anyway. Wonderful and terrible things were happening, and more were still to come. He knew what fear was all about—the scalp cold, the mouth dry, the midnight knock at the door—but he also knew that fear was not the last thing. It was the next to the last thing. The last thing was hope. "You will see him, as he told you," the young man in white said (16:7). If that was true, there was nothing else that mattered. So Mark stopped there.

See also Gabriel.

MARRIAGE

DAY 207 THEY SAY THEY WILL LOVE, comfort, honor each other to the end of their days. They say they will cherish each other and be faithful to each other always. They say they will do these things not just when they feel like it, but even—for better for worse, for richer for poorer, in sickness and in health—when they don't feel like it at all. In other words, the vows they make at a marriage could hardly be more extravagant. They give away their freedom. They take on themselves each other's burdens. They bind their lives together in ways that are even more painful to unbind emotionally, humanly, than they are to unbind legally. The question is, what do they get in return?

They get each other in return. Assuming they have any success at all in keeping their rash, quixotic promises, they never have to face the world quite alone again. There will always be the other to talk to, to listen to. If they're lucky, even after the first passion passes, they still have a kindness and a patience to depend on, a chance to be patient and kind. There is still someone to get through the night with, to wake into the new day beside. If they have children, they can give them, as well as each other, roots and wings. If they don't have children, they each become the other's child.

They both still have their lives apart as well as a life together. They both still have their separate ways to find. But a marriage made in heaven is one where a man and a woman become more richly themselves together than the chances are either of them could ever have managed to become alone. When Jesus changed the water into wine at the wedding in Cana, perhaps it was a way of saying more or less the same thing.

MARY

THE TIME THEIR TWELVE-YEAR-OLD got lost in Jerusalem and they finally found him in the Temple, Mary said, "Behold, DAY 208 thy father and I have sought thee sorrowing" (Luke 2:48), and as things turned out, it was a shadow of things to come.

It's not hard to imagine her sorrowing again when Jesus left a good, steady job in Nazareth to risk his neck wandering around all over creation to proclaim whatever it was he thought he was proclaiming. Part of her sorrow was presumably that she loved him too much for himself instead of for the wild and holy business he thought he'd been called to. Another part must have been that like just about everybody else who was closest to him in Nazareth, she never really understood what he thought he was doing and may well have been one of the ones who, when he went back home once, decided he must be off his rocker. "He is beside himself," they said (Mark 3:21) and tried to lock him up for his own good.

Maybe some of the things he said to her didn't sound as bad in Aramaic as they do in English, but even so, she can't have been too happy about the time she told him the wine was running out at the wedding in Cana, and he said, "Woman, what have you to do with me?" (John 2:4), or the time they came and told him his mother was waiting outside for him, and he said, "Who is my mother?" (Matthew 12:48), adding that whoever did the will of his father who was in heaven, that was who his mother was.

For all the sentimentalizing that their relationship has come in for since, there's no place in the Gospels where he speaks some special, loving word or does some special, loving thing for the woman who gave him birth. You get the idea that he felt he couldn't belong truly to anybody unless he somehow belonged equally to everybody. They were all his mothers and brothers and sisters, and there's no place in the record where he offers her anything more than he offered everybody else.

No place, that is, except at the very end when, cross-eyed with pain, he looked down from where they'd nailed him and said something just for her. Even here he didn't call her his mother, just "woman" again, and he didn't say good-bye to her or anything like that. But it's as if here at last he finally spoke to the awful need he must have always sensed in her. "Behold your son," he said, indicating the disciple who was standing beside her, and then to the disciple, "Behold your mother" (John 19:26–27).

It was his going-away present to her really, somebody to be the son to her that he had had no way of being himself, what with a world to save, a death to die. He would be present in that disciple, he seemed to be saying, for her to live for, and to live for her. Beyond that, he would be present in generation after generation for her to mother, the Mater Dolorosa who seeks him always, and sorrowing, everywhere she goes.

See also Gabriel.

MARY MAGDALENE

I T IS SOMETIMES HELD that Mary Magdalene was the woman Luke tells about whom, to the righteous horror of Simon the Pharisee, Jesus let wash his feet and dry them with her hair despite her highly unsavory reputation, and about whom Jesus said, "I tell you, her sins, which are many, are forgiven because she loved much" (Luke 7:47). It's a powerful story, and it would be nice to think that Mary Magdalene is the one it's about, but unfortunately there's no really good reason for doing so.

When Jesus was on the road with his disciples, he had a group of women with him whom he'd cast evil spirits out of once and who had not only joined up with him, but all chipped in to help meet expenses. One of them was Mary Magdalene, and in her case it was apparently not just one evil spirit that had been cast out but seven.

DAY 209

Just what her problem had been, nobody says, but, helped along by the story in Luke, tradition has it that she'd been a whore. Maybe so. In any case, she seems to have teamed up with Jesus early in the game and to have stuck with him to the end. And beyond.

It's at the end that she comes into focus most clearly. She was one of the women who was there in the background when he was being crucified—she had more guts than most of them had—and she was also one of the ones who was there when they put what was left of him in the tomb. But the time that you see her best is on that first Sunday morning after his death.

John is the one who gives the greatest detail, and according to him it was still dark when she went to the tomb to discover that the stone had been rolled away from the entrance and that, inside, it was empty as a drum. She ran back to wherever the disciples were hiding out to tell them, and Peter and one of the others returned with her to check out her story. They found out that it was true and that there was nothing there except some pieces of cloth the body had been wrapped in. They left then, but Mary stayed on outside the tomb someplace and started to cry. Two angels came and asked her what she was crying about, and she said, "Because they have taken away my lord, and I do not know where they have laid him" (John 20:13). She wasn't thinking in terms of anything miraculous, in other words; she was thinking simply that even in death they wouldn't let him be and somebody had stolen his body.

Then another person came up to her and asked the same questions. Why was she crying? What was she doing there? She decided it must be somebody in charge, like the gardener maybe, and she said if he was the one who had moved the body somewhere else, would he please tell her where it was so she could go there.

Instead of answering her, he spoke her name—Mary—and then she recognized who he was, and though from that instant forward the whole course of human history was changed in so many profound and complex ways that it's impossible to imagine how it would have been different otherwise, for Mary Magdalene the only thing that had changed was that, for reasons she was in no state to consider, her old friend and teacher and strong right arm was alive again. "Rabboni!" she shouted and was about to throw her arms around him for sheer joy and astonishment when he stopped her.

"*Noli me tangere,*" he said. "Touch me not. Don't hold on to me" (John 20:17), thus making her not only the first person in the world to have her heart stop beating for a second to find him alive again when she'd thought he was dead as a doornail, but the first person also to have her heart break a little to realize that he couldn't be touched anymore, wasn't there anymore as a hand to hold on to when the going got tough, a shoulder to weep on, because the life in him was no longer a life she could know by touching it, with her here and him there, but a life she could know only by living it: with her here—old tart and retread, old broken-heart and last, best friend—and with him here too, alive inside her life, to raise her up also out of the wreckage of all that was wrecked in her and dead.

In the meanwhile, he had much to do and far to go, he said, and so did she, and the first thing she did was go back to the disciples to report. "I have seen the Lord," she said, and whatever dark doubts they might have had on the subject earlier, one look at her face was enough to melt them all away like morning mist. *John 20:1–18*

MATTHEW

THE APOSTLE MATTHEW was a tax collector, and one of the Gospels bears his name. Like Mark's, the book was written anonymously and the name attached to it later. Maybe it contains some of Matthew's recollections buried in it somewhere. Maybe not. In any case, it's the man who wrote it who's of chief interest

DAY 210

here, and all we know about him is what his book tells us. He didn't write it from scratch, but included virtually all of Mark in it plus a collection of the sayings of Jesus that seems to have been floating around plus some other material peculiar to him. It's what he did with it all that tells the kind of man he was.

What he did with it especially was to show that if, on the one hand, faith in Jesus was as new as a newborn babe, on the other hand, it was as old as the hills. As very likely a Jew himself, Matthew knew his Torah, and according to him Jesus was what the Torah was all about, whether anybody knew it or not. Much of his life was foretold there, Matthew keeps saying, and he loved to give examples. "Behold, a virgin shall conceive and bear a son, and his name shall be called Emmanuel," the prophet Isaiah had said, and Matthew nailed his idea that Mary was a virgin to that (Matthew 1:23). Jesus was born at Bethlehem, and that's just where the prophet Micah had said he'd be born (2:6). Hosea was the one who predicted the flight into Egypt when Jesus was still on his mother's knee (2:15), and it was Zechariah who said he'd come riding into Jerusalem on a donkey like a king great in his humbleness and humble in his greatness (21:5). But things like this were mere window dressing compared with the main thing Matthew wanted to say.

The main thing he wanted to say was that, although Jesus was born in the sticks and never had two cents to rub together and was ignored by just about everybody who mattered and was strung up in the end between two crooks, he was the same Messiah, the same Christ, the same Anointed of the Lord, that for centuries Israel had been waiting for with tears in its eyes. Everything Matthew wrote was aimed at convincing people that this was so and that to accept it was to find eternal life and that to deny it was to be like the Pharisees to whom Jesus said, "Woe to you . . . sons of those who murdered the prophets . . . you serpents, you brood of vipers, how are you to escape being sentenced to hell?" (23:29–33). Nobody loved the Jews more than Matthew did, writing till he was blue in the face so they would believe and be saved, but nobody was harder on them either. It was Matthew who added to Mark's account the terrible words they spoke when Pilate washed his hands of the whole grim business: "His blood be on us and on our children" (27:25).

Jesus was the Messiah, Matthew said, and he was also a second Moses, giving his Sermon on the Mount just as Moses had brought the tablets down from Mt. Sinai, but taking the fierce old stone and making pure gold of it. "You have heard that it was said 'An eye for an eye and a tooth for a tooth,' but I say to you, do not resist one who is evil" (5:38–39). "You have heard that it was said, 'You shall love your neighbors and hate your enemies,' but I say to you, love your enemies and pray for those who persecute you" (5:43–44). As Matthew saw it, Jesus came not to drown the old law out, as the Jews supposed, but to make it sing anew, like an angel.

It worried him a little the way in Mark's Gospel the Son of God sometimes sounds so much like anybody's son, and he did what he could to make him sound more godly. Where Mark wrote that when Jesus healed the leper, he was "moved with pity" (Mark 1:41), Matthew leaves out the pity and says he just healed him. When Mark says he looked at the people who objected to miracles on the Sabbath "with anger, grieved at their hardness of heart" (Mark 3:5), Matthew leaves that out too. He won't let him "sigh deeply" when they ask him for a sign (Mark 8:12), and Mark's "he could do no mighty work" in his own hometown (Mark 6:5) becomes just "he did not" do any in Matthew (13:58). "Why do you call me good? No one is good but God alone," Jesus says in Mark to the man who greets him that way (Mark 10:18), and Matthew tinkers with it till it reads, "Why do you ask me about what is good?" (19:17). You can't blame him for tinkering really. He can't help retouching the photograph when he loves its subject so—making the warts a little less wartlike, the miracles a little more miraculous—and in the end he lets him at least die like a man as well as like a God with the same dark cry that Mark reports—"My God, my God, why have you let me down?" (27:46).

Mark ends his Gospel with the women tearing out of the empty tomb in terror. Things were happening beyond their power to cope with, "and they said nothing to any one, for they were afraid" (Mark 16:8). But in Matthew the angel tells them not to be. "Don't be afraid," he says (28:5). There was no reason to be afraid, Matthew says. It was all set down right there in the Torah if you just knew how to read it right. Hadn't Isaiah written, "He will not wrangle or cry aloud, nor will any one hear his voice in the streets; he will not break a bruised reed or quench a smoldering wick"? (12:19–20). Such a man as that, so gentle and kind, was bound to come to such an end. There was no need to be afraid. And yet wasn't it written also, "The people who sat in darkness have seen a great light, and for those who sat in the region of the shadow of death, light has dawned" (4:16)? Dawned for the gentle man himself, and for the frightened women, and dawned for everyone else too who would only hear and believe.

The women took the angel's word to heart apparently because, though "they departed quickly from the tomb with fear," Matthew says, they departed also with "great joy" and ran to tell the disciples what had happened because they couldn't hold it in any longer (28:8). And just in case there should be any question as to what their great joy was all about, Matthew ends his Gospel with words that explain it. "Lo, I am with you always," Jesus says, "even unto the end of the world" (28:20), and for once Matthew felt that no Old Testament reference was necessary.

ME

As in "ME FIRST" and "gimme," the pronoun *me* has gotten a bad name over the years. It's other people we're told we should be thinking about. It's giving to them. But taken all by itself—just *me*—there's something rather poignant about it. Only two letters long. Barely one syllable. It looks as though it needs all the help it can get.

DAY 211

"Love your neighbor as yourself," we're told. Maybe before I can love my neighbor very effectively, I have to love me—not in the sense of a blind passion, but in the sense of looking after, of wishing well, of forgiving when necessary, of being my own friend.

MEDITATION

In our minds we are continually chattering with ourselves, and the purpose of meditation is to stop it. To begin with, maybe we try to concentrate on a single subject—the flame of a candle, the row of peas we are weeding, our own breath. When other subjects float up to distract us, we escape them by simply taking note of them and then letting them float away without thinking about them. We keep returning to the in-and-out of our breathing until there is no room left in us for anything else. To the candle flame until we ourselves start to flicker and burn. To the weeds until we become only a pair of grubby hands pulling them. In time we discover that we are no longer chattering.

DAY 212

If we persist, every once and so often we may find ourselves entering the suburbs of a state where we are conscious but no longer conscious of anything in particular, where we have let go of almost everything.

The end of meditation is to become empty enough to be filled with the kind of stillness the Psalmist has in mind when he says, "Be still, and know that I am God" (46:10).

MEMORY

DAY 213   THERE ARE TWO WAYS OF REMEMBERING. One way is to make an excursion from the living present back into the dead past. The old sock remembers how things used to be when you and I were young, Maggie. The faraway look in his eyes is partly the beer and partly that he's really far away.

The other way is to summon the dead past back into the living present. The young widow remembers her husband, and he is there beside her.

When Jesus said, "Do this in remembrance of me" (1 Corinthians 11:24), he was not prescribing a periodic slug of nostalgia.

MEPHIBOSHETH

DAY 214   MEPHIBOSHETH WAS ONLY FIVE YEARS OLD when news came through that his father, Jonathan, and his grandfather, King Saul, had both been killed in battle. Terrified that the child might be next, his nurse snatched him up in her arms and started to run off with him when she tripped and fell in her panic, and the boy was so badly crippled that he never walked right again.

The new king, David, might very well have decided to get rid of him. It was standard procedure then to wipe out your predecessor's entire family when you came to the throne just in case any of them happened to have political ambitions; but maybe because Mephibosheth was a cripple and thus not likely to give him much trouble, or maybe because his father had been David's best friend, or maybe just because he felt sorry for him, or maybe some combination of all these, David decided to be generous. It was the kind of crazy, magnificent gesture he liked to make every once in a while, like the time some soldiers risked their necks breaking through the enemy lines to bring him a cup of cool water from Bethlehem, his hometown, and David won the hearts of everybody by saying, "Shall I drink the blood of the men who went at the risk of their lives?" (2 Samuel 23:15–17), and poured it out on the ground.

In any case, he had Mephibosheth brought to him, and the poor child fell on his face in terror at what for all he knew was going to be the ax, but David told him not to be afraid. He told him that he was to have all the property that rightfully belonged to him and a man named Ziba to look after him, and he also promised him that from then on he was to take all his meals at the king's table as if he was his own son.

Ziba was a sly one, as it turned out, and years later when there was a revolt against David, Ziba told him that Mephibosheth had defected to the other side. What motivated this lie was the hope that David would grant him not only his favor, but also all of Mephibosheth's real estate, and so David did.

After the revolt was successfully put down, however, Mephibosheth showed up and convinced David that Ziba had been lying and he had been on the right side all along, and David seemed to believe him. But poor David—he was so shattered by everything that had happened, especially by the death of his beloved if treacherous Absalom, that he couldn't give the matter his full attention and more or less brushed Mephibosheth off by telling him that he and Ziba could divide the real estate between them for all he cared and to stop pestering him.

It would be sad if the relationship had ended on such an unsatisfactory note—the old king too broken-hearted to care much about anything anymore, and Mephibosheth limping home to work things out somehow with Ziba. But that isn't where it ended.

Before David had a chance to leave, Mephibosheth said that he was so overjoyed that David had driven the rascals out and come through the battle safe and sound that just to celebrate he was prepared to let Ziba take the whole damn place. Whether or not he made good on the offer, or even intended to, hardly matters. It was a crazy and magnificent gesture to make, and maybe David was not too lost in his own grief to realize, however dimly, at whose knees he had learned to make it.   *2 Samuel 9; 16:1–4; 19:24–30*

See also Absalom.

MESSIAH

"W IE MAN'S MACHT, IST'S FALSCH" is a crude German saying that means, freely translated, "Whatever people do, it turns out lousy." The Russians throw out the czars and end up with Stalin. The Americans free their slaves so they can move out into the world as paupers.

Or take the Jews. The nation that God chooses to be the hope of the world becomes the stooge of the world. The nation of priests becomes a nation of international politicians so inept at playing one major power off against another that by the time they're through, Egypt, Assyria, Babylonia, Persia, Rome, all have a chance at wiping their feet on them—the cream of the population deported, the

Temple destroyed, Jerusalem razed. The law of Moses becomes the legalism of the Pharisees, and "Can mortals be righteous before God?" becomes "Is it kosher to wear my dentures on the Sabbath?" The high priests sell out to the army of occupation. The Holy City turns into Miami Beach. Even God is fed up. Nobody knows all this better than the Jews know it. Who else has a Wailing Wall? Read the prophets.

Wie man's macht, ist's falsch. But the Jews went on hoping anyway, and beginning several centuries before the birth of Jesus, much of their hope took the form of an implausible dream that someday God would send them Somebody to make everything right. He was referred to as the Messiah, which means in Hebrew "the Anointed One," that is, the One anointed by God, as a king at his coronation is anointed, only for a bigger job. The Greek word for Messiah is "Christ."

How and when the Messiah would come was debatable. Theories as to what he would be like multiplied and overlapped: a great warrior king like David, a great priest like Melchizedek, a great prophet like Elijah. Who could possibly say? But whatever he was, his name would be called "Wonderful Counselor, Mighty God, Everlasting Father, Prince of Peace," and "of the increase of his government and of peace there would be no end" (Isaiah 9:6–7). Handel set him to music. On Passover eve to this day an extra cup is placed on the table for Elijah in case he stops in to say the Messiah is here at last. The door is left open.

When Jesus of Nazareth came riding into Jerusalem on his mule, a small group of radicals, illiterates, and ne'er-do-wells hailed him as the Messiah, the Christ. Everybody else suggested that you had to draw the line somewhere and advised as public and unpleasant an execution as possible, so nobody would fail to get the point. No one can deny that reason and prudence were on the side of the latter.

Reasons for Drawing the Line Somewhere

1. He wasn't a king, a priest, or a prophet. He was nobody from nowhere. He spoke with an accent.

2. On the one hand, his attitude toward the law was cavalier, to say the least. He said that it wasn't what went into your mouth that mattered, but what came out of it, thus setting back both the kosher industry and the WCTU about a thousand years apiece (Matthew 15:11). Also, some of his best friends were whores and crooks.

3. On the other hand, he not only went further than Moses, but claimed his own to be the higher authority. Moses was against murder. Jesus was against vindictive anger. Moses was against adultery. Jesus was against recreational sex. Moses said love your neighbor. Jesus said love your enemy too. Moses said be good. Jesus said be perfect (Matthew 5:21–48).

4. Who did he think he was anyway?

5. Who *can* be perfect?

6. Who wants to be?

7. He was not only a threat to the established church but to the establishment itself. Jewish orthodoxy and the Pax Romana were both in danger. He could easily have become a Fidel Castro.

8. His fans attributed a great many miracles to him up to and including bringing a corpse back to life, but there was one miracle he couldn't pull off, and that was saving his own skin. He died just as dead on the cross as all the others who had died on it, and some of them held out a lot longer.

9. His fans continue to ascribe a great many miracles to him, including his own resurrection, but the world is in just about as bad shape since his time as before, maybe worse.

As far as I know, there is only one good reason for believing that he was who he said he was. One of the crooks he was strung up with put it this way: "If you are the Christ, save yourself and us" (Luke 23:39). Save us from whatever we need most to be saved from. Save us from each other. Save us from ourselves. Save us from death both beyond the grave and before.

If he is, he can. If he isn't, he can't. It may be that the only way in the world to find out is to give him the chance, whatever that involves. It may be just as simple and just as complicated as that.

See also Jesus, salvation.

MICAH

WHEN MICAH'S MOTHER discovered the silver missing, the last person she suspected was her son Micah, so she laid a curse on the unknown thief's head that was enough to fell an ox. This threw such a scare into Micah that he produced the silver from under his bed and owned up.

DAY 216

To show there were no hard feelings, his mother counteracted the curse with a blessing that was enough to make hair grow on a doorknob. She also said she wanted Micah to have the money anyway, since he seemed to want it so badly, but told him to use it in a good cause. What he did was to have it melted down and made into a religious statue that made the Golden Calf look like an animal cracker and hired a priest just to take care of it. He had the idea that not only was this a good cause, but it was also good business. "Now

I know that the Lord will prosper me," he said (Judges 17:13). That's what he knew.

After a while a bunch of Danite toughs turned up who were so impressed by the silver statue, they decided they'd have to have it. The priest started to make a fuss as they were struggling out the door with it, but when they explained to him that working for a tribe like the Danites got you a lot more in the way of fringe benefits than working for one small-time crook with an Oedipus complex, his scruples were overcome, and they ended up getting not only the statue, but the priest to go with it.   *Judges 17–18*

MINISTER

DAY 217   THERE ARE three basic views of ministers:

1. Ministers are nice people. They'll take a drink if you offer them one, and when it comes to racy stories, they can tell a few right along with the best of them. They preach good sermons, but they're not like those religious fanatics who think they've got to say a prayer every time they pay a call. When it comes to raising money, they're nobody's fool and have all the rich old parishioners eating out of their hands. They have bridged the generation gap by introducing things like a rock group at the eleven-o'clock service and what they call rap sessions on subjects like drugs and sex instead of Sunday school. At the same time they admit privately that, though the kids have a lot going for them, they wish they'd cut their hair properly. They're big on things like civil rights, peace, and the environment. They send their children to private school. They make people feel comfortable in their presence by showing them that they've got their feet on the ground

like everybody else. They reassure them that religion is something you should take seriously, but not go overboard with.

2. Ministers have their heads in the clouds, which is just where you should have your head when your mind is on higher things. Their morals are unimpeachable, and if you should ever happen to use bad language in their presence, you apologize. They have a lovely sense of humor and get a kick out of it every time you ask if they can't do something about all this rainy weather we've been having. They keep things like sex, politics, race, and alcoholism out of their sermons. Their specialty is religion, and they're wise enough to leave other matters to people who know what they're talking about.

3. Ministers are as anachronistic as alchemists or chimney sweeps. Like Tiffany glass or the queen of England, their function is primarily decorative. Although their various perspectives are admittedly limited, rapists and rape victims, drug addicts, victims and perpetrators of child abuse, and the like are all to be listened to for their special insights. The perspective of ministers, on the other hand, is so hopelessly distorted and biased that there is no point in listening to them unless you happen to share it.

The first ministers were the twelve disciples. There is no evidence that Jesus chose them because they were brighter or nicer than other people. In fact the New Testament record suggests that they were continually missing the point, jockeying for position, and, when the chips were down, interested in nothing so much as saving their own skins. Their sole qualification seems to have been their initial willingness to rise to their feet when Jesus said, "Follow me." As Saint Paul put it later, "God chose what is foolish in the world to shame the wise, God chose what is weak in the world to shame the strong" (1 Corinthians 1:27).

When Jesus sent the twelve out into the world, his instructions were simple. He told them to preach the Kingdom of God and to heal (Luke 9:2), with the implication that to do either right was in effect to do both. Fortunately for the world in general and the church in particular, the ability to do them is not dependent on either moral character or IQ. To do them in the name of Christ is to be a minister. In the name of Christ not to do them is to be a bad joke.

See also healing, joke, Reverend.

MIRACLE

DAY 218

A CANCER INEXPLICABLY CURED. A voice in a dream. A statue that weeps. A miracle is an event that strengthens faith. It is possible to look at most miracles and find a rational explanation in terms of natural cause and effect. It is possible to look at Rembrandt's *Supper at Emmaus* and find a rational explanation in terms of paint and canvas.

Faith in God is less apt to proceed from miracles than miracles from faith in God.

See also healing.

MONEY

DAY 219

THE MORE YOU THINK about money, the less you understand it. The paper it's printed on isn't worth a red cent. There was a time you could take it to the bank and get gold or silver for it, but all you'd get now would be a blank stare.

If the government declared that the leaves of the trees were money so there would be enough for everybody, money would be worthless. It has worth only if there is not enough for everybody. It has worth only because the government declares that it has worth and because people trust the government in that one particular although in every other particular they wouldn't trust it around the corner.

The value of money, like stocks and bonds, goes up and down for reasons not even the experts can explain and at moments nobody can predict, so you can be a millionaire one moment and a pauper the next without lifting a finger. Great fortunes can be made and lost completely on paper. There is more concrete reality in a baby's throwing a rattle out of the crib.

There are people who use up their entire lives making money so they can enjoy the lives they have entirely used up.

Jesus says that it's easier for a camel to go through the eye of a needle than for a rich man to enter the Kingdom of God. Maybe the reason is not that the rich are so wicked they're kept out of the place, but that they're so out of touch with reality they can't see it's a place worth getting into.

MORALITY

IT IS NO SECRET that ideas about what is right and what is wrong vary from time to time and place to place. King Solomon would not be apt to see eye to eye with a Presbyterian missionary on the subject of monogamy. For that reason, a popular argument runs, morality is all relative to the tastes of the time and not to be taken any more seriously by the enlightened than tastes in food, dress, architecture, or anything else. At a certain level, this is indisputably so. But there is another level.

DAY 220

In order to be healthy, there are certain rules you can break only at your peril. Eat sensibly, get enough sleep and exercise, avoid bottles marked poison, don't jump out of boats unless you can swim, and so on.

In order to be happy, there are also certain rules you can break only at your peril. Be at peace with your neighbor, get rid of hatred and envy, tell the truth, avoid temptations to evil you're not strong enough to resist, don't murder, steal, and so on.

Both sets of rules are as valid for a third-century Hottentot as for a twentieth-century Norwegian, for a Muslim as for a Methodist bishop, for the emperor Nero as for Marilyn Monroe.

Both sets of rules—the moral as well as the hygienic—describe not the way people feel life ought to be, but the way they have found life is.

See also law.

MOSES

DAY 221

WHENEVER HOLLYWOOD cranks out a movie about Moses, they always give the part to somebody like Charlton Heston in fake whiskers. The truth of it is he probably looked a lot more like Tevye the milkman.

Forty years of tramping around the wilderness with the Israelites was enough to take it out of anybody. When they weren't raising hell about running out of food, they were raising it about running out of water. They were always hankering after the fleshpots of Egypt and making bitter remarks about how they should have stayed home and let well enough alone. As soon as his back was turned, they started whooping it up around the Golden Calf, and when somebody stood up and said he ought to be thrown out, the motion was seconded by thousands. Any spare time he had left after taking care of things like that he spent trying to persuade God not to wipe them out altogether, as they deserved.

And then, of course, there was the hardest blow of all. When he finally had it all but made and got them as far as the top of Mt. Pisgah, where the whole Promised Land stretched out before them as far as the eye could see, God spoke up and said this was the place all right, but for reasons that were never made entirely clear, Moses was not to enter it with them. So he died there in his one hundred and twentieth year, and after a month of hanging around and wishing they'd treated him better, the Israelites went on in without him.

Like Abraham before him and Noah before that, not to mention like a lot of others since, the figure of Moses breathing his last up there in the hills with his sore feet and aching back serves as a good example of the fact that when God puts the finger on people, their troubles have just begun.

And yet there's not a doubt in the world that in the last analysis Moses, like the rest of those tough old birds, wouldn't have had it any different. Hunkered down in the cleft of a rock once, with God's hand over him for added protection, he had been allowed to see the Glory itself passing by and, although all God let him see was the back part, it was something to hold on to for the rest of his life. And then there was one other thing that was even better than that.

Way back when he was just getting started and when out of the burning bush God had collared him for the first time, he had asked God what God's name was, and God had told him, so that from then on he could get in touch with God anytime he wanted. Nobody had ever known God's name before Moses did, and nobody would ever have known it afterward except for his having passed it on; and with that thought in his heart up there on Pisgah, and with that name on his lips, and with the sunset in his whiskers, he became in the end a kind of burning bush himself.

See also Aaron, Korah.

MOTHER

DAY 222
JESUS WAS BY NO MEANS SENTIMENTAL on the subject of mothers. He said that people who loved their mothers more than they loved him were not worthy of him (Matthew 10:37), indicating that duty comes first. And when they told him his mother was outside waiting while he spoke to some group or other, he said that his mother was anybody who did God's will (Matthew 12:50), indicating that his fellow believers came a close second.

To his own mother he could be very abrupt. When she came to him at the wedding in Cana to tell him the wine had given out, he said, "O woman, what have you to do with me? My hour has not yet come" (John 2:4), meaning perhaps that she was to let him alone, that at that early point in his ministry he wasn't ready to be known as a miracle worker. He was speaking his heart to her if not exactly reprimanding her, and it was just "woman" he called her, not "mother."

Some of the last words he ever spoke were in her behalf, however. She was standing at the foot of his cross when he told her in effect that from then on his disciple John would look after her. "Behold your son," he said, indicating him to her (John 19:26). Again it was just "woman" he called her, but her welfare and safekeeping were among the last thoughts he ever had.

Our mothers, like our fathers, are to be honored, the Good Book says. But if Jesus is to be our guide, honoring them doesn't mean either idealizing or idolizing them. It means seeing them both for who they are and for who they are not. It means speaking the truth to them. It means the best way of repaying them for their love is to love God and our neighbor as faithfully and selflessly as at their best our parents have tried to love us. It means seeing they are taken care of to the end of their days.

MOVIES

Victor Laszlo leading the patrons of Rick's Café in the "*Marseillaise*" to drown out the Nazis' "*Wacht am Rhine*" under the direction of Major Strasser—possibly that moment in *Casablanca* had as much impact on the World War II generation as the news of Pearl Harbor or the eloquence of Winston Churchill.

DAY 223

Or the blacks in the Alabama courthouse gallery rising to their feet as Atticus Finch passes by below. Or Dolly Levi sashaying down the grand staircase of the Harmonia Gardens to find Louis Armstrong at the bottom radiant as the sun at noon. Or John Travolta lithe as a panther in his white suit and pompadour dancing in Brooklyn. Or Jimmy Stewart being bailed out by his friends in the last moments of *It's a Wonderful Life*.

In a world where there are no longer books we have almost all of us read, the movies we have almost all of us seen are perhaps the richest cultural bond we have. They go on haunting us for years the way our dreams go on haunting us. In a way they *are* our dreams. The best of them remind us of human truths that would not seem as true without them. They help to remind us that we are all of us humans together.

MUSIC

DAY 224

WHEREAS PAINTERS WORK WITH SPACE—the croquet players on the lawn, behind them the dark foliage of the hedge, above them the sky—musicians work with time, as one note follows another note the way tock follows tick.

Music both asks us and also enables us to listen to certain qualities of time—to the grandeur of time, says Bach, to the poignance of time, says Mozart, to the swing and shimmer of time, says Debussy, or however else you choose to put into words the richness and complexity of what each of them is wordlessly "saying."

We learn from music how to listen to the music of our own time—one moment of our lives following another moment the way the violin passage follows the flute, the way the sound of footsteps on the gravel follows the rustle of leaves in the wind, which follows the barking of a dog almost too far away to hear.

Music helps us to "keep time" in the sense of keeping us in touch with time, not just time as an ever-flowing stream that bears all of us away at last, but time also as a stream that every once in a while slows down and becomes transparent enough for us to see down to the streambed the way, at a wedding, say, or watching the sun rise, past, present, and future are so caught up in a single moment that we catch a glimpse of the mystery that, at its deepest place, time is timeless.

See also art.

MYSTERY

DAY 225

T HERE ARE MYSTERIES you can solve by taking thought. For instance, a murder mystery whose mysteriousness must be dispelled in order for the truth to be known.

There are other mysteries that do not conceal a truth to think your way to, but whose truth is itself the mystery. The mystery of your self, for example. The more you try to fathom it, the more fathomless it is revealed to be. No matter how much of your self you are able to objectify and examine, the quintessential, living part of your self will always elude you, that is, the part that is conducting the examination. Thus you do not solve the mystery, you live the mystery. And you do that not by fully knowing yourself, but by fully being yourself.

To say that God is a mystery is to say that you can never nail him down. Even on Christ the nails proved ultimately ineffective.

MYSTICISM

DAY 226

M YSTICISM IS WHERE RELIGIONS START. Moses with his flocks in Midian, Buddha under the Bo tree, Jesus up to his knees in the waters of Jordan—each of them is responding to Something of which words like *Shalom, Nirvana, God* even, are only pallid souvenirs. Religion as ethics, institution, dogma, ritual, Scripture, social action—all of this comes later and in the long run maybe counts for less. Religions start, as Frost said poems do, with a lump in the throat—to put it mildly—or with a bush going up in flames, a rain of flowers, a dove coming down out of the sky. "I have seen things," Aquinas told a friend, "that make all my writings seem like straw."

Most people have also seen such things. Through some moment of beauty or pain, some sudden turning of their lives, most of them have caught glimmers at least of what the saints are blinded by. Only then, unlike the saints, they tend to go on as though nothing has happened.

We are all more mystics than we choose to let on, even to ourselves. Life is complicated enough as it is.

MYTH

DAY 227　THE RAW MATERIAL OF A MYTH, like the raw material of a dream, may be something that actually happened once. But myths, like dreams, do not tell us much about that kind of actuality. The creation of Adam and Eve, the Tower of Babel, Oedipus—they do not tell us primarily about events. They tell us about ourselves.

In popular usage, a myth has come to mean a story that is not true. Historically speaking, that may well be so. Humanly speaking, a myth is a story that is always true.

NAAMAN

NAAMAN WAS A FIVE-STAR GENERAL in the Syrian army and also a leper. His wife had working for her a little Jewish slave girl who mentioned one day that there was a prophet named Elisha back home who could cure leprosy as easily as a toad cures warts. So Naaman took off for Israel with a letter of introduction from the king and a suitcase full of cash and asked Elisha to do his stuff.

Elisha told him to go dunk in the Jordan seven times, and after some initial comments to the effect that there were rivers back in Syria that made the Jordan look like a leaky faucet, Naaman went and did what he was told. When he came out of the water, his complexion was positively radiant. Naaman was so grateful that he converted on the spot and reached into his suitcase for an inch of fifties, but Elisha said he was a prophet of Yahweh, not a dermatologist, and refused to take a cent.

Elisha had a servant named Gehazi, however, who had different ideas. He hot-footed it after Naaman and told him that Elisha had changed his mind. He said that if Naaman would like to make a small contribution to charity, he, Gehazi, would make sure it got into the right hands. Naaman was only too pleased to hand out the fifties, and Gehazi went home and deposited them in his personal checking account.

When Elisha got wind of it, he told Gehazi that the healing power of God was not for sale to the highest bidder and, to press his point home, transferred Naaman's leprosy to him. For the sake of Naaman's newfound faith in Yahweh as above all a God of love and mercy, it would be nice to believe that news of Elisha's over-reaction never reached him in Syria.   *2 Kings 5*

See also Elisha.

NAKEDNESS

DAY 229   EVERYBODY KNOWS WHAT EVERYBODY else looks like with no clothes on, but there are few of us who would consider going around in public without them. It is our sexuality that we're most concerned to hide from each other, needless to say, although one sometimes wonders why. Males and females both come with more or less standard equipment, after all. There would be no major surprises.

It started, of course, with Adam and Eve. Before they ate the apple, "the man and his wife were both naked, and were not ashamed," Genesis tells us, and it was only afterward that "they sewed fig leaves together and made themselves aprons" (2:25; 3:7). In other words, part of knowing evil as well as good was to know sex as a way of making objects of each other as well as a way of making love, and we have all felt guilty about it ever since. *Pudenda*, deriving from the Latin for "that of which we ought to be ashamed," is etymology at its most depressing.

People go around dressed to the teeth, and in our minds we go around undressing them. Again one wonders why. It's not just to see their bodies, surely. We already know what those look like. If our most abandoned fantasies came true and we were actually to have our way with the bodies that attract us most, I suspect it wouldn't even be that either. We already know just what bodies can do and what they can't.

Maybe our hunger to know each other fully naked is in the last analysis simply our hunger to know each other fully. I want to know you with all your defenses down, all your pretenses set aside, all your secrets laid bare. Then maybe I will be brave enough to lay myself bare, so that at last we can be naked together and unashamed.

NARCOTICS

WHETHER THEY MAKE YOU FEEL SILLY or dreamy or bursting with cosmic energy, whether they induce euphoria or hallucinations, whether they give you a sense of being all-powerful and all-knowing or a sense of drifting through space like the dawn, all narcotics offer you a temporary reprieve from reality. Needless to say, that's what makes narcotics in particular and drugs in general so addictive. Everybody wants out from time to time, and they provide a way. They provide an adventure. Most of all, maybe, they provide a vacation from being yourself.

DAY 230

It was Karl Marx who called religion the opiate of the masses, and the metaphor was not intended to be complimentary. Religion is only a way of making the poor forget the bitter reality of their life on earth by giving them pipe dreams of pie in the sky by and by. That's what Marx meant by his comparison, and the history of the church has frequently confirmed his analysis. There are other ways of comparing them, however.

For instance, whereas people who do drugs get a temporary reprieve from a reality they often find too hard to live with, religious people claim to find a new kind of life grounded in a Reality they find increasingly hard to live without. They claim also that, although narcotics may provide you with an adventure, the life of faith is an adventure in itself, because once you start out on that path, there's no telling where it may take you next.

Finally, they would say that if by dulling or sharpening or altering your senses you can get a vacation from being yourself, by coming to your senses you can little by little—often quite painfully at first, but more and more gratefully as time goes by—become yourself. That much of the pie, anyway, can be yours this side of the sky.

NATHAN

DAY 231 JUST ABOUT EVERY KING seems to have had a prophet to help keep him honest. Saul had Samuel, Ahab had Elijah, Hezekiah had Isaiah, Jehoiakim and Zedekiah seem to have shared Jeremiah, and so on. King David was the one who had Nathan. There is nothing of Nathan's in writing so it's impossible to grade him on literary skill, but when it comes to the ability to be a thorn in the king's flesh, he gets a straight A. The best example is, of course, the most famous.

David had successfully gotten rid of Uriah the Hittite by assigning him to frontline duty, where he was soon picked off by enemy snipers. After a suitable period of mourning, David then proceeded to marry Uriah's gorgeous young widow, Bathsheba. The honeymoon had hardly started rolling before Nathan came around to describe a hardship case he thought David might want to do something about.

There were these two men, Nathan said, one of them a big-time rancher with flocks and herds of just about everything that has four legs and a tail and the other the owner of just one lamb he was too soft-hearted even to think about in terms of chops and mint jelly. He had it living at home with himself and the family, and he got to the point where he even let it lap milk out of his own bowl and sleep at the foot of his bed. Then one day the rancher had a friend drop in unexpectedly for a meal and, instead of taking something out of his own overstuffed freezer, he got somebody to go over and commandeer the poor man's lamb, which he and his friend consumed with a garnish of roast potatoes and new peas.

When Nathan finished, David hit the roof. He said anybody who'd pull a stunt like that ought to be taken out and shot. At the very least he ought to be made to give back four times what the lamb was worth. And who was the greedy, thieving slob anyway, he wanted to know.

"Take a look in the mirror the next time you're near one," Nathan said. It was only the opening thrust. By the time Nathan was through, it was all David could do just to pick up the receiver and tell room service to get a stiff drink up to the bridal suite.

2 Samuel 12:1–15

NATHANIEL

PHILIP COULD HARDLY WAIT to tell somebody, and the first person he found was Nathaniel. Ever since Moses they'd been saying the Messiah was just around the corner, and now, by God, if

DAY 232

he hadn't finally turned up. Who would have guessed where? Who would have guessed who?

"Jesus of Nazareth," Philip said. "The son of Joseph." But he could hear his words fall flat even as he was saying them. It wasn't as if he'd said it was the head rabbi or somebody.

"Can anything good come out of Nazareth?" Nathaniel said. Or Podunk maybe? *Brooklyn?*

Philip told him to come take a look for himself then, but Jesus got a look at Nathaniel first as he came puffing down the road toward him, nearsighted and earnest, with his yarmulke on crooked, his dog-eared Torah under his arm.

"Behold, an Israelite indeed, in whom is no guile," Jesus said. Nathaniel was sweating like a horse. His thick specs were all fogged up. His jaw hung open. He said, "How do you know me?" His astonishment made him stammer.

"Before Philip called you," Jesus said, "when you were under the fig tree, I saw you."

It was all it took apparently. "Rabbi!" Nathaniel's long black overcoat was too tight across the shoulders and you could hear a seam split somewhere as he made an impossible bow. "You are the Son of God," he said. "You are the King of Israel."

"Because I said I saw you under the fig tree, do you believe?" Jesus said. There was more to it than parlor tricks. He said, "You shall see greater things than these." But all Nathaniel could see for the moment, not daring to look up, were his own two shoes, pigeon-toed in the dust.

"You will see heaven opened," he heard Jesus say, "the angels of God ascending and descending upon the Son of man." When Nathaniel decided to risk a glance, the sun almost blinded him.

What Nathaniel did see finally was this. It was months later, years. One evening he and Peter and a few of the others took the boat out fishing. They didn't get a nibble between them but stuck it out all night. It was something to do anyway. It passed the time. Just at dawn, in that queer half-light, somebody showed up on the beach and cupped his mouth with his hands. "Any luck?" The answer was no in more ways than one, and they said it. Then give it another try, the man said. Reel in the nets and cast them off the starboard side this time. There was nothing to lose they hadn't lost already, so they did it, and the catch had to be seen to be believed, had to be felt, the heft of it almost swamping them as they pulled it aboard.

Peter saw who the man was first and heaved himself overboard like a side of beef. The water was chest-high as he plowed through it, tripping over his feet in the shallows so he ended up scrambling ashore on all fours. Jesus was standing there waiting for him by a little charcoal fire he had going. Nathaniel and the others came ashore, slowly, like men in a dream, not daring to speak for fear they'd wake up. Jesus got them to bring him some of their fish, and then they stood around at a little distance while he did the cooking. When it was done, he gave them the word. "Come and have breakfast," he said, and they all came over and sat down beside him in the sand.

Nathaniel's name doesn't appear in any of the lists of the twelve apostles, but there are many who claim he was also known as Bartholomew, and that name does appear there. It would be nice to think so. On the other hand, he probably considered it honor enough just to have been on hand that morning at the beach, especially considering the unfortunate remark he'd made long ago about Nazareth.

They sat there around the fire eating their fish with the sun coming up over the water behind them, and they were all so hushed and glad and peaceful that anybody passing by would never have guessed that, not long before, their host had been nailed up on a hill outside the city and left there to die without a friend to his name.

John 1:43–51; 21:1–14

NATURE

DAY 233 — AN UNNATURAL MOTHER means one who doesn't behave the way mothers are supposed to behave, and a natural affection is the kind of affection that's right on the mark, unlike the other kinds that make respectable flesh crawl just to think about them. When somebody does or is asked to do something abominable, you can say that it is against nature because nature is not abominable. Natural foods, natural colors, natural flavors, the natural look, and so on are currently the advertising industry's highest endorsement. The idea of Mother Nature represents the same view of things—nature as nurturing, pure, beneficent, on the side of the good.

Unfortunately, Adam and Eve took nature with them when they fell. You've only to look at the sea in a November gale. You've only to consider the staggering indifference of disease, or the field at Antietam, or a cook boiling a lobster, or the statistics on child abuse. You've only to remember your own darkest dreams.

But the dream of Eden is planted deep in all of us too. A parade of goldenrod by the road's edge. The arc of a baseball through the summer sky. The way a potter's hand cradles the clay. They all cry aloud of the might-have-been of things, and the may-be-still.

NAVE

DAY 234 — THE NAVE IS THE CENTRAL PART of the church from the main front to the chancel. It's the part where the laity sit, and in great Gothic churches it's sometimes separated from the choir and clergy by a screen. It takes its name from the Latin *navis,* meaning "ship," one reason being that the vaulted roof looks rather like an inverted keel. A more interesting reason is that the church itself is thought of as a ship or Noah's ark. It's a resemblance worth thinking about.

In one as in the other, just about everything imaginable is aboard, the clean and the unclean both. They are all piled in together helter-skelter, the predators and the prey, the wild and the tame, the sleek and beautiful ones and the ones that are ugly as sin. There are sly young foxes and impossible old cows. There are the catty and the piggish and the peacock-proud. There are hawks and there are doves. Some are wise as owls, some silly as geese; some meek as lambs and others ravening wolves. There are times when they all cackle and grunt and roar and sing together, and there are times when you could hear a pin drop. Most of them have no clear idea just where they're supposed to be heading or how they're supposed to get there or what they'll find if and when they finally do, but they figure the people in charge must know and in the meanwhile sit back on their haunches and try to enjoy the ride.

It's not all enjoyable. There's backbiting just like everywhere else. There's a pecking order. There's jostling at the trough. There's growling and grousing, bitching and whining. There are dogs in the manger and old goats and black widows. It's a regular menagerie in there, and sometimes it smells to high heaven like one.

But even at its worst, there's at least one thing that makes it bearable within, and that is the storm without—the wild winds and terrible waves and in all the watery waste, no help in sight.

And if there is never clear sailing, there is at least shelter from the blast, a sense of somehow heading in the right direction in spite of everything, a ship to keep afloat, and, like a beacon in the dark, the hope of finding safe harbor at last.

NEBUCHADNEZZAR

NEBUCHADNEZZAR, KING OF BABYLON, was a real horror. The ingenuities of his torture chamber made those of Vlad the Impaler look like parlor games. When King Zedekiah of Israel rebelled against him, for instance, he had his eyes put out—which anybody could have thought of—but the master touch was that just before this was done, he had Zedekiah's sons killed before him in some appropriately loathsome way, so that in his blindness he'd have that last sight to live with for the rest of his days.

And then there was the famous trio of Shadrach, Meshach, and Abednego. They were all three of them employees of the Babylonian civil service, but as Jews they believed there was one God only, and his name was Yahweh. Therefore when Nebuchadnezzar had a ninety-foot idol made out of twenty-four-karat gold and commanded everybody to grovel at its feet—or else—Shadrach, Meshach, and Abednego tried to get themselves registered as conscientious objectors. Nebuchadnezzar lost no time in ordering them to be thrown into a flaming, fiery furnace prepared especially for the occasion.

He ordered the furnace to be heated to seven times its normal temperature, had the three trussed up in their long black overcoats, galoshes, and derby hats, and then took his seat in the front row center. The fire was so hot that the men who tossed them in were burned to a crisp in the process. This wasn't supposed to be part of the act, and neither was what happened next. First of all, Nebuchadnezzar could see that there were four men in the furnace, instead of three, and that the fourth was an angel. Second, they were all obviously fireproof.

Nebuchadnezzar was so undone that he called to them to come

out, and when they emerged with not even their earlocks singed, he pardoned them on the spot and remarked that Yahweh was clearly a God you didn't fool around with. He then went a step further by issuing a new command to the effect that from that day forward, anybody caught treating Yahweh with anything but the highest respect was to be torn limb from limb and have his house burned down, in that order.

Yahweh was presumably pleased by this sudden conversion of Nebuchadnezzar's, but he may have had the sense that there were still a few rough edges to take care of before the job was complete.

Daniel 3; 2 Kings 25:7

See also Daniel, Judith.

NEHEMIAH

N EHEMIAH BROKE DOWN and wept when he found out that DAY 236 the walls of Jerusalem were still in ruins from when the Babylonians had pulled them down over a century earlier. The Persians had replaced the Babylonians as the number-one superpower by then, and, as luck would have it, Nehemiah was one of the king of Persia's right-hand men. So, waiting till the king was in a mellow mood after his second planter's punch, he went and asked for permission to go home to Jerusalem and supervise its refortification. The king said not to stay too long, but gave him the go-ahead anyway. To strengthen his hand when he got to Jerusalem, he even had him made governor.

It took Nehemiah twelve years to get the job done, and it was tough sledding all the way. The Samaritans thought he was rebuilding the walls to keep them out and so did their friends. Others made a fuss because they were suspicious of a Jewish governor who worked for Persia. A man named Tobiah said that any wall Nehemiah was likely to build would fall to pieces the first time a fox stubbed his toe on it (Nehemiah 4:3). The construction crews threatened to walk off the job because back on the farm what the weeds hadn't taken over, the neighbors had. The Jerusalem Jews tended to be freer and easier about religion than Nehemiah was, so they objected to him as a narrow-minded, holier-than-thou Puritan prude. And so on. But after twelve years the walls somehow got put back in working order anyway, Nehemiah threw a big celebration, and then he went back to Persia.

After another twelve years, he showed up in Jerusalem to see how things had been getting on and almost had a heart attack. The walls were strong as ever, but inside the walls everything had gone to pot. Tobiah, the man who'd made the remark about the fox, was living like a king in the Temple, while a lot of priests were out on the street corners selling apples. Everybody went to work on the Sabbath just like any other day, and all the big stores were open, not to mention the bars, and if people bothered to go to religious services at all, they could hardly hear a word over the spiel of the Tyrian fish peddlers. Worst of all in Nehemiah's eyes, there were a lot of Jewish boys who'd not only married foreign girls, but had picked up their foreign ways to such an extent that most of their kids didn't even know Hebrew.

Once again Nehemiah rose to the occasion. He tossed Tobiah out on his ear and had the place fumigated. He took the priests off the streets. He reinstated the Blue Laws with a vengeance. He sent the fish peddlers packing. He had the city gates locked from Saturday night till Monday morning. As for the boys who'd married wrong, he reminded them how even the great Solomon had gotten into trouble over his taste for imported cheesecake, and to make sure they wouldn't forget, he "contended with them and cursed them and beat some of them and pulled out their hair" (Nehemiah 13:25). By the time he was through, he had Jerusalem looking like a convention of hard-shell Baptists.

The ones who called Nehemiah a blue-nosed Puritan weren't entirely off base, of course, but you can't help admiring him anyway. It's too bad that one of his favorite prayers had to be "Remember for my good, O my God, all that I have done for this people" (Nehemiah 5:19; compare 13:14, 31). It would be nice to think he'd done it all for love. But even when he went wrong, he went wrong for the right reasons mostly, and when his time finally came, it's at least ten to one that God didn't fail to remember.

The Book of Nehemiah

NEIGHBOR

WHEN JESUS SAID to love your neighbor, a lawyer who was present asked him to clarify what he meant by *neighbor*. He wanted a legal definition he could refer to in case the question of loving one ever happened to come up. He presumably wanted something on the order of: "A neighbor (hereinafter referred to as the party of the first part) is to be construed as meaning a person of Jewish descent whose legal residence is within a radius of no more than three statute miles from one's own legal residence unless there is another person of Jewish descent (hereinafter to be referred to as the party of the second part) living closer to the party of the first part than one is oneself, in which case the party of the second part is to be construed as neighbor to the party of the first part and one is oneself relieved of all responsibility of any sort or kind whatsoever."

DAY 237

Instead, Jesus told the story of the Good Samaritan (Luke 10:25–37), the point of which seems to be that your neighbor is to be construed as meaning anybody who needs you. The lawyer's response is left unrecorded.

See also love.

NEUROTICS

DAY 238   A MINISTER BEGAN TO PREACH by saying, "To start with, I'm just as neurotic as everybody else," and there was an audible sigh of relief from the entire congregation. Anxiety, depression, hypochondria, psychosomatic aches and pains, fear of things like heights and crowds—there's almost nobody who can't lay claim to at least a few of them. They involve an utterly fruitless expenditure of energy. They result in an appalling waste of time. Yet maybe there's something to be said for them anyhow.

Neurotics don't lose their sense of reality like people who think they're a poached egg or that somebody's going to blow poison gas under the door while they're asleep. You might even say that they have a heightened sense of reality. They sense everything that's really there and then some. They don't understand why the peculiar things that are going on inside their heads are going on, but at least they're more or less in touch with what's going on inside their heads and realize not only that they're peculiar themselves, but that so are lots of other people. That's probably why neurotics are apt to be more sympathetic than most and, unless their particular neurosis happens to be nonstop talking or antisocial behavior, why they make such good listeners.

You wouldn't want one of them operating on your brain or flying you across the Andes in a jet or in charge of things when there's a red alert, but when it comes to writing poems and novels or painting pictures or even preaching sermons, it's hard to beat them. Their overactive imaginations, which are a curse elsewhere, are a blessing there. Personally speaking, their oversensitivity may be their undoing, but professionally it's one of their strongest cards. They may see and hear and feel more than is good for them, but there's no question that, with the exception of their immediate families, it's good for everybody else.

"A thorn was given me in the flesh, a messenger of Satan, to harass me, to keep me from being too elated," Saint Paul wrote to his friends (2 Corinthians 12:7). Nobody knows just what the problem was that he was referring to, but you don't have to read many of his Letters to suspect that he would have been among those who sighed with relief at the minister's opening confession. His violent swings of mood from deep depression to exaltation. His passionate likes and dislikes. His boasting. His dark sense of guilt. Almost certainly it was some sort of neurosis that was bugging him. Three times he prayed to God to get rid of it for him, he said, but God never did. Maybe it's not so hard to guess why.

A psychological cure would no doubt have greatly enriched Paul's own life at the time but would have greatly impoverished generations of his readers' lives ever since. "Through his wounds we are healed" are words to be reserved only for the most grievous Wound, the holiest Healing (Isaiah 53:5). But maybe in some small measure they can be applied to people like Paul too. Their very hang-ups and crotchets and phobias and general quirkiness give their kind—and, through them, give us—insights into the human heart that few can match. It's a high price for them to pay for our comfort and edification, but where they come closest to a kind of oddball holiness of their own is the feeling they give you sometimes that even if they could get out of paying it, they wouldn't.

NEWS

WHEN THE EVENING NEWS comes on, hundreds of thousands of people all over the earth are watching it on their TV screens or listening to it on their radios. Disasters and scandals, scientific breakthroughs and crimes of passion, perpetual wars and the perpetual search for peace—people sit there by the millions half dazed by the things that go to create each particular day. Maybe they even try to make some kind of sense of it or, if they're not up to that, at least try to come to some sort of terms with it, try to figure out how it's apt to affect them for good or ill.

There is also, of course, the news that rarely if ever gets into the media at all, and that is the news of each particular day of each particular one of us. That is the news we're so busy making that we seldom get around to sitting down and thinking it over. If it takes some extraordinary turn we might, but the unextraordinary, commonplace events of each day as they come along we tend to let slip by almost unnoticed. That is, to put it mildly, a pity. What we are letting slip by almost unnoticed are the only lives on this planet we're presumably ever going to get.

We're all of us caught up in our own small wars, both hot and cold. We have our crimes and passions, our failures and successes. We make our occasional breakthroughs. God knows we are searching for peace. It's all apt to happen so quietly and on so small a scale we hardly realize it's happening. Only an unanswered letter. A phone conversation. A tone of voice. A chance meeting at the post office. An unexpected lump in the throat. Laughing till we cry. But these things are what it's all about. These things are what we are all about.

Maybe there's nothing on earth more important for us to do than sit down every evening or so and think it over, try to figure it out if we can, at least try to come to terms with it. The news of *our* day. Where it is taking us. Where it is taking the people we love. It is, if nothing else, a way of saying our prayers.

NICODEMUS

NICODEMUS HAD HEARD ENOUGH about what Jesus was up to in Jerusalem to make him think he ought to pay him a visit and find out more. On the other hand, as a VIP with a big theological reputation to uphold, he decided it might be just as well to pay it at night. Better to be at least fairly safe than to be sorry, he thought, so he waited till he thought his neighbors were all asleep.

DAY 240

So Nicodemus was fairly safe, and, at least at the start of their nocturnal interview, Jesus was fairly patient. What the whole thing boiled down to, Jesus told him, was that unless you got born again, you might as well give up.

That was all very well, Nicodemus said, but just how were you supposed to pull a thing like that off? How especially were you supposed to pull it off if you were pushing sixty-five? How did you get born again when it was a challenge just to get out of bed in the morning? He even got a little sarcastic. Could one "enter a second time into the mother's womb?" he asked (John 3:4), when it was all one could do to enter a taxi without the driver's coming around to give him a shove from behind?

A gust of wind happened to whistle down the chimney at that point, making the dying embers burst into flame, and Jesus said being born again was like that. It wasn't something you *did*. The wind did it. The Spirit did it. It was something that happened, for God's sake.

"How can this be?" Nicodemus asked (John 3:9), and that's when Jesus really got going.

Maybe Nicodemus had six honorary doctorates and half a column in *Who's Who*, Jesus said, but if he couldn't see something as plain as the nose on his face, he'd better go back to kindergarten.

Jesus said, "I'm telling you God's so in love with this world that he's sent me down, so if you don't believe your own eyes, then maybe you'll believe mine, maybe you'll believe me, maybe you won't come sneaking around scared half to death in the dark anymore, but will come to, come clean, come to *life*."

What impressed Nicodemus even more than the speech was the quickening of his own breathing and the pounding of his own heart. He hadn't felt like that since his first kiss, since the time his first child was born.

Later on, when Jesus was dead, he went along with Joseph of Arimathea to pay his last respects at the tomb in broad daylight. It was a crazy thing to do, what with the witch-hunt that was going on, but he decided it was more than worth it.

When he heard the next day that some of the disciples had seen Jesus alive again, he wept like a newborn child.   *John 3:1–21; 19:38–42*

See also born again, Joseph of Arimathea.

NOAH

DAY 241   THE WATERS HAD ALL DRAINED off and the ground was dry again when God hung a rainbow in the sky to remind him he'd promised "that never again shall all flesh be cut off by the waters of a flood" (Genesis 9:11). The way he explained it to Noah, "I will look upon it and remember the everlasting covenant between God and every living creature that is upon the earth" (9:13).

In one way, then, it gave Noah a nice warm feeling to see the rainbow up there, but in another way it gave him an uneasy twinge. If God needed the rainbow as a reminder, he thought, that could mean that, if someday God didn't happen to look in the right direction or had something else on his mind, he might forget his promise and the heavy drops would start pattering down on the roof a second time.

Noah could never forget the first time—how little by little the waters had risen, first just spreading in over the kitchen linoleum and trickling down the cellar stairs, but eventually floating newspapers and family photographs off tables and peeling wallpaper off walls until people were driven to the rooftops, where they sat wrapped in blankets with their transistor radios on their laps looking up for a break in the clouds and reassuring each other that this must be the clearing shower at last. He remembered the animals he'd had to leave behind—the old sow with her flaxen lashes squealing on top of a hen house as the ripples lapped at her trotters, the elephants awash up to their hips, a marmalade cat with one ragged ear clinging to a TV aerial as a pair of parakeets in a wicker cage floated by over what had once been the elementary-school gym.

He also remembered the endless days in the ark—the miserable food, the seasickness, the smells. When the downpour finally stopped, he sent birds out to see if they could find any dry land anywhere, and he remembered watching them fly away until they were no bigger than flyspecks on a windowpane, remembered the feeling in his stomach when they finally flew back having found no place to roost.

He remembered especially one of the doves and how, when he saw it returning, he had reached out over the rail, and it had landed on the calluses of his upturned palm. With his eyes closed and tears on his cheeks, he had touched his lips to its feathers, and as he felt the panic of its bird's heart, it had seemed to him that the whole world was just as fragile and as doomed.

But then, after weeks, another dove came back with a sprig of olive in its beak, and the tops of the mountains began to reappear out of the watery waste, and now at last the great, glittering rainbow arched above him, and the great promise echoed in his ears. "Never again," God had said, and Noah clung on to those words like a raft in a high sea.

With the rainbow tied around his little finger to jog his memory, surely God would never forget what he'd said. No matter what new meanness people might think up, surely the terrible thing would never happen again. As an expert in hoping against hope, the old sailor told himself that the worst was over and that as sure as God made little green apples, a new, green world would blossom up out of the sodden wreckage of the old.

He then planted the first vineyard and invented wine. The way he figured it, wine would help him forget the dark past and, if all went well, would be like the champagne at a wedding that you toast the future with. And if all did not go well, if doubts and fears began to gather like rain clouds in his heart, then wine would help him ride out the storm within as before he'd ridden out the forty days and forty nights.

In the meantime, he would keep his eye on the rainbow and his hand near the corkscrew and try to be fruitful and multiply just the way God had told him and his seven-time great-grandfather Adam before him.

Genesis 6–9

See also Ham.

NUMBERS

IT'S EXTRAORDINARY how many numbers we carry around in our heads—countless telephone and fax numbers, account numbers, street numbers, ID numbers, ZIP codes, area codes, and so on and so forth.

DAY 242

Numbers are lifeless and boring abstractions, yet for each of us there are some that are so charged that, if we happen to be paying attention, they can make our hearts skip a beat. The year somebody we loved was born or died. A telephone number we may not have called for twenty years. The number of steps there were to climb to our bedroom as a child. The age we were when we first fell in love.

Uninteresting as they are in themselves, numbers remind us that, if we have our wits about us, almost anything we look at has treasure buried in it.

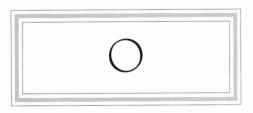

OBEDIENCE

DAY 243

IN RECENT TIMES *obedience* has become a bad word. It seems incompatible with good words like *independence, individualism,* and *freedom.* The emphasis is all on doing your own thing and doing it your own way. What you're supposed to obey is authority, and authority has come to be confused with "the authorities"—people in uniform or with Ph.D.s or earning ten times a year more than you do. Who wants to obey *them?*

Many parents have given up asking their children to obey them and just hope they won't burn the house down. In religious circles, obedience, like its partners poverty and chastity, tends to be associated largely with monasticism. If the mother superior or the abbot tells you to do something, you better do it. Otherwise you let your own conscience be your guide and take no guff from anybody. The phrase *obeying your conscience* is gradually being replaced by *listening to your conscience.*

It is generally supposed that to obey somebody is necessarily to do something for somebody else's sake. However, when Jesus asks people to obey above everything the law of love, it is above everything for their own sakes that he is asking them to obey it.

See also freedom, law of love.

OBSERVANCE

A RELIGIOUS OBSERVANCE can be a wedding, a christening, a Memorial Day service, a bar mitzvah, or anything like that you might be apt to think of. There are lots of things going on at them. There are lots of things you can learn from them if you're in a receptive state of mind. The word *observance* itself suggests what is perhaps the most important thing about them. DAY 244

A man and a woman are getting married. A child is being given a name. A war is being remembered and many deaths. A youngster is coming of age.

It is life that is going on. It is always going on, and it is always precious. It is God that is going on. It is you who are there that is going on.

As Henry James advised writers, be one on whom nothing is lost. *Observe!!* There are few things as important, as religious, as that.

OCEAN

THEY SAY THAT whenever the great Protestant theologian Paul Tillich went to the beach, he would pile up a mound of sand and sit on it gazing out at the ocean with tears running down his cheeks. One wonders what there was about it that moved him so. DAY 245

The beauty and power of it? The inexpressible mystery of it? The futility of all those waves endlessly flowing in and ebbing out again? The sense that it was out of the ocean that life originally came and that when life finally ends, it is the ocean that will still remain? Who knows?

In his theology Tillich avoided using the word *God* because it seemed to him too small, denoting only another being among beings. He preferred to speak instead of the Ground of Being, of God as that which makes being itself possible, as that because of which existence itself exists. His critics complain that he is being too metaphysical. They say they can't imagine praying to anything so abstract and remote.

Maybe Tillich himself shared their difficulty. Maybe it was when he looked at the ocean that he caught a glimpse of the One he was praying to. Maybe what made him weep was how vast and overwhelming it was and yet at the same time as near as the breath of it in his nostrils, as salty as his own tears.

OLD AGE

DAY 246

OLD AGE IS NOT, as the saying goes, for sissies. There are some lucky ones who little by little slow down to be sure, but otherwise go on to the end pretty much as usual. For the majority, however, it's like living in a house that's in increasing need of repairs. The plumbing doesn't work right anymore. There are bats in the attic. Cracked and dusty, the windows are hard to see through, and there's a lot of creaking and groaning in bad weather. The exterior could use a coat of paint. And so on. The odd thing is that the person living in the house may feel, humanly speaking, much as always. The eighty-year-old body can be in precarious shape, yet the spirit within as full of beans as ever. If that leads senior citizens to think of all the things they'd still love to do but can't anymore, it only makes things worse. But it needn't work that way.

Second childhood commonly means something to steer clear of, but it can also mean something else. It can mean that if your spirit is still more or less intact, one of the benefits of being an old crock is that you can enjoy again something of what it's like being a young squirt.

Eight-year-olds, like eighty-year-olds, have lots of things they'd love to do but can't because they know they aren't up to them, so they learn to *play* instead. Eighty-year-olds might do well to take notice. They can play at being eighty-year-olds, for instance. Stiff knees and hearing aids, memory loss and poor eyesight are no fun, but there are those who marvelously survive them by somehow managing to see them as, among other things and in spite of all, a little funny.

Another thing is that, if part of the pleasure of being a child the first time round is that you don't have to prove yourself yet, part of the pleasure of being a child the second time round is that you don't have to prove yourself any longer. You can be who you are and say what you feel, and let the chips fall where they may.

Very young children and very old children also have in common the advantage of being able to sit on the sideline of things. While everybody else is in there jockeying for position and sweating it out, they can lean back, put their feet up, and like the octogenarian King Lear "pray, and sing, and tell old tales, and laugh at gilded butterflies."

Very young children and very old children also seem to be in touch with something that the rest of the pack has lost track of. There is something bright and still about them at their best, like the sun before breakfast. Both the old and the young get scared sometimes about what lies ahead of them, and with good reason, but you can't help feeling that whatever inner goldenness and peace they're in touch with will see them through in the end.

ONAN

DAY 247   THE ANCIENT LAW was that if a man died, his brother was supposed to have a child by his widow so the line wouldn't become extinct. Therefore, when Er died, it was up to his brother Onan to perform the duty with Er's widow, Tamar. Because Onan knew that the child to be born wouldn't really be his, he refused and "spilled his semen on the ground" instead (Genesis 38:9). As a result, God killed him.

This story is dismal enough in itself, but later generations have made it more so. Onanism has become a euphemism for masturbation, and the punishment Onan received has been interpreted as meaning that God is, to say the least, against it. Actually what God was against was that Onan had disobeyed the law of levirate marriage and had done so on the unedifying grounds that he didn't want any children of his running around with another man's name. Presumably the punishment would have been just as severe if, instead of doing what he did, he'd simply caught the next bus out of town.

According to Dr. Kinsey, some 92 percent of all males have masturbated, as have some 62 percent of all women. The only damage to come of it seems to be the crippling sense of guilt and terror inculcated by well-meaning, pious folk who, forgetting their own sexual past, say that it makes you go crazy or blind or have your hair fall out.

There seem to be no scriptural grounds for condemning masturbation in itself. Like sex in general, if it is practiced to the exclusion of a loving relationship with other human beings, it is an infraction of the law of love and is its own punishment. On the other hand, if it's practiced as a temporary expedient until the right person comes along, it is harmless. It was not for his sexuality that Onan was punished, but for his stinginess and selfishness and general cussedness.   *Genesis 38:1–10*

ONESIMUS

S AINT PAUL WAS SERVING one of his periodic sentences behind bars when he met Onesimus. Onesimus was a slave who belonged to a Christian friend named Philemon, and why he was in jail nobody knows. Maybe he was a runaway. Maybe Philemon had charged him with theft. Anyway, when Onesimus had done his stretch and was about to be sprung, Paul wrote a short letter for him to give to his master, Philemon, when he got back home.

DAY 248

While they were doing time together, Paul wrote, not only had he made a Christian out of Onesimus, but he had also made him one of his best friends. The boy was like a son to him, Paul said, and sending him back was like "sending my very heart" (Philemon 1:12). Onesimus means "useful," and Paul plays on the name by saying he's become so useful to him that he doesn't know what he'll do without him. He doesn't come right out and say what he wants Philemon to do, but the hint could hardly be broader. "I would have been glad to keep him with me in order that he might serve me on your behalf during my imprisonment for the gospel," he wrote, "but I preferred to do nothing without your consent." In case that wasn't enough, he added, "Yes, my brother, I want some benefit from you in the Lord. Refresh my heart in Christ." In the meanwhile he hopes that Philemon will receive the boy back "no longer as a slave but more . . . as a beloved brother" (1:13–20).*

It's not known whether or not Philemon took the hint and let Onesimus return to be the old saint's comfort for what time was left him, but there's at least one good reason for believing that such was the case. Years later, when Paul was long since dead, another saint by the name of Ignatius was in jail. The bishop of Ephesus had sent some friends to visit him, and Ignatius wrote asking if a couple of them could be allowed to stay. Ignatius in his letter used some of the same language that Paul had used in his to Philemon, almost as if he was trying to remind him of something. And what was the name of the bishop he wrote to? It was Onesimus.

There's no proof that he was the same slave boy grown old and venerable with a mitre on his head, but it's very tempting to believe so. If he was, then he refreshed the hearts of not just one old saint, but two, and was more true to his name, *useful*, than Paul ever lived to discover.   *Philemon*

---

*Cf. John Knox, *Philemon Among the Letters of Paul* (Chicago: University of Chicago Press, 1935).

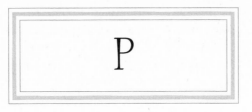

PARABLE

DAY 249

A PARABLE IS A SMALL STORY with a large point. Most of the ones Jesus told have a kind of sad fun about them. The parables of the Crooked Judge (Luke 18:1–8), the Sleepy Friend (Luke 11:5–8), and the Distraught Father (Luke 11:11–13) are really jokes in their way, at least part of whose point seems to be that a silly question deserves a silly answer. In the Prodigal Son (Luke 15:11–32), the elder brother's pious pique when the returning Prodigal gets the red-carpet treatment is worthy of Molière's *Tartuffe*, as is the outraged legalism of the Laborers in the Vineyard (Matthew 20:1–16) when Johnny-come-lately gets as big a slice of the worm as the early bird. The point of the Unjust Steward is that it's better to be a resourceful rascal than a saintly schlemiel (Luke 16:1–8); and of the Talents that, spiritually speaking, playing the market will get you further than playing it safe (Matthew 25:14–30).

Both the sadness and the fun are at their richest, however, in the parable of the Great Banquet (Luke 14:16–24). The "beautiful people" all send in their excuses, of course—their real estate, their livestock, their sex lives—so the host sends his social secretary out into the streets to bring in the poor, the maimed, the blind, the lame.

The string ensemble strikes up the overture to *The Bartered Bride*, the champagne glasses are filled, the cold pheasant is passed round, and there they sit by candlelight with their white canes and their empty sleeves, their orthopedic shoes, their sleazy clothes, their aluminum walkers. A woman with a harelip proposes a toast. An old man with the face of Lear on the heath and a party hat does his best to rise to his feet. A deaf-mute thinks people are starting to go home and pushes back from the table. Rose petals float in the finger bowls. The strings shift into the *Liebestod*.

With parables and jokes both, if you've got to have them explained, don't bother.

See also prayer.

PARENTS

DAY 250

"HONOR YOUR FATHER and your mother," says the Fifth Commandment (Exodus 20:12). Honor them for having taken care of you before you were old enough to take care of yourself. Honor them for the sacrifices they made on your behalf, including the ones you would have kept them from making if you'd had the chance. Honor them for having loved you.

But how do you honor them when, well-intentioned as they may have been, they made terrible mistakes with you that have shadowed your life ever since? How do you honor them when, far from loving you or taking care of you, they literally or otherwise abandoned you? How do you honor them when physically or sexually or emotionally they abused you?

The answer seems to be that you are to honor them even so.

Honor them for the pain that made them what they were and kept them from being what they might otherwise have become. Honor them because there were times when, even at their worst, they were doing the best they knew how to do. Honor them for the roles they were appointed to play—father and mother—because even when they played them abominably or didn't play them at all, the roles themselves are holy the way priesthood is holy even when the priest is a scoundrel. Honor them because, however unthinkingly or irresponsibly, they gave you your life.

PATRIOTISM

ALL "ISMS" RUN OUT IN THE END, and good riddance to most of them. Patriotism, for example. DAY 251

If patriots are people who stand by their country right or wrong, Germans who stood by Adolf Hitler and the Third Reich should be adequate proof that we've had enough of them.

If patriots are people who believe not only that anything they consider unpatriotic is wrong, but that anything they consider wrong is unpatriotic, the late Senator Joseph McCarthy and his backers should be enough to make us avoid them like the plague.

If patriots are people who believe things like "Better Dead Than Red," they should be shown films of Hiroshima and Nagasaki on August 6 and 9, 1945, respectively, and then be taken off to the funny farm.

The only patriots worth their salt are the ones who love their country enough to see that in a nuclear age it is not going to survive unless the world survives. True patriots are no longer champions of any one country in particular, but champions of the human race. It is not the homeland that they feel called on to defend at any cost, but the planet earth as home. If in the interest of making sure we don't blow ourselves off the map once and for all, we end up relinquishing a measure of national sovereignty to some international body, so much the worse for national sovereignty.

There is only one sovereignty that matters ultimately, and it is of another sort altogether.

PAUL

DAY 252

HE WASN'T MUCH TO LOOK AT. "Bald-headed, bowlegged, strongly built, a man small in size, with meeting eyebrows, with a rather large nose." Years after his death that's the way the apocryphal *Acts of Paul and Thecla* describes him, and Paul himself quotes somebody who had actually seen him: "His letters are strong, but his bodily presence is weak" (2 Corinthians 10:10). It was no wonder.

"Five times I have received at the hands of the Jews the forty lashes less one," he wrote. "Three times I have been beaten with rods. Once I was stoned. Three times I have been shipwrecked. A night and a day I have been adrift at sea. In danger from rivers . . . robbers . . . my own people . . . Gentiles. In toil and hardship, in hunger and thirst . . . in cold and exposure" (2 Corinthians 11:24–27). He also was sick off and on all his life and speaks of a "thorn in the flesh" that God gave him "to keep me from being too elated" (2 Corinthians 12:7). Epilepsy? Hysteria? Who knows? The wonder of it is that he was able to get around at all.

But get around he did. Corinth, Ephesus, Thessalonica, Galatia, Colossae, not to mention side trips to Jerusalem, Cyprus, Crete, Malta, Athens, Syracuse, Rome—there was hardly a whistle-stop in the Mediterranean world that he didn't make it to eventually, and sightseeing was the least of it. He planted churches the way Johnny Appleseed planted trees. And whenever he had ten minutes to spare he wrote letters. He bullied. He coaxed. He comforted. He cursed. He bared his soul. He reminisced. He complained. He theologized. He inspired. He exulted. Punch-drunk and Christ-drunk, he kept in touch with everybody. The postage alone must have cost him a fortune, not counting the energy and time. And where did it all start? On the road, as you might expect. He was still in charge of a Pharisee goon squad in those days and was hell-bent for Damascus to round up some troublemaking Christians and bring them to justice. And then it happened.

It was about noon when he was knocked flat by a blaze of light that made the sun look like a forty-watt bulb, and out of the light came a voice that called him by his Hebrew name twice. "Saul," it said, and then again "Saul. Why are you out to get me?" and when he pulled himself together enough to ask who it was he had the honor of addressing, what he heard to his horror was, "I'm Jesus of Nazareth, the one you're out to get." We're not told how long he lay there in the dust then, but it must have seemed at least six months. If Jesus of Nazareth had what it took to burst out of the grave like a guided missile, he thought, then he could polish off one bowlegged Christian-baiter without even noticing it, and Paul waited for the ax to fall. Only it wasn't an ax that fell. "Those boys in Damascus," Jesus said. "Don't fight them. Join them. I want you on my side," and Paul never in his life forgot the sheer lunatic joy and astonishment of that moment. He was blind as a bat for three days afterward, but he made it to Damascus anyway and was baptized on the spot. He was never the same again, and neither, in a way, was the world (Acts 9:1–6; 22:4–16; 26:9–18).

Everything he ever said or wrote or did from that day forward was an attempt to bowl over the human race as he'd been bowled over himself while he lay there with dust in his mouth and road apples down the front of his shirt: "Don't fight them, join them. He wants you on his side." *You*, of all people. *Me*. Who in the world, who in the solar system, the galaxy, could ever have expected it? He knew it was a wild and crazy business—"the folly of what we preach," he said—but he preached it anyway. "A fool for Christ's sake" he called himself as well as weak in his bodily presence, but he knew that "God's foolishness is wiser than human wisdom, and God's weakness is stronger than human strength" (1 Corinthians 1:18–25). There were times he got so carried away that his language went all out of whack. Infinitives split like atoms, syntax exploded, participles were left dangling.

"By grace you have been saved," he wrote to the Ephesians, and *grace* was his key word. *Grace*. Salvation was free, *gratis*. There was nothing you had to do to earn it and nothing you *could* do to earn it. "This is not your own doing, it is the gift of god—not the result of works, so that no one may boast," and God knows he'd worked, himself, and boasted too—worked as a Pharisee, boasting about the high marks he'd racked up in heaven till the sweat ran down and Christian heretics dropped like flies—only to find en route to Damascus that he'd been barking up the wrong tree from the start, trying to beat and kick his way through a door that had stood wide open the whole time. "For we are *his* workmanship, created in Christ Jesus for good works," he wrote; in other words, good works were part of it, all right, but after the fact, not before (Ephesians 2:8–10).

Little by little the forgiven person became a forgiving person, the person who found he or she was loved became capable of love, the slob that God had had faith in anyway became de-slobbed, faithful, and good works blossomed from his branches, from her branches, like fruit from a well-watered tree. What fruit? Love, Paul wrote the boys and girls in Galatia. Love was the sweetest and tenderest. And then "joy, peace, patience, kindness, goodness, faithful-ness, gentleness, self-control" till his typewriter ribbon was in tat-ters and he had to take to a pencil instead (Galatians 5:22–23).

And *Christ* was his other key word, of course. *Christ*—the key to the key. He never forgot how he'd called him by name—twice, to make sure it got through—and "while we were yet sinners, Christ died for us," he wrote out for the Romans (Romans 5:6) and for the Galatians again, "I have been crucified with Christ"—all that was dried up in him, full of hate and self-hating, self-serving and sick, all of it behind him now, dead as a doornail—so that "it is no longer I who live, but Christ who lives in me" (Galatians 2:20). And then, to the Philippians by registered mail, return receipt requested: "For me to live is Christ" (Philippians 1:21), and to the Ephesians, for fear they'd feel neglected if the mail carrier came empty-handed, "You he made alive when you were dead" (Ephesians 2:1). Alive like him.

But there were other times too. Sometimes the depression was so great he could hardly move the pencil across the page. "I don't understand my own actions," he said. "For I don't do what I want, but I do the very thing I hate. . . . I can will what is right, but I can't do it. For I don't do the good I want, but the evil I don't want is what I do. . . . For I delight in the law of God in my inmost self, but I see in my members another law at war with the law of my mind and making me captive to the law of sin. . . . Wretched man that I am! Who will deliver me from this body of death?" He sat there by himself, aiming his awful question at the plaster peeling off his walls, and maybe it was only ten minutes or maybe it was ten years before he had the heart to scratch out the answer: "Thanks be to God through Jesus Christ our Lord," he said (Romans 7:15–25).

It got him going again, and on the next page he was back in his old stride with a new question. "If God is for us, who is against us?"

He worked on that one for a minute or two and then gave it another try. "Who shall separate us from the love of Christ? Shall tribulation, or distress, or persecution, or famine, or nakedness, or peril, or sword?" It was the story of his life, needless to say, and at last he'd laid the groundwork for an answer he could get his back into. "*No!*" he wrote, the tip of his pencil point breaking off, he bore down so hard. "In all these things we are more than conquerors through him who loved us. For I am sure that neither death, nor life, nor angels, nor principalities, nor things present, nor things to come, nor powers, nor height, nor depth, nor anything else in all creation, will be able to separate us from the love of God in Christ Jesus our Lord" (Romans 8:31–39). He sat there, with his cauliflower ear and a lump on his forehead the size of an egg from the last time the boys had worked him over, and when he reached for the drawer to get out an envelope, he found that his hand was shaking so badly he could hardly open it.

The ups and the downs. The fights with his enemies and the fights with his friends. The endless trips with a fever and diarrhea. Keeping one jump ahead of the sheriff. Giving his spiel on windy street corners with nobody much to hear him most of the time except some underfed kids and a few old women and some yokels who didn't even know the language. Where was it all going to get him in the end? Where was it all going to get all of them, any of them, in the end? When you came right down to it, what was God up to, for God's sweet sake, sending them all out—prophets, apostles, evangelists, teachers, the whole tattered bunch—to beat their gums and work themselves into an early grave?

God was making a body for Christ, Paul said. Christ didn't have a regular body anymore, so God was making him one out of anybody he could find who looked as if he or she might just possibly do. He was using other people's hands to be Christ's hands and other people's feet to be Christ's feet, and when there was someplace where Christ was needed in a hurry and needed bad, he put the finger on some maybe not all that innocent bystander and got that person to go and be Christ in that place for lack of anybody better.

And how long was the whole great circus to last? Paul said, why, until we all become *human beings* at last, until we all "come to maturity," as he put it; and then, since there had been only one really *human* being since the world began, until we all make it to where we're like him, he said—"to the measure of the stature of the fullness of Christ" (Ephesians 4:11–13). Christs to each other, Christs to God. All of us. Finally. It was just as easy, and just as hard, as that.

Nobody's sure whether he ever got to Spain the way he'd planned or not, but either before he went or soon after he got back, he had his final run-in with the authorities, and the story is that they took him to a spot about three miles out of Rome and right there on the road, where he'd spent most of his life including what was in a way the beginning of his life, they lopped off his head.

At the end of its less than flattering description of his personal appearance, the *Acts of Paul and Thecla* says that "at times he looked like a man, and at times he had the face of an angel." If there is a God in heaven, as even in his blackest moments Paul never doubted there was, then bald-headed and bowlegged as he was, with those eyebrows that met and that oversized nose, it was with angel eyes that he exchanged a last long glance with his executioners.

See also Agrippa, Eutychus, Felix, Onesimus, Pauline Letters, Stephen.

PAULINE LETTERS

P AUL'S MADS WERE MADDER and his blues bluer, his pride prouder and his humbleness humbler, his strengths stronger DAY 253 and his weaknesses weaker than almost anybody else's you'd be apt to think of; and the splash he made when he fell for Christ is audible still. It is little wonder that from the start he was a genius at making enemies.

As his own Letters indicate, his contemporaries accused him of being insincere, crooked, yellow, physically repulsive, unclean, bumbling, and off his rocker. Since then the charges against him have tended to narrow down to one; that is, that he took the simple and beautiful gospel of Jesus and loused it up with obscure, divisive, and unnecessary theological subtleties.

Anybody who thinks the gospel of Jesus is simple should go back and take a look at it. "Love your neighbor." "Be ye perfect." "Resist not evil." "I and the Father are one." "Follow me." The only thing that's simple about the gospel is the language.

How? Why? Whence? Whither? These are the questions Paul digs into with all the gentleness and tact of a pneumatic drill. Jesus exploded on the scene like a bomb and blew the world in general and the world of Judaism in particular sky-high. It was left to Paul to try to sort out the pieces.

He wrote the church at Corinth what he got for his pains: "Five times I have received at the hands of the Jews the forty lashes less one. Three times I have been beaten with rods. Once I was stoned. Three times I have been shipwrecked. A night and a day I have been adrift at sea. In danger from rivers . . . robbers . . . my own people . . . Gentiles. In toil and hardship, through many a sleepless night, in hunger and thirst . . . in cold and exposure . . ." (2 Corinthians 11:24–27). One hears the whines and boasts of Shylock. One wishes he hadn't been the one who had to say it. But he says it and means it. And then he says, "I will not boast except of my weakness," and he means that too. The God who could work through the likes of him, he says, must be a God and a half.

So with a cauliflower ear and a split lip and whatever he meant by the thorn in the flesh that God gave "to keep me from being too elated" (2 Corinthians 12:7), he went his way and wrote his marvelous punch-drunk, Christ-drunk Letters. Jesus lit the fire, and Paul used it to forge for him a church.

See also eternal life, justification, sanctification.

PEACE

PEACE HAS COME TO MEAN THE TIME when there aren't any   DAY 254
wars or even when there aren't any major wars. Beggars can't be choosers; we'd most of us settle for that. But in Hebrew peace, *shalom*, means fullness, means having everything you need to be wholly and happily yourself.

One of the titles by which Jesus is known is Prince of Peace, and he used the word himself in what seem at first glance to be two radically contradictory utterances. On one occasion he said to the disciples, "Do not think that I have come to bring peace on earth; I have not come to bring peace, but a sword" (Matthew 10:34). And later on, the last time they ate together, he said to them, "Peace I leave with you; my peace I give to you" (John 14:27).

The contradiction is resolved when you realize that, for Jesus, peace seems to have meant not the absence of struggle, but the presence of love.

PECULIAR TREASURES

ZACCHEUS STOOD BARELY FIVE FEET TALL with his shoes   DAY 255
off and was the least popular man in Jericho. He was head tax

collector for Rome in the district and had made such a killing out of it that he was the richest man in town as well as the shortest. When word got around that Jesus would soon be passing through, he shinnied up into a sycamore tree so he could see something more than just the backs of other people's heads, and that's where he was when Jesus spotted him.

"Zaccheus," Jesus said, "get down out of there in a hurry. I'm spending tonight with *you*" (Luke 19:5), whereupon all Jericho snickered up their sleeves to think he didn't have better sense than to invite himself to the house of a man nobody else would touch with a ten-foot pole.

But Jesus knew what he was doing. Zaccheus was taken so completely aback by the honor of the thing that, before Jesus had a chance to change his mind, Zaccheus promised not only to turn over 50 percent of his holdings to the poor, but to pay back, four to one, all the cash he'd extorted from everybody else. Jesus was absolutely delighted. "Today salvation has come to this house," he said (Luke 19:9), and since that was his specialty after all, you assume he was right.

Zaccheus makes a good one to end the biblical characters with because in a way he can stand for the whole cast of biblical characters who precede him. He's a sawed-off little social disaster with a big bank account and a crooked job, but Jesus welcomes him aboard anyway, and that's why he reminds you of all the others too.

There's Aaron whooping it up with the Golden Calf the moment his brother's back is turned, and there's Jacob conning everybody including his own father. There's Jael driving a tent peg through the head of an overnight guest, and Rahab, the first of the red-hot mamas. There's Nebuchadnezzar with his taste for roasting the opposition, and Paul holding the lynch mob's coats as they go to work on Stephen. There's Saul the paranoid, and David the stud, and those mealy-mouthed friends of Job's who would probably have succeeded in boring him to death if Yahweh hadn't stepped in just in the nick of time. And then there are the ones who betrayed the people who loved them best such as Absalom and poor old Peter, such as Judas even.

Like Zaccheus, they're all of them peculiar as hell, to put it quite literally, and yet you can't help feeling that, like Zaccheus, they're all of them somehow treasured too. Why are they treasured? Who knows? But maybe you can say at least this about it—that they're treasured less for who they are and for what the world has made them than for what they have it in them at their best to be, because ultimately, of course, it's not the world that made them at all. "All the earth is mine!" says Yahweh, "and all that dwell therein," adds Psalm 24, and in the long run, presumably, that goes for you and me too.

Luke 19:1–10

PETER

EVERYBODY KNOWS PETER started out as a fisherman. He lived with his wife in Capernaum, where they shared a house with his mother-in-law and his brother Andrew. He and Andrew had their own boat and were in business with a couple of partners named James and John, Zebedee's sons. The first time Jesus laid eyes on him, he took one good look and said, "So you're Simon, the son of John" (John 1:42), and then said that from then on he'd call him Cephas, which is Aramaic for Peter, which is Greek for "rock."

DAY 256

A rock isn't the prettiest thing in creation or the fanciest or the smartest, and if it gets rolling in the wrong direction, watch out, but there's no nonsense about a rock, and once it settles down, it's pretty much there to stay. There's not a lot you can do to change a rock or crack it or get under its skin, and, barring earthquakes, you can depend on it about as much as you can depend on anything. So Jesus called him the Rock, and it stuck with him the rest of his life. Peter the Rock. He could stop fishing for fish, Jesus told him. He'd been promoted. From there on out people were to be his business. Now he could start fishing for them.

There was a lot of talk going around about who Jesus was and who he wasn't, and Jesus himself seemed just as glad to steer clear of the subject. Then one day he brought it up himself, and the disciples batted it around for a while. There were some people who said he was John the Baptist come back from the grave, they told him, or maybe Elijah, or Jeremiah, or some other prophet who thought he'd see what he could do a second time around. There were all kinds of half-baked theories, they said. Then Jesus put it to them straight: "Who do *you* say that I am?" Nobody wanted to stick his neck out, and the silence was deafening till Peter broke it or till it washed up against the rock that Peter was and broke itself. "You're the Christ," he said, "the Son of the living God" (Matthew 16:15–16).

It took a lot of guts to say, and Jesus knew it did. If it was true, it was enough to blow the lid off everything. If it wasn't true, you could get yourself stoned to death as a blasphemer for just thinking it. But Peter said it anyway, and Jesus made up for him the only beatitude he ever made up for a single individual and said, "Blessed are you, Simon Bar-Jona," which means Simon, son of John, and seems to have been what he always called him when he really meant business. Then he went back to Peter the Rock again and told him that he was the rock he wanted to build his church on and that as soon as he got to heaven, he was to be the one to decide who else got in. "I will give you the keys of the kingdom," Jesus said (Matthew 16:17–19). It was another promotion.

But if Peter was the only one Jesus ever gave a beatitude of his own to, he was also the only one he ever gave hell to, at least in quite such a direct way. It happened not long afterward. Jesus was saying that to be the Christ, the Son of the living God, wasn't going to be a bed of roses all the way, and the time wasn't far off when he'd suffer the tortures of the damned in Jerusalem and be killed. Peter couldn't take it. "God forbid, Lord. This shall never happen," he said, and that's when Jesus lit into him. "Get behind me, Satan," he said, because the rock that Peter was at that point was blocking the grim road that Jesus knew he had to take whether he or Peter or anybody else wanted it that way or not, because God wanted it that way, and that was that. "Get behind me Satan!" he said. "You are a stumbling block to me; for you are setting your mind not on divine things but on human things" (Matthew 16:21–23).

It wasn't the last time Peter said the wrong thing either, or asked the wrong question, or got the wrong point, or at least failed to do the thing that was right. The day he saw Jesus walking on the water and tried to walk out to him himself, for instance. He was just about to go under for the third time, because rocks have never been much good at floating, when Jesus came to the rescue (Matthew 14:28–31). Once when Jesus was talking about forgiveness, Peter asked how many times you were supposed to forgive any one person—seven times maybe?—and Jesus turned on him and said that after you'd forgiven him seventy times seven you were just starting to get warmed up (Matthew 18:21–22). Another time Jesus was talking about heaven, and Peter wanted to know what sort of special deal people like himself got, people who'd left home and given everything up the way he'd given everything up to follow Jesus; and Jesus took it easy on him that time, because a rock can't help being a little thick sometimes, and said he'd get plenty, and so would everybody else (Matthew 19:27–30).

And then there were the things he did or failed to do, those final, miserable days just before the end. At their last supper, when Jesus started to wash the disciples' feet, it was Peter who protested—"*You* wash *my* feet!"—and when Jesus explained that it showed how they were all part of each other and servants together, Peter said, "Lord, not my feet only but my hands and my head!" and would probably have stripped down to the altogether if Jesus hadn't stopped him in time (John 13:5–11). At that same sad meal, Jesus said he would have to be going soon, and because Peter didn't get what he meant or couldn't face it, he asked about it, and Jesus explained what he meant was that he was going where nobody on earth could follow him. Peter finally got the point then and asked *why* he couldn't follow. "I'll lay down my life for you," he said, and then Jesus said to him the hardest thing Peter had ever heard him say. "Listen, listen," he said, "the cock won't crow till you've betrayed me three times" (John 13:36–38), and that's the way it was, of course—Peter sitting out there in the high priest's courtyard keeping warm by the fire while, inside, the ghastly interrogation was in process, and then the girl coming up to ask him three times if he wasn't one of them, and his replying each time that he didn't know what in God's name she was talking about. And then the old cock's wattles trembling scarlet as up over the horizon it squawked the rising sun, and the tears running down Peter's face like rain down a rock (Matthew 26:69–75).

According to Paul, the first person Jesus came back to see after Easter morning was Peter. What he said and what Peter said nobody will ever know, and maybe that's just as well. Their last conversation on this earth, however, is reported in the Gospel of John.

It was on the beach, at daybreak. Some of the other disciples were there, and Jesus cooked them breakfast. When it was over, he said to Peter (only again he called him Simon, son of John, because if ever he meant business, this was it), "Simon, son of John, do you love me?" and Peter said he did. Then Jesus asked the same question a second time and then once again, and each time Peter said he loved him—three times in all, to make up for the other three times.

Then Jesus said, "Feed my lambs. Feed my sheep," and you get the feeling that this time Peter didn't miss the point (John 21:9–19). From fisher of fish to fisher of people to keeper of the keys to shepherd. It was the Rock's final promotion, and from that day forward he never let the head office down again.

See also Ananias, Mark, Nathaniel.

PHYSICIANS

WE GO TO PHYSICIANS with whatever ails us. We take off what the nurse asks us to and sit there until they appear. DAY 257
Who knows what the examination will reveal, but we try to prepare ourselves for the worst. It is not just our bodies that we are putting on the line, but maybe even our chance for survival. We are no longer in control of our future but, like children, can only wait for a grownup to determine it. Stripped of our dignity and self-confidence no less than of most of our clothes, we perhaps don't feel quite so vulnerable anywhere else on earth.

When physicians finally step through the door and start checking us over, we hang not just on every word they speak but on the look in their eyes and the tone of their voices for some clue to what they make of us. When they finally tell us, we listen as though our lives depend on it, which quite possibly they do. If they know their business, in just the touch of their hand there is healing.

Several times in the Gospels, Jesus indirectly refers to himself as a physician (e.g., Matthew 9:12; Luke 4:23). It is a richly touching and suggestive image.

PILATE

As the Roman governor, Pilate had the last word. He could have saved Jesus if he'd wanted to, and all indications are that for various reasons that's what he'd like to have done.

In the first place, after personally interrogating him, he decided that no wrong had been done and said so. "I find no crime in this man," he told the chief priests (Luke 23:4). Period. Maybe the man had committed some religious faux pas in their eyes, but the religion of the Jews was nothing to him, and he couldn't have cared less. In fact, as a sophisticated Roman, religion in general was not his cup of tea, and he'd been quite frank about it to Jesus himself during their interview. When Jesus told him he'd come to bear witness to the truth, Pilate's reply was, "What is truth?" (John 18:38). Truth was for people who had time to worry about truth. Pilate was a busy man. In the second place, on the basis of a troubling dream she'd had, Pilate's wife begged him "to have nothing to do with that righteous man" (Matthew 27:19), and, sophisticated or not sophisticated, that gave him pause. A woman's intuition was not something you sneezed at, especially if you happened to be married to her. In the third place, his main job as a colonial administrator was to keep peace in the colonies at any price, and the last thing he wanted to do was to stir up a hornets' nest by making a martyr out of some local hero.

Nevertheless, when it became clear that he would stir up an even nastier hornets' nest by setting the man free, and when, in addition to that, the Jews pointed out that no true friend of Caesar's would ever be soft on a man who had set himself up as a king to rival Caesar, Pilate prudently gave in to the pressures and said to go ahead and crucify him if that's what they had their hearts set on.

To make it perfectly clear that he wanted no part in the dirty business, however, he said, "I am innocent of this man's blood," and, as a dramatic gesture that not even the dullest colonial clod among them could fail to understand, stepped out in front of the crowd and went through a ritual hand washing in a basin of water he'd had them fill especially for that purpose (Matthew 27:24). And in a sense he was right. Insofar as he'd done all he reasonably could to save the man—even offering to let them crucify Barabbas instead, if it was just a show they were after—he was, in a manner of speaking, innocent. The crucifixion took place against his advice and better judgment.

In this connection, you can't help thinking about that other famous hand washer, Lady Macbeth. Unlike Pilate, Lady Macbeth had committed murder herself, and what she kept trying to wash away in her sleep, long after her hands themselves were clean as a whistle, was her tormenting sense of guilt over the terrible thing she had done. She never succeeded, of course, but God is merciful, and one can hope that in the long run he did the job for her.

Pilate's case is different and worse. For him, it was not so much the terrible thing he'd done as the wonderful thing he'd proved incapable of doing. He could have stuck to his guns and resisted the pressure, and told the chief priests to go to hell, where they were obviously heading anyway. He could have spared the man's life. Or if that is asking too much, he could have spared him at least the scourging and catcalls and the appalling way he died. Or if that is still asking too much, he could have spoken some word of comfort when there was nobody else in the world with either the chance or the courage to speak it. He could have shaken his hand. He could have said good-bye. He could have made some two-bit gesture that, even though it would have made no ultimate difference, to him would have made all the difference.

But he didn't do it, he didn't do it, and on that basis alone you can almost believe the sad old legend is true that again and again his body rises to the surface of a mountain lake and goes through the motion of washing its hands as he tries to cleanse himself not of something he'd done, for which God could forgive him, but of something he might have done but didn't, for which he could never forgive himself.   *Matthew 27:15–26*

See also Barabbas, Herod Antipas.

PLAY

DAY 259   WHEN KING DAVID'S WIFE berates him for making a fool of himself by leaping and dancing before the ark of the Lord, he protests by saying that it seemed exactly the right thing to do, considering all the Lord had done for him. "Therefore will I play before the Lord," he tells her (2 Samuel 6:14–21).

When God describes how he will rescue Jerusalem from his wrath and make it new again, "a city of truth" (Zechariah 8:3), he conveys the glory of it by saying, "And the streets of the city shall be full of boys and girls playing in the streets" (8:5).

When the Psalmist praises God for creating "this great and wide sea, wherein are creeping things innumerable," he makes special mention of Leviathan, "whom," as he says, "thou hast made to play therein" (104:25–26).

The king, the boys and girls, the whale—they are none of them accomplishing anything. They are none of them providing anything. There's nothing edifying or educational or particularly help-ful in what they are doing, nothing that you'd be likely to think of as religious. They haven't a thought in their heads. They are just *playing*, that's all. They are letting themselves go and having a mar-velous time at it.

David has sweat pouring down his face and his eyes are aflame. The boys and girls are spinning like tops. The whale has just shot a thirty-foot spout into the air and is getting ready to heave its entire one hundred and fifty tons into the air after it.

What is the wind doing in the hayfield? What is Victoria Falls up to, or the surf along the coast of Maine? What about the fire going wild in the belly of the stove, or the rain pounding on the roof like the "Hallelujah Chorus," or the violet on the windowsill leaning toward the sun?

What, for that matter, is God up to, getting the whole thing started in the first place? Hurling the stars around like confetti at a parade, gathering the waters together into the seas like a woman gathering shells, calling forth all the creatures of earth and air like a man calling "Swing your partner!" at a hoedown.

"Be fruitful and multiply!" God calls, and creator and creature both all but lose track of which is which in the wonder of their playing.

POLITICS

YOU CAN'T HELP WONDERING what would happen if a person running for the presidency decided to set politics in the flag-waving, tub-thumping, ax-grinding sense aside and to speak, in-stead, candidly, thoughtfully, truthfully out of his or her own heart.

DAY 260

Suppose a candidate were to stand up before the reporters and the TV cameras and the usual bank of microphones and say some-thing like this:

"The responsibilities of this office are so staggering that any-body who doesn't approach them with knees knocking is either a fool or a lunatic. The literal survival of civilization may depend on the decisions that either I or one of the other candidates make during the next four years. The general welfare and peace of mind of millions of people will certainly depend on them. I am only a human being. If I have my strengths, I also have my weaknesses. I can't promise that I'll always do the right thing for this country. I can only promise that it will always be this country rather than my own political fortunes that I'll try to do the right thing for. I believe in this country at its best, but I also believe that we have made many tragic mistakes. I am willing to entertain the possibility that our assumptions about the Arabs, for example, may be as wrong as their assumptions about us, and my major objective, if elected, will be to explore that possibility with them at the highest levels of gov-ernment and in the most radical, searching, and unrelenting ways I can devise. I believe that the survival and well-being of the human race as a whole is more important than the partisan interests of any group, including both theirs and our own."

There are many who would undoubtedly say that such a state-ment is naive, dangerous, unrealistic, and un-American, and that anybody making it couldn't get elected dogcatcher. I can't help be-lieving, however, that there are others who would find it such a note of sanity, honesty, and hope in the political quagmire that they would follow the person who made it to the ends of the earth.

POVERTY

DAY 261   I N A SENSE WE ARE ALL HUNGRY and in need, but most of us don't recognize it. With plenty to eat in the deep freeze, with a roof over our heads and a car in the garage, we assume that the empty feeling inside must be just a case of the blues that can be cured by a Florida vacation, a new TV, an extra drink before supper.

The poor, on the other hand, are under no such delusion. When Jesus says, "Come unto me all ye who labor and are heavy laden, and I will give you rest" (Matthew 11:28), the poor stand a better chance than most of knowing what he's talking about and knowing that he's talking to them. In desperation they may even be willing to consider the possibility of accepting his offer. This is perhaps why Jesus on several occasions called them peculiarly blessed.

See also riches.

PRAISE

YOU PRAISE THE HEARTBREAKING beauty of Jessye Norman singing the *Vier Letzte Lieder* of Richard Strauss. You praise the new puppy for making its offering on the lawn for once instead of on the living-room rug. Maybe you yourself are praised for some generous thing you have done. In each case, the praise that is handed out is a measured response. It is a matter of saying something to one degree or another complimentary, with the implication that if Jessye Norman's voice had sprung a leak or the puppy hadn't made it outside in time or your generous deed turned out to be secretly self-serving, a different sort of response altogether would have been called for.

The way Psalm 148 describes it, praising God is another kettle of fish altogether. It is about as measured as a volcanic eruption, and there is no implication that under any conceivable circumstances it could be anything other than what it is. The whole of creation is in on the act—the sun and moon, the sea, fire and snow, Holstein

DAY 262

cows and white-throated sparrows, old men in walkers and children who still haven't taken their first step. Their praise is not chiefly
a matter of *saying* anything, because most of creation doesn't deal
in words. Instead, the snow whirls, the fire roars, the Holstein bel-
lows, the old man watches the moon rise. Their praise is not something that at their most complimentary they say, but something
that at their truest they are.

We learn to praise God not by paying compliments, but by paying attention. Watch how the trees exult when the wind is in them.
Mark the utter stillness of the great blue heron in the swamp.
Listen to the sound of the rain. Learn how to say "Hallelujah" from
the ones who say it right.

PRAYER

DAY 263

WE ALL PRAY whether we think of it as praying or not. The
odd silence we fall into when something very beautiful is
happening, or something very good or very bad. The "Ah-h-h-h!"
that sometimes floats up out of us as out of a Fourth of July crowd
when the skyrocket bursts over the water. The stammer of pain at
somebody else's pain. The stammer of joy at somebody else's joy.
Whatever words or sounds we use for sighing with over our own
lives. These are all prayers in their way. These are all spoken not just
to ourselves, but to something even more familiar than ourselves
and even more strange than the world.

According to Jesus, by far the most important thing about praying is to keep at it. The images he uses to explain this are all rather
comic, as though he thought it was rather comic to have to explain
it at all. He says God is like a friend you go to borrow bread from at
midnight. The friend tells you in effect to drop dead, but you go on

knocking anyway until finally he gives you what you want so he can go back to bed again (Luke 11:5–8). Or God is like a crooked judge who refuses to hear the case of a certain poor widow, presumably because he knows there's nothing much in it for him. But she keeps on hounding him until finally he hears her case just to get her out of his hair (Luke 18:1–8). Even a stinker, Jesus says, won't give his own child a black eye when the child asks for peanut butter and jelly, so how all the more will God when *his* children . . . (Matthew 7:9–11)?

Be importunate, Jesus says—not, one assumes, because you have to beat a path to God's door before God will open it, but because until you beat the path maybe there's no way of getting to *your* door. "Ravish my heart," John Donne wrote. But God will not usually ravish. He will only court.

Whatever else it may or may not be, prayer is at least talking to yourself, and that's in itself not always a bad idea.

Talk to yourself about your own life, about what you've done and what you've failed to do, and about who you are and who you wish you were and who the people you love are and the people you don't love too. Talk to yourself about what matters most to you, because if you don't, you may forget what matters most to you.

Even if you don't believe anybody's listening, at least you'll be listening.

Believe Somebody is listening. Believe in miracles. That's what Jesus told the father who asked him to heal his epileptic son. Jesus said, "All things are possible to him who believes." And the father spoke for all of us when he answered, "Lord, I believe; help my unbelief!" (Mark 9:14–29).

What about when the boy is not healed? When, listened to or not listened to, the prayer goes unanswered? Who knows? Just keep praying, Jesus says. Remember the sleepy friend, the crooked judge.

Even if the boy dies, keep on beating the path to God's door, because the one thing you can be sure of is that, down the path you beat with even your most half-cocked and halting prayer, the God you call upon will finally come.

See also healing, Job.

PREDESTINATION

DAY 264   PREDESTINATION IS THE THEORY that since God knows everything else, he must also know whether each one of us is going to end up in heaven or in hell, and therefore the die is cast before we even cast it.

Theorizing about God this way is like an isosceles triangle trying to theorize the Great Pyramid of Cheops into the two dimensions of the printed page.

The fact that I know you so well that I know what you're going to do before you do it does not mean that you are not free to do whatever you damn well please.

Logic is only *cigol* spelled backward.

PRIDE

DAY 265   PRIDE IS SELF-LOVE, and in that sense a Christian is enjoined to be proud; another way of saying "Love your neighbor as yourself" is to say "Love yourself as your neighbor." That doesn't mean your pulse is supposed to quicken every time you look in the mirror any more than it's supposed to quicken every time your neighbor passes the window. It means simply that the ability to work for your own good despite all the less than admirable things you know about yourself is closely related to the ability to work for your neighbors' good despite all the less than admirable things you know about them. It also means that just as in this sense love of self and love of neighbor go hand in hand, so do dislike of self and dislike of neighbor. For example: (a) the more I dislike my neighbors, the more I'm apt to dislike myself for disliking them, and them for making me dislike myself, and so on; and (b) I am continually tempted to take out on my neighbors the dislike I feel for myself, just the way if I crack my head on a low door I'm very apt to kick the first cat, child, or chair unlucky enough to catch my bloodshot eye.

Self-love, or pride, is a sin when, instead of leading you to share with others the self you love, it leads you to keep your self in perpetual safe-deposit. You not only don't accrue any interest that way, but you become less and less interesting every day.

See also humility.

PRINCIPLES

PRINCIPLES ARE WHAT PEOPLE HAVE instead of God.   DAY 266
To be a Christian means among other things to be willing, if necessary, to sacrifice even your highest principles for God's or your neighbor's sake the way a Christian pacifist must be willing to pick up a baseball bat if there's no other way to stop a man from savagely beating a child.

Jesus didn't forgive his executioners on principle, but because in some unimaginable way he was able to love them.

Principle is an even duller word than *religion.*

See also idolatry.

PROPHET

DAY 267   P ROPHET MEANS "SPOKESMAN," not "fortune-teller." The one
whom in their unfathomable audacity the prophets claimed
to speak for was the Lord and Creator of the universe. There is no
evidence to suggest that anyone ever asked a prophet home for
supper more than once.

One day some city boys followed along behind the prophet
Elisha calling him "Bald-head!" Elisha summoned two she-bears,
who tore forty-two of the city boys limb from limb. He then continued on his way to keep an appointment at Mt. Carmel (2 Kings
2:23–25).

The prophet Jeremiah showed a clay pot to a crowd of Judeans
and told them it represented Judah. Then he smashed it to smithereens and told them that this was a mild version of what God had in
mind to do to them (Jeremiah 19). He was right.

In a dream, the prophet Ezekiel ate a copy of the Bible, thumb
index and all, to show how sweet as honey was the word of God
(Ezekiel 3:1–3).

In the time of the prophet Amos, the Israelites looked forward
eagerly to the day when the Lord would finally come and deliver
them from all their afflictions. Amos told them they had better
start looking forward to something else, because when the day came,
the Lord was going to settle a lot of people's hash all right, but the
hash that would be settled first was Israel's. Quoting God, Amos
went on to say, "Your great cathedrals bore me just as stiff as your
TV evangelists, and your prayer breakfasts at the White House cause
me no less abdominal discomfort than your dashboard Virgins. *Justice* is what I want, not photo opportunities, and *righteousness* like
an ever-flowing stream" (Amos 5:21–24). Jeremiah was thrown into

a cistern, and the rumor is that Isaiah was sawed in half. It is not recorded how Amos got his.

When the unknown prophet who wrote the last chapters of Isaiah pondered the question of what the chosen people were chosen *for*, his answer was that they were chosen not to overwhelm the world in triumph, but to suffer and die for the world in love. One thinks of the gas ovens of Auschwitz and of Anne Frank. One thinks of the anti-Semitic joke and the restricted neighborhood. One also thinks of Jesus of Nazareth, who, when he went back to his hometown, chose this prophet to read from in the local synagogue (Luke 4:16–19). It is the words of this prophet that perhaps describe Jesus best—"a man of sorrows, and acquainted with grief" (Isaiah 53:3). *Acquainted* with grief. The way Jesus described his mission in the world was "to give his life as a ransom for many" (Mark 10:45).

The prophets were drunk on God, and in the presence of their terrible tipsiness, no one was ever comfortable. With a total lack of tact, they roared out against phoniness and corruption wherever they found them. They were the terror of kings and priests. The prophet Nathan tells King David to his face that he is a crook and an adulterer (2 Samuel 12:1–15). The prophet Jeremiah goes straight to the Temple itself and says, "Do not trust in these deceptive words, 'This is the Temple of the Lord, the Temple of the Lord, the Temple of the Lord'" (Jeremiah 7:4). It was like a prophet to say it three times, just to make sure.

No prophet is on record as having asked for the job. When God put the finger on Isaiah, Isaiah said, "How long, O Lord?" (Isaiah 6:11), and couldn't have been exactly reassured by the answer he was given. Jeremiah pled that he was much too young for that type of work (Jeremiah 1:6). Moses sounded like a prophet when he pointed out to God that he'd never been much good at public speaking and the chances were that Pharaoh wasn't going to give him so much as the time of day (Exodus 4:1–13). Like Abraham Lincoln's story about the man being ridden out of town on a rail, if it hadn't been for the honor of the thing, the prophets would all have rather walked.

Most of the prophets went a little mad before they were through, if they weren't a little mad to begin with. Ezekiel kept seeing wheels with eyes around the rims. John the Baptist ate bugs. You can hardly blame them.

Karl Marx, Friedrich Nietzsche, Jonathan Swift, and Malcolm X were all prophets in their own way. So was Ayn Rand. So are Gloria Steinem and Rosa Parks.

Like Robert Frost's, a prophet's quarrel with the world is deep down a lover's quarrel. If they didn't love the world, they probably wouldn't bother to tell it that it's going to hell. They'd just let it go. Their quarrel is God's quarrel.

PSYCHOTHERAPY

DAY 268

AFTER ADAM AND EVE ate the forbidden fruit, God came strolling through the cool of the day and asked them two questions: "Where are you?" and "What is this that you have done?" Psychotherapists, psychologists, psychiatrists, and the like have been asking the same ones ever since.

"Where are you?" lays bare the present. Adam and Eve are in hiding, that's where they are. What is it they want to hide? From whom do they want to hide it? What does it cost them to hide it? Why are they so unhappy with things as they are that they are trying to conceal it from the world by hiding, and from themselves by covering their nakedness with aprons?

"What is this that you have done?" lays bare the past. What did they do to get this way? What did they hope would happen by doing it? What did they fear would happen? What did the serpent do? What was it that made them so ashamed?

God is described as cursing them then, but in view of his actions at the end of the story and right on through the end of the New Testament, it seems less a matter of vindictively inflicting them with the consequences than of honestly confronting them with the consequences. Because of who they are and what they have done, this is the result. There is no undoing it. There is no going back to the garden.

But then comes the end of the story, where God with his own hands makes them garments of skins and clothes them. It is the most moving part of the story. They can't go back, but they can go forward clothed in a new way—clothed, that is, not in the sense of having their old defenses again, behind which to hide who they are and what they have done, but in the sense of having a new understanding of who they are and a new strength to draw on for what lies before them to do now.

Many therapists wouldn't touch biblical teachings with a ten-foot pole, but in their own way, and at their best, they are often following them.

PURGATORY

AccORDING TO ROMAN CATHOLIC doctrine, some people go to heaven when they die, some people go to hell, and some people, although they will get to heaven eventually, have to make a preliminary detour through purgatory, where the sins that still

DAY 269

cling to them are purged away through suffering. Protestants reject this notion, partly because of the unpleasant odor it developed during the Middle Ages, when, if you put so much cash on the line, the church guaranteed to arrange at least a substantial reduction in your purgatorial sentence, and partly because of the general Protestant view that when you are saved by God, that means among other things that you are saved from torment, however edifying, after death.

What is persuasive about the Catholic view is the implication that even with God on their side people do not attain to what Saint Paul calls "maturity, the measure of the full stature of Christ" (Ephesians 4:13) overnight. At best the job is unlikely to be more than the slimmest fraction done by the time they die.

An Anglican prayer for someone who has died includes the words "grant that, increasing in knowledge and love of thee, he [or she] may go from strength to strength, in the life of perfect service, in thy heavenly kingdom." Increasing in knowledge. From strength to strength. Whichever side of the grave you are talking about, life with God apparently involves growth and growing pains.

The sacrament of bread and wine administered to the dying is known as the *viaticum*, which means provision for a journey, or one for the road. Whether or not you think of it in connection with purgatory, *viaticum* suggests that many a high adventure still awaits you and many a cobbled street before you finally reach the fountain in the square.

QUEEN OF HEAVEN

THE GREEKS CALLED HER ARTEMIS and the Syrians Atargatis. The Egyptians worshiped her as Isis and the Assyrians as Ishtar. In Jeremiah's day the women kneaded dough to make cakes in her likeness and burned incense to her. In the book of Revelation she became "a woman clothed with the sun, with the moon under her feet, and on her head a crown of twelve stars" (12:1). She is the goddess of heaven and earth who answers petitions, heeds sighs, and loves mercy. She is the lady of nurture and fertility who restores life to the earth at springtime.

In the Judeo-Christian tradition, God has been thought of largely as King, Father, Judge, Lord of Hosts, and the like, and these exclusively male metaphors testify to the experience of God as all-powerful, just, demanding obedience, benign, and so on. But there are other dimensions of the experience that they clearly leave out. Whatever else the Roman Catholics' adoration of the Virgin Mary may be, in this respect at least it helps restore the balance.

It is from the ancients that Rome borrowed the title they honor Mary with: *Regina Coeli*, or Queen of Heaven. God is Mother as well as Father—compassionate, forgiving, life-giving, endlessly creative, and nourishing. She brings us forth from her womb. We take love at her breast.

See also Mary.

QUEEN OF SHEBA

DAY 271

THE QUEEN OF SHEBA decided to go see for herself if King Solomon was all he was cracked up to be, and, court etiquette being what it was, she didn't go empty-handed. She brought enough camels to stock six zoos and gold and jewels enough to fill a dozen steamer trunks and so many spices that when the wind blew the wrong way, it almost knocked you off your feet. She also anointed herself from head to toe with Chanel No. 5, fastened on herself as many feathers, ribbons, and diamonds as there were places to fasten them, and when she arrived in Jerusalem, it was like a Mardi Gras parade.

Since part of what Solomon was famous for was his skill at riddles, she brought a number of those along too. "Which came first, the chicken or the egg?" and "What goes up a chimney down, but won't go down a chimney up?" were among the easier ones, and the others were real shin-crackers. Solomon knocked them all off one right after another without even batting an eye and said it was like shooting fish in a barrel. He then offered to give her a guided tour of the palace.

He showed her wine cellars that made her feathers tremble with excitement and storerooms full of marvelous things to eat that had her mouth watering all over her upper diamonds. He showed her his personal wardrobe, remarking that most of it was last season's stuff, and the uniforms of all his butlers, bodyguards, chamber-maids, and cupbearers, together with an estimate of what it cost per year just to have them dry-cleaned. He showed her a dining-room table that could seat the whole State Department down to the last undersecretary's secretary, plus the gold plates he used when he wanted to put on the dog and the massive silver service he kept for when he wanted just a quiet evening at home with the family. When he took her to the place where he kept burnt offer-ings for Yahweh, she thought they'd wandered into the Chicago stockyards by mistake. By the time they'd finished, the queen was so undone that she had to excuse herself and go to her room, where she took off her girdle, put her feet up, and had her lady's maids apply cold compresses until the bell rang for supper. As the book of 1 Kings sums it up, "There was no more spirit in her" (1 Kings 10:5).

After supper she rallied enough to make a little speech. Seeing was believing, she said, but she still thought her contact lenses must need readjustment. She'd heard plenty before she came, but she now knew she hadn't heard the half of it. She couldn't say which he was better at, cracking riddles or picking wives, and the fifty of them or so who were present because they weren't pregnant at the time applauded politely. She said Yahweh must be tickled pink to have a king like Solomon on the payroll. Then she sat down, but not before making him a bread-and-butter present of as much of the gold and jewels and spices and camels as she thought she wouldn't be needing herself on the trip home.

Solomon responded by giving her so much in return that it made what she'd given him look like something she'd picked up at a tag sale, and when she got back to Sheba, it was some years before she ventured forth again.   *1 Kings 10:1–13*

See also Solomon.

QUESTIONS

O N HER DEATHBED, Gertrude Stein is said to have asked, "What is the answer?" Then, after a long silence, "What is the question?" Don't start looking in the Bible for the answers it gives. Start by listening for the questions it asks.

We are much involved, all of us, with questions about things that matter a good deal today but will be forgotten by this time tomorrow—the immediate wheres and whens and hows that face us daily at home and at work—but at the same time we tend to lose track of the questions about things that matter always, life-and-death questions about meaning, purpose, and value. To lose track of such deep questions as these is to risk losing track of who we really are in our own depths and where we are really going. There is perhaps no stronger reason for reading the Bible than that somewhere among all those India-paper pages there awaits each one of us, whoever we are, the one question that (though for years we may have been pretending not to hear it) is the central question of our individual lives. Here are a few of them:

- For what will it profit them if they gain the whole world but forfeit their life? (Matthew 16:26)
- Am I my brother's keeper? (Genesis 4:9)
- If God is for us, who can be against us? (Romans 8:31)
- What is truth? (John 18:38)
- How can anyone be born after having grown old? (John 3:4)
- What do people gain from all the toil at which they toil under the sun? (Ecclesiastes 1:3)
- Whither shall I go from thy Spirit? (Psalm 139:7)

- Who is my neighbor? (Luke 10:29)
- What shall I do to inherit eternal life? (Luke 10:25)

When you hear the question that is your question, then you have already begun to hear much. Whether you can accept the Bible's answer or not, you have reached the point where at least you can begin to hear it too.

QUIET

A N EMPTY ROOM IS SILENT. A room where people are not speaking or moving is quiet. Silence is a given, quiet a gift. Silence is the absence of sound and quiet the stilling of sound. Silence can't be anything but silent. Quiet chooses to be silent. It holds its breath to listen. It waits and is still.

"In returning and rest you shall be saved," says God through the prophet Isaiah, "in quietness and confidence shall be your strength" (Isaiah 30:15). They are all parts of each other. We return to our deep strength and to the confidence that lies beneath all our misgiving. The quiet there, the rest, is beyond the reach of the world to disturb. It is how being saved sounds.

DAY 273

QUIRINIUS

S AINT LUKE SAYS THAT JESUS was born in the year "when Quirinius was governor of Syria" (Luke 2:2), although it is indicated elsewhere that at the same time Herod the Great was king. Since Quirinius wasn't governor until ten years or so after Herod was dead, the two dates can't really be reconciled, although for centuries

DAY 274

scholars eager to defend scriptural accuracy in all things have knocked themselves out trying to reconcile them.

So maybe Luke made a mistake. The inspiration of the Scriptures is no more undermined by the fact that their chronology isn't infallible than the inspiration of Shakespeare is undermined by the fact that he thought there was a seacoast in Bohemia.   *Luke 2:2*

See also Herod the Great.

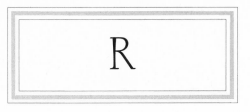

RACHEL

THE LIFE OF JACOB'S WIFE RACHEL was never an easy one. In the first place, she had Laban for a father, and in the second place, she had Jacob for a husband. And then, of course, she also had her sister, Leah.

Rachel was the younger and prettier of the two girls, and Laban told Jacob that if he worked hard for seven years for him, he could have her. So Jacob worked hard for seven years, but when the wedding night rolled around at last, Laban sneaked Leah in in Rachel's place, and it wasn't till Jacob got a good look at her the next morning that he realized he'd been had. Leah was a nice girl, but she had weak eyes, and Rachel was the one he'd lost his heart to anyway. Laban gave some kind of shaky explanation about how it was an old family custom for the oldest daughter to get married first no matter what, and Jacob had to work another seven years before Rachel was finally his in addition to Leah.

To be married to two sisters simultaneously is seldom recommended even under the best of circumstances, and in this case it was a disaster. For a long time Rachel couldn't have babies, and Leah had four. When they weren't fighting with each other, they were fighting with Jacob, and when Jacob wasn't fending them off, he was trying to outcheat his crooked father-in-law, Laban, with the result that in the end the whole situation blew up, and Jacob cleared out with both his wives plus Laban's household gods, which Rachel pinched for luck just as they were leaving because luck was what she felt she was running out of. It wasn't long afterward that Rachel died on the road giving birth to a son whom she lived just long enough to name Benoni, which means "Son of my sorrow," although Jacob changed it to Benjamin later on.

Even in death her problems weren't over. From her sons and Leah's the twelve tribes of Israel descended, and the whole story of the Old Testament is basically the story of how for years to come they were always getting into one awful mess after another with God, with their neighbors, and with themselves. Centuries later, when the Babylonians carried them off into exile, it was Jeremiah who said that even in her tomb she was grieving still. "A voice is heard in Ramah, lamentation and bitter weeping," he said. "Rachel is weeping for her children" (Jeremiah 31:15).

But Rachel's children were also God's children, according to Jeremiah, and the last words were God's too. "Is Ephraim my dear son?" God said, naming one of them to stand for them all. "Is he my darling child?" And then God answered his own question in a way that even to Rachel, with her terrible luck, must have brought some hope. "Therefore my heart yearns for him," God said, "and as often as I speak against him, I do remember him still" (Jeremiah 31:20).

Genesis 29–31; 35

See also Jacob, Jeremiah, Laban.

RACISM

I N 1957 WHEN GOVERNOR FAUBUS of Arkansas refused to de-DAY 276
segregate the schools in Little Rock, if President Eisenhower with
all his enormous prestige had personally led a black child up the
steps to where the authorities were blocking the school entrance, it
might have been one of the great moments in history. It is heartbreaking to think of the opportunity missed.

Nothing in American history is more tragic surely than the relationship of the black and white races. Masters and slaves both were
dehumanized. The Jim Crow laws carried the process on for decades
beyond the Emancipation. The Ku Klux Klan and its like keep going
forever. Politically, economically, socially, and humanly, blacks continue to be the underdog. Despite all the efforts of both races to rec-
tify the situation and heal the wounds, despite all the progress that
has been made, it is still as hard for any black to look at any white
without a feeling of resentment as it is for any white to look at any
black without a feeling of guilt.

"There is neither Jew nor Greek, there is neither slave nor free,
there is neither male nor female; for you are all one in Christ Jesus,"
Paul wrote to the Galatians (3:28), and many a white and many a
black must have read his words both before the Civil War and
since, perhaps even given them serious thought. If more whites had
taken them to heart, were to take them to heart today, you can't
help speculating on all the misery—past, present, and to come—
that both races would have been or would be spared.

Many must have taken them to heart, but then simply not done
what their hearts directed. The chances are they weren't bad people
or unfeeling people all in all. Like Eisenhower, they simply lacked

the moral courage, the creative vision that might have won the day. The Little Rock schools were desegregated in the end anyhow by a combination of legal process and armed force, but it was done without some gesture of courtesy, contrition, or compassion that might have captured the imagination of the world.

RAHAB

DAY 277   RAHAB RAN AN UNPRETENTIOUS little establishment in the red-light district of Jericho and was known for, among other things, her warm and generous heart. That is perhaps why, when Joshua was getting ready to attack, the spies he sent in to case the joint made a beeline for her.

When the king of Jericho found out they were there, he rang Rahab up and over the din of the piano player downstairs managed to get it across to her who they were and that she was to turn them in on the double if not quicker. Rahab replied that, though it was true some customers answering his description had been there that evening, she'd thought they were just a couple of butter-and-egg men out for a good time and had kissed them good-bye not more than twenty minutes earlier. If he got a move on, he could probably still catch them.

She then went up to the roof where she had the spies stashed away and told them what had happened. She said that as far as she was concerned, the customer was always right, and she had no intention of squealing on them. She also said she felt it in her bones that with Yahweh on his side, Joshua was going to find Jericho a pushover when the attack began. All she asked in return for her services was that, when the boys came marching in, they'd give her and her family a break.

The spies were only too happy to agree, she let them down with a rope, and they beat it back to headquarters to report to Joshua. A few days later, when Joshua went through Jericho like a dose of salts, he saw to it that Rahab and her family got out before he burned the place down, and they lived happily ever after.

Matthew lists Rahab as one of the ancestresses of the Lord Jesus Christ (Matthew 1:5), and that may be one reason why there was something about free-wheeling ladies with warm and generous hearts that he was never quite able to resist.   *Joshua 2; 6*

REBEKAH

R EBEKAH'S MARRIAGE TO ISAAC was a family arrangement DAY 278
rather than a love match, and all the love she had in her to give she seems to have lavished on her son Jacob.

When she overheard old Isaac say that he was going to give Jacob's twin brother, Esau, the paternal blessing and make him his heir, she was almost beside herself. She ran and told Jacob what was up and said he'd better get to Isaac before Esau did or Esau would get the blessing and everything that went with it and Jacob wouldn't get a blessed thing. Jacob objected that, blind as Isaac was, he would still be able to tell the brothers apart because Esau was a hairy man whereas he, Jacob, had all he could do just to raise a toothbrush mustache. Just one touch, Jacob said, and the old duffer would know that something fishy was going on.

Rebekah thought fast and, after dressing Jacob up in one of Esau's best suits, produced some bearskin gloves for him to put on his hands and an extra pelt to wrap around his neck. The trick worked beautifully. Isaac thought it was Esau kneeling before him, and Jacob carried the day.

When the cat was finally out of the bag, Esau first burst into tears and then announced that, by the time he got through with Jacob, not even his mother would recognize him. But again Rebekah thought fast. She told Jacob what his brother had in mind and persuaded him to get out of town while he could still walk. Jacob took the advice, and the bitter irony of it is that if Rebekah ever saw the apple of her eye again, it is at least not so recorded.

It is also not recorded when or where or in what state of mind Rebekah finally died, but there is a note to the effect that when the time came, they buried the lonely old woman in a cave at Machpelah. Years later Jacob was buried there too, and if she had any way of knowing about it, one can imagine her happy at last to be lying there side by side with the beloved boy for whose sake she had betrayed not only Isaac, her husband, and Esau, her son, but God himself, in whose name the fateful blessing had been given.

Genesis 24–27

See also Isaac.

RELIGION

DAY 279 THE WORD *religion* points to that area of human experience where one way or another we come upon Mystery as a summons to pilgrimage; where we sense beyond and beneath the realities of every day a Reality no less real because it can only be hinted at in myths and rituals; where we glimpse a destination that we can never fully know until we reach it.

Since the Reality that religion claims to deal with is beyond space and time, we cannot use normal space-and-time language (i.e., nouns and verbs) to describe it directly. We must fall back on the language of metaphor and resign ourselves to describing it at best indirectly.

It is obvious that this is what we are doing when we say Jesus is the "Son of God," or the Lord is our "shepherd," or the Kingdom of God is "within you." It is not so obvious that this is what we are doing—but we are doing it no less—when we say, "God exists." This does not mean that God "exists" literally as you and I do—that is, exists now and not then, here and not there, and stands out of (*ex* + *sistere*) some prior reality. It is at best a crude metaphor.

To say that God "does not exist" may be a better metaphor to suggest the nature of God's reality. But since it also is bound to be taken literally, it is better not to say it.

RELIGIOUS BOOKS

THERE ARE POETRY BOOKS and *poetic* books—the first a book with poems in it, the second a book that may or may not have poems in it, but that is in some sense a poem itself.

DAY 280

In much the same way there are *religion* books and *religious* books. A *religion* book is a book with religion in it in the everyday sense of religious ideas, symbols, attitudes, and—if it takes the form of fiction—with characters and settings that have overtly religious associations and implications. There are good religion books like *The Scarlet Letter* by Nathaniel Hawthorne or *Wise Blood* by Flannery O'Connor, and there are miserable ones like most of what is called "Christian" fiction.

A *religious* book may not have any religion as such in it at all, but to read it is in some measure to experience firsthand what a *religion* book can only tell about. A *religion* book is a canvas. A *religious* book is a transparency. With a *religious* book it is less what we see in it than what we see through it that matters. John Irving's *A Prayer for Owen Meany* would be an example. *Huckleberry Finn* would be another.

Writers of *religious* books tend to achieve most when they are least conscious of doing so. The attempt to be religious is as doomed as the attempt to be poetic. Thus in the writing, as in the reading, a *religious* book is an act of grace—no less rare, no less precious, no less improbable.

REMEMBER

DAY 281

WHEN YOU REMEMBER ME, it means that you have carried something of who I am with you, that I have left some mark of who I am on who you are. It means that you can summon me back to your mind even though countless years and miles may stand between us. It means that if we meet again, you will know me. It means that even after I die, you can still see my face and hear my voice and speak to me in your heart.

For as long as you remember me, I am never entirely lost. When I'm feeling most ghostlike, it's your remembering me that helps remind me that I actually exist. When I'm feeling sad, it's my consolation. When I'm feeling happy, it's part of why I feel that way.

If you forget me, one of the ways I remember who I am will be gone. If you forget me, part of who I am will be gone.

"Jesus, remember me when you come into your kingdom," the good thief said from his cross (Luke 23:42). There are perhaps no more human words in all of Scripture, no prayer we can pray so well.

REPENTANCE

To repent is to come to your senses. It is not so much something you do as something that happens. True repentance spends less time looking at the past and saying, "I'm sorry," than to the future and saying, "Wow!"

DAY 282

RETIREMENT

Somewhere around the age of sixty-five, many people decide it's time to stop working and start just enjoying life. The trouble, of course, is that they're apt to discover that with nothing much to do except play golf, travel, catch up on their reading, watch TV, and so on, life isn't all that enjoyable. They need something to give themselves to the way they once gave themselves to their jobs. The question is, give themselves to what? Maybe they could do worse than give themselves to the world that needs them as much as they need the world.

DAY 283

This may involve things like volunteer work at the hospital or delivering meals on wheels or heading the library-fund drive, but the place where giving yourself to the world starts is simply paying attention to the world—to the people you've been saying hello to for years without really knowing them, to the elementary-school kids hanging upside down on the jungle gym, to the woman taxi driver with the face of a Boston bull and no teeth to speak of who waits for fares at the bus stop, to the old vets marching down Main Street on Memorial Day.

If retirees just learn to keep their eyes open, the chances are they will find themselves more involved, fulfilled, challenged, and nourished than all the years they spent with their noses to the grindstone. And enjoying themselves more too.

REVELATION

DAY 284

THERE ARE TWO DIFFERENT WAYS of describing how you came to know something. One way is to say *you found it out*. The other way is to say *it occurred to you*. Reason is involved in both. To say you *found out* that so-and-so was the best friend you had suggests that you reasoned your way to such a conclusion. To say it *occurred to you* suggests that, although the conclusion was not reached by reason, it was not incompatible with it.

It occurred to you as distinct from *you found out* suggests knowledge given as distinct from knowledge earned. It suggests inner meaning as distinct from outer semblance. For example, I *found out* that Francis of Assisi gave all his money to the poor, called the sun his brother, and preached sermons to birds. But *it occurred to me* that he must be a saint. Or an idiot.

Revelation means knowledge as grace. Nobody has ever managed to *find out* much if anything about God.

Classic Buddhism is reasonable, *found out*, and doesn't claim to be otherwise. In the Four Noble Truths, Buddha puts it in a nutshell. Like the family doctor, he diagnoses our ailment and prescribes a cure. He says (1) that the name of our ailment is life, which causes great pain because we know that it always falls to pieces in the end. He says (2) that if we didn't like life so much, we wouldn't mind having it fall to pieces in the end. Therefore, he says, (3) the way to get cured of the ailment is to stop clinging to life as though it were a prize instead of a fatal disease. Finally (4) he outlines eight steps for getting out of life and into Nirvana.

Classic Christianity, on the other hand, is not primarily reasonable or something we have *found out* or worked out for ourselves. Christ came. He healed people. He forgave people their sins and said to love everybody including your enemy. He died in a peculiarly unpleasant way, forgiving his executioners. Christianity was born when *it occurred* to some of the ones who had known him that his kind of life was the only kind worth living, and that in some invisible way Christ was still around to help them live it.

Nobody figured Christianity out. It happened. That is what it means to call it a *revealed* religion—not incompatible with reason maybe, if you give it some thought, but not arrived at primarily by reason either.

See also theology.

REVEREND

DAY 285

R EVEREND IS A TITLE OF RESPECT to be used only in the third person, if then. Speak *about* the Reverend Susan Smith if you have to, but never go up to her and say, "That's telling them, Reverend!" any more than you'd go up to a senator and say, "How are things in Washington, Honorable?"

Reverend means "to be revered." Ministers are not to be revered for who they are in themselves, but for who it is they represent, just as the Spanish ambassador is seated at the hostess's right not because of his *beaux yeux,* but because he represents the king.

See also minister.

RICHES

DAY 286

T HE TROUBLE WITH BEING RICH is that since you can solve with your checkbook virtually all of the practical problems that bedevil ordinary people, you are left in your leisure with nothing but the great human problems to contend with: how to be happy, how to love and be loved, how to find meaning and purpose in your life.

In desperation the rich are continually tempted to believe that they can solve these problems too with their checkbooks, which is presumably what led Jesus to remark one day that for a rich man to get to heaven is about as easy as for a Mercedes to get through a revolving door.

RIGHTEOUSNESS

DAY 287   Y OU HAVEN'T GOT IT RIGHT!" says the exasperated piano teacher. Junior is holding his hands the way he's been told. His fingering is unexceptionable. He has memorized the piece perfectly. He has hit all the proper notes with deadly accuracy. But his heart's not in it, only his fingers. What he's playing is a sort of music, but nothing that will start voices singing or feet tapping. He has succeeded in boring everybody to death, including himself.

Jesus said to his disciples, "Unless your righteousness exceeds that of the scribes and Pharisees, you will never enter the kingdom of heaven" (Matthew 5:20). The scribes and Pharisees were playing it by the book. They didn't slip up on a single do or don't. But they were getting it all wrong.

Righteousness is getting it all *right*. If you play it the way it's supposed to be played, there shouldn't be a still foot in the house.

RITUAL

DAY 288   A WEDDING. A HANDSHAKE. A kiss. A coronation. A parade. A dance. A meal. A graduation. A ritual is the ceremonial acting out of the profane in order to show forth its sacredness. A sacrament is the breaking through of the sacred into the profane.

A sacrament is God offering his holiness to us. A ritual is our raising up the holiness of our humanity to God.

See also sacrament.

RUTH

R UTH WAS A MOABITE GIRL who married into a family of Israelite transplants living in Moab because there was a famine going on at home. When her young husband died, her mother-in-law, Naomi, decided to pull up stakes and head back for Israel where she belonged. The famine was over by then, and there was no longer anything to hold her where she was, her own husband having died about the same time that Ruth's had. She advised Ruth to stay put right there in Moab and to try to snag herself another man from among her own people.

DAY 289

She was a strong-willed old party, and when Ruth said she wanted to go to Israel with her, she tried to talk her out of it. Even if by some gynecological fluke she managed to produce another son for Ruth to marry, she said, by the time he was old enough, Ruth would be ready for the geriatric ward. But Ruth had a mind of her own too, besides which they'd been through a lot together, what with one thing and another, and home to her was wherever Naomi was. "Where you go, I go, and where you live, I live," Ruth told her, "and if your God is Yahweh, then my God is Yahweh too" (Ruth 2:10–17). So Naomi gave in, and when the two of them pulled in to Bethlehem, Naomi's hometown, there was a brass band to meet them at the station.

Ruth had a spring in her step and a fascinating Moabite accent, and it wasn't long before she caught the eye of a prosperous farmer named Boaz. He was a little long in the tooth, but he still knew a pretty girl when he saw one, and before long, in a fatherly kind of way, he took her under his wing. He told the hired hands not to give her any trouble. He helped her in the fields. He had her over for a meal. And when she asked him one day in her disarming Moabite way why he was being so nice to her, he said he'd heard how good she'd been to Naomi, who happened to be a distant cousin of his, and as far as he was concerned, she deserved nothing but the best.

Naomi was nobody's fool and saw which way the wind was blowing long before Ruth did. She was dead set on Ruth's making a good catch for herself, and since it was obvious she'd already hooked old Boaz whether she realized it or not, all she had to do was find the right way to reel him in. Naomi gave her instructions. As soon as Boaz had a good supper under his belt and had polished off a nightcap or two, he'd go to the barn and hit the sack. Around midnight, she said, Ruth should slip out to the barn and hit the sack too. If Boaz's feet just happened to be uncovered somehow, and if she just happened to be close enough to keep them warm, that probably wouldn't be the worst thing in the world either (Ruth 3:1–5). But she wasn't to go too far. Back in Jericho, Boaz's mother, Rahab, had had a rather seamy reputation for going too far professionally, and anything that reminded him of that might scare him off permanently.

Ruth followed her mother-in-law's advice to the letter, and it worked like a charm. Boaz was so overwhelmed that she'd pay attention to an old crock like him when there were so many young bucks running around in tight-fitting jeans that he fell for her hook, line, and sinker and, after a few legal matters were taken care of, made her his lawful wedded wife.

They had a son named Obed after a while, and Naomi came to

take care of him and stayed on for the rest of her life. Then in time Obed had a son of his own named Jesse, and Jesse in turn had seven sons, the seventh of whom was named David and ended up as the greatest king Israel ever had. With Ruth for his great-grandmother and Naomi for his grandfather's nurse, it was hardly a wonder.

The Book of Ruth

See also Rahab.

SABBATH

DAY 290 For Jews the Sabbath is the seventh day, Saturday, and for most Christians it is the first day, Sunday. In either case, it is a day set aside from the other six as the day God himself blessed and hallowed, "because on it God rested from all his work which he had done in creation" (Genesis 2:3).

Banks and post offices are closed, and most businesses shut down. In some states you can't buy a drink, and the regular weekday newscasters are replaced by substitutes. Religiously inclined people may go to church. Otherwise life goes on much as always. The shopping malls are usually just as crowded as on any other day, many of the roads are even more so, and newspapers swell to grotesque proportions. Insofar as it is still treated as a day of rest, the rest is apt to consist of people knocking themselves out on tennis courts, golf courses, and hiking trails or doing things like mowing the lawn, painting the back porch, paying bills, or taking a long afternoon nap.

You think of God resting after the creation was finally all created. You think of the deep hush of it, like the hush between breakers at the beach. You think of the new creation itself resting—the gray squirrel ceasing to twitch and chatter, the kingfisher settling down on the branch by the pond, the man and the woman standing still in the garden. You think of God blessing this one day of the seven and hallowing it, making it holy.

The room is quiet. You're not feeling tired enough to sleep or energetic enough to go out. For the moment there is nowhere else you'd rather go, no one else you'd rather be. You feel at home in your body. You feel at peace in your mind. For no particular reason, you let the palms of your hands come together and close your eyes. Sometimes it is only when you happen to taste a crumb of it that you dimly realize what it is that you're so hungry for you can hardly bear it.

SACRAMENT

A SACRAMENT IS WHEN something holy happens. It is transparent time, time you can see through to something deep inside time. DAY 291

Generally speaking, Protestants have two official sacraments (the Lord's Supper, Baptism) and Roman Catholics have these two plus five others (Confirmation, Penance, Extreme Unction, Ordination, and Matrimony). In other words, at such milestone moments as seeing a baby baptized or being baptized yourself, confessing your sins, getting married, dying, you are apt to catch a glimpse of the almost unbearable preciousness and mystery of life.

Needless to say, church isn't the only place where the holy happens. Sacramental moments can occur at any moment, at any place, and to anybody. Watching something get born. Making love. A walk on the beach. Somebody coming to see you when you're sick. A meal with people you love. Looking into a stranger's eyes and finding out they are not a stranger's.

If we weren't blind as bats, we might see that life itself is sacramental.

See also baptism, Lord's Supper, music, ritual.

SACRIFICE

DAY 292   To SACRIFICE SOMETHING is to make it holy by giving it away for love.

SAINT

DAY 293   IN HIS HOLY FLIRTATION WITH THE WORLD, God occasionally drops a pocket handkerchief. These handkerchiefs are called saints.

Many people think of saints as plaster saints, men and women of such paralyzing virtue that they never thought a nasty thought or did an evil deed their whole lives long. As far as I know, real saints never even come close to characterizing themselves that way. On the contrary, no less a saint than Saint Paul wrote to Timothy, "I am foremost among sinners" (1 Timothy 1:15), and Jesus himself prayed God to forgive him his trespasses, and when the rich young man addressed him as "good Teacher," answered, "No one is good but God alone" (Mark 10:18).

In other words, the feet of saints are as much of clay as everybody else's, and their sainthood consists less of what they have done than of what God has for some reason chosen to do through them. When you consider that Saint Mary Magdalene was possessed by seven devils, that Saint Augustine prayed, "Give me chastity and continence, but not now," that Saint Francis started out as a high-living young dude in downtown Assisi, and that Saint Simeon Stylites spent years on top of a sixty-foot pillar, you figure that maybe there's nobody God can't use as a means of grace, including even ourselves.

The Holy Spirit has been called "the Lord, the giver of life" and, drawing their power from that source, saints are essentially life-givers. To be with them is to become more alive.

SALOME

ONE OF THE LESS OFFENSIVE ACTS of Herod Antipas was to walk off with his brother's wife, Herodias—at least there may have been something like love in it—but it was against the law, and since John the Baptist was a stickler for legalities, he gave Herod a hard time over it. Needless to say, this didn't endear him to Herodias, who urged her husband to make short work of him. Herod said he'd be only too pleased to oblige her, but unfortunately John was a strong man with a strong following, and it might lead to unpleasantness.

DAY 294

Then one day he threw himself a birthday party, possibly because he couldn't locate anybody who felt like throwing it for him, and one of the guests was Herodias's daughter from her former marriage. Her name was Salome, and she was both Herod's stepdaughter and his niece. As it happened, she was also a whiz at dancing. Sometime during the evening she ripped off a little number that so tickled Herod that, carried away by the general hilarity of the occasion as he was, he told her he'd give her anything she wanted up to and including half of his kingdom. Since she already had everything a girl could want and was apparently not eager for all the headaches that taking over half the kingdom would undoubtedly involve, she went out and told her mother, Herodias, to advise her what she ought to ask for.

It didn't take Herodias twenty seconds to tell her. "The head of John," she snapped out, so that's what Salome went back and told Herod, adding only that she would prefer to have it served on a platter. No sooner was it brought to her than she got rid of it like a hot potato by handing it over to her mother. It's not hard to see why.

Salome disappears from history at that point, and you can only hope that she took the platter with her to remind her that she should be careful where she danced that particular dance in the future, and that she should never ask her mother's advice again about anything, and that even when you cut a saint's head off, that doesn't mean you've heard the last of him by a long shot.

Mark 6:17–22

See also Herod Antipas.

SALVATION

DAY 295 S ALVATION IS AN EXPERIENCE first and a doctrine second.
Doing the work you're best at doing and like to do best, hearing great music, having great fun, seeing something very beautiful, weeping at somebody else's tragedy—all these experiences are related to the experience of salvation because in all of them two things happen: (1) you lose yourself, and (2) you find that you are more fully yourself than usual.

A closer analogy is the experience of love. When you love somebody, it is no longer yourself who is the center of your own universe. It is the one you love who is. You forget yourself. You deny yourself. You give of yourself, so that by all the rules of arithmetical logic there should be less of yourself than there was to start with. Only by a curious paradox there is more. You feel that at last you really *are* yourself.

The experience of salvation involves the same paradox. Jesus put it like this: "Those who find their life will lose it, and those who lose their life for my sake will find it" (Matthew 10:39).

You give up your old self-seeking self for somebody you love and thereby become yourself at last. You must die with Christ so that you can rise with him, Paul says. It is what baptism is all about.

You do not love God so that, tit for tat, he will then save you. To love God is to be saved. To love anybody is a significant step along the way.

You do not love God and live for him so you will go to heaven. Whichever side of the grave you happen to be talking about, to love God and live for him is heaven.

It is a gift, not an achievement.

You can make yourself moral. You can make yourself religious. But you can't make yourself love.

"We love," John says, "because he first loved us" (1 John 4:19).

Who knows how the awareness of God's love first hits people. We all have our own tales to tell, including those of us who wouldn't believe in God if you paid us. Some moment happens in your life that you say yes to right up to the roots of your hair, that makes it worth having been born just to have happen. Laughing with somebody till the tears run down your cheeks. Waking up to the first snow. Being in bed with somebody you love.

Whether you thank God for such a moment or thank your lucky stars, it is a moment that is trying to open up your whole life. If you turn your back on such a moment and hurry along to business as usual, it may lose you the ball game. If you throw your arms around such a moment and bless it, it may save your soul.

How about the person you know who as far as you can possibly tell has never had such a moment—one of those soreheads and slobs of the world, the ones the world has hopelessly crippled? Maybe for that person the moment that has to happen is you.

It is a process, not an event.

See also baptism, eternal life, justification, sanctification, sin.

SAMUEL

DAY 296

SAMUEL WAS A COMBINATION PROPHET, judge, and one-man band. When the old curmudgeon wasn't out in the field trying to fight off the Philistine guerrillas, he was riding his circuit trying to keep the tribes of Israel honest, and when he wasn't doing that, he was giving them hell for cheating on Yahweh every time a new fertility god showed up with a come-hither look in his eye. When he reached retirement age, he might have turned things over to his sons, but they were a bunch of crooks who sold justice to the highest bidder, and the Israelites said maybe he'd better get them a king instead. They'd never had one before, but they felt the time had come. Samuel threw a fit.

He said there was only one king worth the time of day, and Yahweh was his name. He also told them kings were a bad lot from the word go and didn't spare them a single sordid detail. They were always either drafting you into their armies or strong-arming you into taking care of their farms. They took your daughters and put them to work in their kitchens and perfume factories. They filled their barns with your livestock and got you to slave for them till you dropped in your tracks. What was more, if the Israelites chose a king, Yahweh would wash his hands of them and good riddance. Samuel had it on the highest authority. But the Israelites insisted, and since Samuel didn't have the pep he'd once had, he finally gave in.

The king he dug up for them was a tall drink of water named Saul. He was too handsome for his own good, had a rich father, and when it came to religion tended to go off the deep end. Samuel had him in for a meal and, after explaining the job to him, anointed him with holy oil against his better judgment and made him the first king Israel ever had. He regretted this action till the day he died, and even in his grave the memory of it never gave him a moment's peace.   *1 Samuel 8–11*

See also Agag, Saul, witch of Endor.

SANCTIFICATION

IN "BEAUTY AND THE BEAST," it is only when the Beast discovers that Beauty really loves him in all his ugliness that he himself becomes beautiful.   DAY 297

In the experience of Saint Paul, it is only when we discover that God really loves us in all our unloveliness that we ourselves start to become godlike.

Paul's word for this gradual transformation of a sow's ear into a silk purse is *sanctification*, and he sees it as the second stage in the process of salvation.

Being sanctified is a long and painful stage because with part of themselves sinners prefer their sin, just as with part of himself the Beast prefers his glistening snout and curved tusks. Many drop out with the job hardly more than begun, and among those who stay with it there are few if any who don't drag their feet most of the way.

But little by little—less by taking pains than by taking it easy—the forgiven person starts to become a forgiving person, the healed person to become a healing person, the loved person to become a loving person. God does most of it. The end of the process, Paul says, is eternal life.

See also eternal life, justification.

SARAH

DAY 298

QUANTITATIVELY SPEAKING, you don't find all that much laughter in the Bible, but, qualitatively, there's nothing quite like it to be found anywhere else. There are a couple of chapters in the book of Genesis that positively shake with it. Sarah was never going to see ninety again, and Abraham had already hit one hundred, and when the angel told them that the stork was on its way at last, they both of them almost collapsed. Abraham laughed "till he fell on his face" (Genesis 17:17), and Sarah stood cackling behind the tent door so the angel wouldn't think she was being rude as the tears streamed down her cheeks. When the baby finally came, they even called him "Laughter"—which is what Isaac means in Hebrew—because obviously no other name would do.

Laughter gets mixed up with all sorts of things in the Bible and in the world too, things like sneering, irony, making fun of, and beating the competition hollow. It also gets mixed up with things like comedians and slipping on banana peels and having the soles of your feet tickled. There are times when you laugh to keep from crying, like when the old wino staggers home in a party hat, or even in the midst of crying, like when Charlie Chaplin boils his shoe for supper because he's starving to death. But 100 percent, bonded, aged-in-the-wood laughter is something else again.

It's the crazy parrot squawks that issue out of David as he spins like a top in front of the ark (2 Samuel 6:16–21). It's what the Psalms are talking about where they say, "When the Lord had rescued

Zion, then our mouth was filled with laughter" (126:1–2), or where they get so excited they yell out, "Let the floods clap their hands, let the hills sing for joy together!" because the Lord has come through at last (98:8). It's what the Lord himself is talking about when he says that on the day he laid the cornerstone of the earth "the morning stars sang together, and all the sons of God shouted for joy" (Job 38:7), and it's what the rafters ring with when the Prodigal comes home and his old crock of a father is so glad to see him he almost has a stroke and "they began to make merry" and kept on making merry till the cows came home (Luke 15:24). It's what Jesus means when he stands in that crowd of cripples and loners and oddballs and factory rejects and says, "Blessed are you that weep now, for you shall laugh" (Luke 6:21). Nobody claims there's a chuckle on every page, but laughter's what the whole Bible is really about. Nobody who knows a hat from home plate claims that getting mixed up with God is all sweetness and light, but ultimately it's what that's all about too.

Sarah and her husband had had plenty of hard knocks in their time, and there were plenty more of them still to come, but at that moment when the angel told them they'd better start dipping into their old-age pensions for cash to build a nursery, the reason they laughed was that it suddenly dawned on them that the wildest dreams they'd ever had hadn't been half wild enough.

Genesis 17; 18; 21

See also Hagar.

SAUL

S AUL, THE FIRST KING OF ISRAEL, had three things going against him almost from the beginning. One of them was the prophet Samuel, another was a young man named David, and the third and worst was himself. DAY 299

Samuel never thought Israel should have had a king in the first place and told him so at regular intervals. After Saul defeated the Amalekites, Samuel said the rules of the game were that he should take the whole pack of them plus their king and all their livestock and sacrifice them to Yahweh. When Saul decided to sacrifice only the swaybacks and runts of the litter, keeping the cream of the crop and the king for himself, Samuel said it was the last straw and that Yahweh was through with him for keeps. Samuel then snuck off and told a boy named David that he was to be the next king, and the sooner the better. In the meanwhile, however, they both kept the matter under their hats.

Saul was hit so hard by the news that Yahweh was through with him that his whole faith turned sour. The God he'd always loved became the God who seemed to have it in for him no matter what he did or failed to do, and he went into such a state of depression that he could hardly function. The only person who could bring him out of it was this same David. He was a good-looking young redhead with a nice voice and would come and play songs on his lyre till the king's case of the horrors was under at least temporary control. Saul lost his heart to him eventually, and when the boy knocked out the top Philistine heavyweight, their relationship seemed permanently cinched.

It wasn't. David could charm the birds out of the trees, and soon all Israel was half in love with him. "Saul has slain his thousands and David his ten thousands," the ladies would dither every time he rounded the bend in his fancy uniform (1 Samuel 18:7), and Saul began to smolder. It was one day when David was trying to chase his blues away with some new songs that he burst into flame. He heaved his spear at him and just missed by a quarter of an inch. When his own son and heir, Jonathan, fell under David's spell too, that did it. It was love-hate from then on.

Saul hated David because he needed him, and he needed him because he loved him, and when he wasn't out to kill him every chance he got, he was hating himself for his own evil disposition. One day he went into a cave to take a leak, not knowing that David was hiding out there, and while he was taking forty winks afterward, David snipped off a piece of his cloak. When David produced the snippet later to prove he could have tried to kill him in return but hadn't, Saul said, "Is this your voice, my son David?" and wept as if his heart would break (1 Samuel 24). It was exactly what, in the end, his heart did.

He was told in advance that he was going to lose the battle of Gilboa and die in the process, but in spite of knowing that, or maybe because of it, he went ahead and fought it anyway.

There are two versions of what happened to him then. One is that after being badly wounded by arrows, he persuaded a young Amalekite to put him out of his misery. The other is that he took his own sword and fell on it. In either case, it is hard to hold it against him for tendering back to the God he had once loved a life that for years he had found unbearable.   *1 Samuel 9–30*

See also Agag, Goliath, Jonathan, Samuel, witch of Endor.

SCIENCE

S CIENCE IS THE INVESTIGATION of the physical universe and its ways, and consists largely of weighing, measuring, and putting things in test tubes. To assume that this kind of investigation can unearth solutions to all our problems is a form of religious faith whose bankruptcy has only in recent years started to become apparent.   DAY 300

There is a tendency in many people to suspect that anything that can't be weighed, measured, or put in a test tube is either not real or not worth talking about. That is like a blind person's suspecting that anything that can't be smelled, tasted, touched, or heard is probably a figment of the imagination.

A scientist's views on such subjects as God, morality, and life after death are apt to be about as enlightening as a theologian's views on the structure of the atom or the cause and cure of the common cold.

The conflict between science and religion, which reached its peak toward the end of the nineteenth century, is like the conflict between a podiatrist and a poet. One says that Susie Smith has fallen arches. The other says she walks in beauty like the night. In his own way each is speaking the truth. What is at issue is the kind of truth you're after.

SECOND COMING

DAY 301   JUST BEFORE THE FINAL BENEDICTION, the New Testament ends with the prayer, "Come, Lord Jesus!" (Revelation 22:20). When he came the first time, he came so unobtrusively that except for Mary and Joseph and a handful of shepherds, nobody much knew or cared. But he says he will come a second time.

Who knows how he will come, or when, or where. He says himself, "Of that day and hour no one knows, not even the angels of heaven, nor the Son, but the Father only" (Matthew 24:36). People who in search of a timetable try to crack the book of Revelation like a code are on a wild goose chase. People who claim that all who join their sect will be saved and all others lost are wrong. The ones who will be saved, Jesus says, are the ones who feed the hungry, welcome the stranger, clothe the naked, and visit the sick and the prisoners (Matthew 25:31–46). If you love, in other words, you're in. If you don't, you're out. It doesn't seem to matter to him whether you're a Jehovah's Witness, a Jesuit, or a Jew.

In one of the more outlandish of his outlandish images, he says he will come like a thief in the night (Matthew 24:42–43). We must be ready at all times therefore. We can never be sure when he will break into the world as into a house, when he will break into our lives.

No one can say just what will happen when that day comes, but that it will be a day to remember there is no doubt. The dead will be raised. The Last Judgment will take place. The present age will end and the new age begin. In Dante's vision, the redeemed will shine like a great white rose unfolding petal by petal in the light of glory. In John's, the new Jerusalem will come down out of heaven like a bride.

"My grace is sufficient for you, for my power is made perfect in weakness," the risen Christ said to his servant Paul (2 Corinthians 12:9). It is in that hope only that we dare say "Amen" to the prayer that brings all Scripture to a close.

SECRETS

WE TEND TO THINK RIGHT AWAY of dark secrets—things we did or failed to do that we have never managed to forgive ourselves for; fierce hungers that we have difficulty admitting even to ourselves; things that happened to us long ago too painful to speak of; doubts about our own worth as human beings, doubts about the people closest to us, about God if we believe in God; and fear—the fear of death, the fear of life.

DAY 302

But there are also happy secrets, the secrets we keep like treasure less because we don't want to share them with the world for fear of somehow tarnishing them than because they are so precious we have no way of sharing them adequately. The love we feel for certain people, some of them people we scarcely know, some of them people who do not suspect our love and wouldn't know how to respond to it if they did. The way our hearts leap at certain things that the chances are wouldn't make anybody else so much as turn a hair—the sound of a particular voice on the telephone, a dog-eared book we read as children, the first snow, the sight of an old man smoking his pipe on the porch as we drive by.

We are our secrets. They are the essence of what makes us ourselves. They are the rich loam out of which, for better or worse, grow the selves by which the world knows us. If we are ever to be free and whole, we must be free from their darkness and have their spell over us broken. If we are ever to see each other as we fully are, we must see by their light.

"Search me, O God, and know my heart!" cries out the great Psalm 139, which is all about the hiding and baring of secrets. "Try me and know my thoughts . . . for darkness is as light to thee." Even our darkness.

It is the secret prayer of us all.

SENSES

DAY 303   TASTE AN APPLE. Taste salt.
See the sunlight on the wall, the deer track in the snow.
Hear the luffing of the sail.

Smell the rose, the dead mouse behind the wainscoting, the child's hair.

Touch the hand that is touching your hand.

Although we have been taught better, it is easier to assume that nothing that lies beyond the reach of our five senses is entirely real than to acknowledge that what we know about reality through the five senses is roughly the equivalent of what an ant crawling across the front page of the *New York Times* knows about the state of the world.

SERMON

DON'T PREACH TO ME!" means "Don't bore me to death with your offensive platitudes!" Respectable verbs don't get into that kind of trouble entirely by accident.

DAY 304

Sermons are like jokes; even the best ones are hard to remember. In both cases that may be just as well. Ideally the thing to remember is not the preachers' eloquence but the lump in your throat or leap of your heart or the thorn in your flesh that appeared as much in spite of what they said as because of it.

Paul said, "Woe to me if I do not preach the gospel!" (1 Corinthians 9:16). Jesus said, "If any of you put a stumbling block before one of these little ones who believe in me, it would be better for you if a great millstone were fastened around your neck and you were drowned in the depth of the sea" (Matthew 18:6). People who preach sermons without realizing that they're heading straight for Scylla and Charybdis ought to try a safer and more productive line of work.

SEX

CONTRARY TO MRS. GRUNDY, sex is not sin. Contrary to Hugh Hefner, it's not salvation either. Like nitroglycerin, it can be used either to blow up bridges or heal hearts.

DAY 305

At its roots, the hunger for food is the hunger for survival. At its roots the hunger to know a person sexually is the hunger to know and be known by that person humanly. Food without nourishment doesn't fill the bill for long, and neither does sex without humanness.

Adultery, promiscuity (either heterosexual or homosexual), masturbation—one appealing view is that anything goes as long as nobody gets hurt. The trouble is that human beings are so hopelessly psychosomatic in composition that whatever happens to the *soma* happens also to the *psyche*, and vice versa.

Who is to say who gets hurt and who doesn't get hurt, and how? Maybe the injuries are all internal. Maybe it will be years before the X rays show up anything. Maybe the only person who gets hurt is you.

In practice Jesus was notoriously soft on sexual misbehavior. Some of his best friends were hustlers. He saved the woman taken in adultery from stoning. He didn't tell the woman at the well that she ought to marry the man she was living with. Possibly he found their fresh-faced sensualities closer to loving God and humanity than the thin-lipped pieties of the Pharisees. Certainly he shared the Old Testament view that the body in all its manifestations was basically good because a good God made it.

But he also had some hard words to say about lust (Matthew 5:27–28), and told the adulterous woman to go and sin no more. When the force of a person's sexuality is centrifugal, pushing further and further away as *psyches* the very ones being embraced as *somas*, this sexuality is of the Devil. When it is centripetal, it is of God.

See also sin.

SIMEON

JESUS WAS STILL IN DIAPERS when his parents brought him to the Temple in Jerusalem "to present him to the Lord" (Luke 2:22), as the custom was, and offer a sacrifice, and that's when old Simeon spotted him. Years before, he'd been told he wouldn't die till he'd seen the Messiah with his own two eyes, and time was running out. When the moment finally came, one look through his cataract lenses was all it took. He asked if it would be all right to hold the baby in his arms, and they told him to go ahead but be careful not to drop him.

"Lord, now lettest thou thy servant depart in peace, according to thy word, for mine eyes have seen thy salvation," he said (Luke 2:29), the baby playing with the fringes of his beard. The parents were pleased as punch, and so he blessed them too for good measure. Then something about the mother stopped him, and his expression changed.

What he saw in her face was a long way off, but it was there so plainly he couldn't pretend. "A sword will pierce through your soul," he said (Luke 2:35).

He would rather have bitten off his tongue than said it, but in that holy place he felt he had no choice. Then he handed her back the baby and departed in something less than the perfect peace he'd dreamed of all the long years of his waiting.   *Luke 2:22–35*

SIMON MAGUS

SIMON MAGUS LIVED in Samaria and was the Houdini of his day. He made small boys climb ropes and disappear. He sawed pretty girls in half. He pulled rabbits out of hats and levitated volunteers from the audience. And he made a good thing of it too. He got top billing, drove a BMW convertible to work, and wore nothing but silk next to his skin.

Then one day Philip came to town on a preaching junket, and Simon Magus got religion in a big way. When the altar call was given, he was the first to come forward. He then got himself baptized, and Philip added him to the team.

After a while the apostle Peter came down from the head office in Jerusalem to see how things were going, and before he was through, he conferred the power of healing on some of them by laying his hands on their heads. The healings struck Simon Magus as the most spectacular trick he had ever seen in his life, and he offered Peter hard cash if he'd lay his hands on him.

God didn't belong to the magicians' union, Peter told him, and as for the hard cash, he knew what he could do with it. He said that maybe if Simon Magus repented, God would overlook what had happened, but he didn't make the prospects sound too hopeful. There might still be hell to pay.

Knowing when he'd been upstaged, Simon Magus begged Peter to use his influence with the Lord to get him off the hook and then steered clear of the old fisherman for the remainder of his visit.

Acts 8:5–24

SIN

DAY 308　THE POWER OF SIN IS CENTRIFUGAL. When at work in a human life, it tends to push everything out toward the periphery. Bits and pieces go flying off until only the core is left. Eventually bits and pieces of the core itself go flying off until in the end nothing at all is left. "The wages of sin is death" is Saint Paul's way of saying the same thing.

Other people and (if you happen to believe in God) God or (if you happen not to) the world, society, nature—whatever you call the greater whole of which you're part—sin is whatever you do, or fail to do, that pushes them away, that widens the gap between you and them and also the gaps within your self.

For example, the sin of the Pharisee is not just (a) his holier-than-thou attitude, which pushes other people away, but (b) his secret suspicion that his own holiness is deficient too, which pushes part of himself away, and (c) his possibly not so subconscious feeling that anybody who expects him to be all that holy must be a cosmic SOB, which pushes Guess Who away.

Sex is sinful to the degree that, instead of drawing you closer to other human beings in their humanness, it unites bodies but leaves the lives inside them hungrier and more alone than before.

Religion and unreligion are both sinful to the degree that they widen the gap between you and the people who don't share your views.

The word *charity* illustrates the insidiousness of sin. From meaning "a free and loving gift" it has come to mean "a demeaning handout."

Original sin means we all originate out of a sinful world, which taints us from the word go. We all tend to make ourselves the center of the universe, pushing away centrifugally from that center everything that seems to impede its freewheeling. More even than hunger, poverty, or disease, it is what Jesus said he came to save the world from.

See also salvation.

SLEEP

DAY 309   SLEEP IS A SURRENDER, a laying down of arms. Whatever plans you're making, whatever work you're up to your ears in, whatever pleasures you're enjoying, whatever sorrows or anxieties or problems you're in the midst of, you set them aside, find a place to stretch out somewhere, close your eyes, and wait for sleep.

All the things that make you the particular person you are stop working—your thoughts and feelings, the changing expressions of your face, the constant moving around, the yammering will, the relentless or not so relentless purpose. But all the other things keep on working with a will and purpose of their own. You go on breathing in and out. Your heart goes on beating. If some faint thought stirs somewhere in the depths of you, it's converted into a dream so you can go on sleeping and not have to wake up to think it through before it's time.

Whether you're just or unjust, you have the innocence of a cat dozing under the stove. Whether you're old or young, homely or fair, you take on the serenity of marble. You have given up being in charge of your life. You have put yourself into the hands of the night.

It is a rehearsal for the final laying down of arms, of course, when you trust yourself to the same unseen benevolence to see you through the dark and to wake you when the time comes—with new hope, new strength—into the return again of light.

SLOTH

SLOTH IS NOT TO BE CONFUSED with laziness. Lazy people, DAY 310
people who sit around and watch the grass grow, may be
people at peace. Their sun-drenched, bumblebee dreaming may be
the prelude to action or itself an act well worth the acting.

Slothful people, on the other hand, may be very busy people.
They are people who go through the motions, who fly on automatic pilot. Like somebody with a bad head cold, they have mostly
lost their sense of taste and smell. They know something's wrong
with them, but not wrong enough to do anything about. Other
people come and go, but through glazed eyes they hardly notice
them. They are letting things run their course. They are getting
through their lives.

SMELL

MY BROTHER AND I were walking up a flight of stairs some- DAY 311
where when I suddenly stopped and asked him what the
smell reminded him of. Without a moment's hesitation he said our
grandparents' house in Pittsburgh when we were children, and he
was right. It was a comforting kind of smell, faint but unmistakable—freshly laundered sheets, applesauce simmering with nut-
meg in it, old picture books. More than any sight or taste or sound,
it brought back in its totality the feeling of being a child there all
those years ago—the excitement of it, the peace of it, the unutter-
able magic of it.

Dogs have it right. Frantically zigzagging along, their tails in a
frenzy, they miss nothing as they go, not a hydrant or trash can or

curbstone, not a tree or hedge or flower pot. And it's not just the good smells that send them into raptures either, but smells we would recoil from in horror. "O taste and see that the Lord is good," says the Psalmist (34:8), to which their refrain is, "Oh sniff and smell!" More fragrant even than grandparents' houses is the Quarry they track with their noses to the ground.

SNOBS

DAY 312   SNOBS ARE PEOPLE who look down on other people, but that does not justify our looking down on them. Who can say what dark fears of being inferior lurk behind their superior airs or what they suffer in private for the slights they dish out in public?

Don't look down on them for looking down on us. Look at them, instead, as friends we don't know yet and who don't yet know what they are missing in not knowing us.

SOLOMON

DAY 313   KING SOLOMON WAS A PRODUCT of the scandalous liaison between King David and Uriah's wife, Bathsheba. It was not an auspicious beginning. He was then brought up in that hotbed of oriental intrigue and ostentation that was his father's court, and that was less than conducive to the development of sound moral character. He also spent his formative years under the thumb of his beautiful but conniving mother, who had browbeaten David on his deathbed into giving him the throne in the first place. It is a wonder he turned out as well as he did.

He was the first of the big-time spenders, and the menu that he and his retinue consumed per diem reads like the inventory of

General Foods: a thousand measures of flour and meal plus ten oxen, twenty steers, and one hundred sheep, not to mention a garnishing of harts, gazelles, roebucks, and butterball chickens for when their jaded palates were in need of reupholstering. He had forty thousand horses with twelve thousand horsemen to keep them in shape, and recent excavations of his stables indicate that these figures aren't as far out of line as they might seem. His building program isn't to be overlooked either.

He put up a temple in Jerusalem that had to be seen to be believed. It stood three stories high, and you entered it through a soaring porch of Egyptian design that was flanked by two thirty-foot free-standing bronze columns with carved lilies on top. It had cedar ceilings, cypress floors, and olive-wood doors, and the amount of gold they used to trim it inside and out would have bankrupted Fort Knox. Seven years was what it took him to finish this job for God, and he then proceeded to build a palace for himself, which took thirteen. It was composed of the House of the Forest of Lebanon, the Hall of Pillars, the Hall of the Throne, and the Hall of Judgment. These were for show. He also had them knock together a nice little place for his personal use and another for his wife, the daughter of Pharaoh.

The daughter of Pharaoh was not his only wife. Perhaps the reason they preferred separate bedrooms was that he had six hundred and ninety-nine more. Just in case they all happened to be busy at the same time some evening, he also had three hundred other ladies who were ready to drop everything for him at a moment's notice. Some of these were Moabites or Ammonites, some were Edomites or Sidonians, and there were five or six dozen Hittites thrown in to round things out. It was a regular smorgasbord.

Somehow he found time to run the country too, and in some ways he didn't make too bad a job of it. His reign lasted forty years, and Israel was at peace the whole time. He made advantageous treaties with both Egypt and Tyre, and in partnership with Hiram, king of Tyre, maintained a fleet of oceangoing ships that did a brisk export-import business with a number of Mediterranean ports, dealing in things like gold, silver, ivory, apes, and peacocks. He also made a killing as a horse trader.

Unfortunately the price for all this ran pretty high, and it was his subjects who had to pick up the tab. In order to finance his building program he had to bleed them white with tolls and taxes. In order to get people to run the bulldozers and bench saws, he had to press them into forced labor gangs. You don't keep seven hundred wives and three hundred lady friends happy on peanuts either, and it was the people who had to foot that bill too. When some of them revolted in the north under the leadership of Jeroboam, he managed to quash it successfully, but instead of solving the problem, that just postponed it.

Furthermore, his taste for foreign ladies got him into more kinds of trouble than just financial. They worshiped a whole carnival of fancy foreign gods, and in his old age Solomon decided to play it safe by seeing to it that not one of them went neglected. He put up expensive altars to Ashtoreth of the Sidonians, Milcom of the Ammonites, and Chemoth of the Moabites, to name just a few, and Yahweh was so furious he said it was only for the sake of his father, David, that he didn't settle Israel's hash right then and there. As it was, he said he'd wait a few years.

In spite of everything, Solomon was famous for his great wisdom. There wasn't a riddle he couldn't crack with one hand tied behind him, and he tossed off so many *bon mots* in the course of a day that it reached the point where people figured that if anything clever was said anywhere, it must have been Solomon who originally said it, and the whole book of Proverbs was ascribed to his hand. His judgments in court were also praised to the skies, the most famous of them involving a couple of chippies each of whom claimed to be the mother of the same child, to which Solomon proposed the simple solution of slicing the child down the middle and giving each one half. When the first girl said that was fine by her and the second girl said she'd rather lose the case, Solomon awarded the child to the second girl, and it was all over Jerusalem within the hour.

But wisdom is more than riddles and wisecracks and courtroom coups, and in most things that mattered King Solomon was among the wisest fools who ever wore a crown. He didn't even have the wit to say *"Après moi, le déluge"* in Hebrew and was hardly cold in his grave when revolution split the country in two. From there on out the history of Israel was an almost unbroken series of disasters.

1 Kings 3–11

See also Bathsheba, Hiram, queen of Sheba.

SPIRIT

THE WORD *spirit* has come to mean something pale and shapeless, like an unmade bed. School spirit, the American spirit, the Christmas spirit, the spirit of '76, the Holy Spirit—each of these points to something that you know is supposed to get you to your feet cheering, but that you somehow can't rise to. The adjective *spiritual* has become downright offensive. If somebody recommends a person as spiritual you tend to avoid that person, and usually with good reason. *Inspiring* is even worse. *Inspirational* is worse still. Inspirational books are almost invariably for the birds.

Like its counterparts in Hebrew and Greek, the Latin word *spiritus* originally meant "breath" (as in *expire, respiratory,* and so on), and breath is what you have when you're alive and don't have when

DAY 314

you're dead. Thus spirit = breath = life, the aliveness and power of your life, and to speak of your spirit (or soul) is to speak of the power of life that is in you. When your spirit is unusually strong, the life in you unusually alive, you can breathe it out into other lives, become literally in-spiring.

Spirit is highly contagious. When people are very excited, very happy, or very sad, you can catch it from them as easily as measles or a yawn. You can catch it from what they say or from what they do or just from what happens to the air of a room when they enter it without saying or doing anything. Groups also have a spirit, as anybody can testify who has ever been caught up in the spirit of a football game, a political rally, or a lynch mob. Spirit can be good or bad, healing or destructive. Spirit can be transmitted across great distances of time and space. For better or worse, you can catch the spirit of people long dead (Saint Thérèse of Lisieux or the Marquis de Sade), of people whose faces you have never seen and whose languages you cannot speak.

God also has a spirit—*is* Spirit, says the apostle John (4:24). Thus God is the power of the power of life itself, has breathed and continues to breathe life into his creation. In-spires it. The spirit of God, Holy Spirit, Holy Ghost, is highly contagious. When Peter and his friends were caught up in it at Jerusalem on Pentecost, everybody thought they were drunk even though the sun wasn't yet over the yardarm (Acts 2). They were.

See also Trinity.

STEPHEN

DAY 315 AFTER JESUS DIED, it took a while for his followers to settle down and get organized, and the process was no easier then than it has been ever since. One problem that came up early in the game was how to take care of the poor, especially the widows who couldn't support themselves. The apostles decided to appoint a group to handle this side of things, and one of the ones they appointed was Stephen.

His career was a short one. In addition to doing what he could for the poor, he also did what he could to spread the word about Jesus, the one who'd gotten him interested in the poor in the first place. He healed, and he preached, and he talked about how his own life had been changed, and it wasn't long before the Jewish authorities called him on the mat to defend his far-out views as best he could. As far as they were concerned, he was a bad apple.

Stephen made them a long speech, the gist of which was that from year one the Jews had always been an ornery lot, "stiff-necked," he said, and circumcised as all get-out in one department, but as cussed and mean as everybody else in all the others (Acts 7:51). They'd given Moses a hard time in the wilderness, he said, and there hadn't been a saint or prophet since whom they hadn't had it in for. The way they'd treated Jesus was the last and worst example of how they were always not just missing the boat, but doing their damnedest to sink it. The authorities were naturally enraged and illustrated the accuracy of Stephen's analysis of them by taking him out and stoning him to death.

Stoning somebody to death, especially somebody as young and healthy as Stephen, isn't easy. You don't get the job done with the first few rocks and broken bottles, and even after you've got the person down, it's a long, hot business. To prepare themselves for the workout, they stripped to the waist and got somebody to keep an eye on their things till they were through. The one they got was a young fire-breathing archconservative Jew named Saul, who was there because he thoroughly approved of what they were doing.

It was a scene that Saul never forgot. Years later when he'd become a Christian himself and was under arrest much as Stephen had been, he spoke of it. He wasn't called Saul anymore by then, but Paul, the apostle to the Gentiles, the great letter-writing saint, and he still remembered how it had been that day when he'd stood guard over the pile of coats and ties and watched a young man's death.

Stephen was the first person to shed blood for the new faith he loved more than his life, and as Saul-who-was-to-become-Paul watched the grim process, it never occurred to him that by the grace of God the time was not far off when he himself would be another.

Acts 6–7; 22:20

See also Paul.

STORY

DAY 316

IT IS WELL TO REMEMBER what the ancient creeds of the Christian faith declare credence in.

"God of God, Light of Light . . . for us and for our salvation came down from heaven . . . born of the Virgin Mary . . . suffered . . . crucified . . . dead . . . buried . . . rose again . . . sitteth on the right hand of God . . . shall come again, with glory, to judge both the quick and the dead." That is not a theological idea or a religious system. It is a series of largely flesh-and-blood events that happened, are happening, will happen in time and space. For better or worse, it is a story.

It is well to remember because it keeps our eyes on the central fact that the Christian faith *always* has to do with flesh and blood, time and space, more specifically with your flesh and blood and mine, with the time and space that day by day we are all of us involved with, stub our toes on, flounder around in trying to look as if we have good sense. In other words, the truth that Christianity claims to be true is ultimately to be found, if it's to be found at all, not in the Bible, or the church, or theology—the best they can do is point to the truth—but in our own stories.

If the God you believe in as an idea doesn't start showing up in what happens to you in your own life, you have as much cause for concern as if the God you don't believe in as an idea does start showing up.

It is absolutely crucial, therefore, to keep in constant touch with what is going on in your own life's story and to pay close attention to what is going on in the stories of others' lives. If God is present anywhere, it is in those stories that God is present. If God is not present in those stories, then they are scarcely worth telling.

SUICIDE

THE MOST FAMOUS SUICIDE in the Old Testament is King Saul's. He was doing battle with the Philistines. The Philistines won the day. They killed his three sons, and he himself was wounded by archers. Fearing that he would be captured by the enemy and made a mockery of if he survived, he asked his armor-bearer to put him out of his misery. When the armor-bearer refused, he fell on his own sword (1 Samuel 31:4).

DAY 317

Judas Iscariot's is of course the most famous one in the New Testament. When Jesus was led off to Pilate and condemned to death, Judas took his thirty pieces of silver and tried to return them to the Jewish authorities on the grounds that Jesus was innocent and he had betrayed him. The authorities refused to take them. They said that was his problem, and Judas, throwing the silver to the ground, went off and hanged himself (Matthew 27:3–5).

Taking your own life is not mentioned as a sin in the Bible. There's no suggestion that it was considered either shameful or cowardly. When, as in the case of Saul and Judas, pain, horror, and despair reach a certain point, suicide is perhaps less a voluntary act than a reflex action. If you're being burned alive with a loaded pistol in your hand, it's hard to see how anyone can seriously hold it against you for pulling the trigger.

SUPERSTITION

DAY 318   SUPERSTITION IS THE SUSPICION that things are seldom what they seem and usually worse. Breaking a mirror foreshadows a graver misfortune than having to buy a new one. Inviting thirteen for dinner involves a greater risk than not having enough to go round. The superstitious person may be more nearly right in being wrong than the person who takes everything at face value. If a black cat crosses your path and all you see is a black cat, you need to have more than your eyes examined. What is crossing your path with four legs and a hoisted tail is the dark and inscrutable mystery of creation itself.

SUSANNA

DAY 319   SUSANNA AND BATHSHEBA had a number of points in common. Both of them were very beautiful, both were married, and both had the fatal habit of taking their baths out of doors. Both of them also had the misfortune to arouse, through no fault of their own, the baser passions of the male animal. But there the resemblance ends. How Bathsheba responded to the advances of King David is recorded under her name. Susanna was a different kind of woman.

In her case, it was not a young king who lusted after her charms, but a couple of old goats. They were not only friends of her husband's, but judges to boot, and in both capacities they ought to have known better. Each of them, unknown to the other, used to keep himself in a state of perpetual excitement by spying on her as she took her noonday strolls in her husband's garden, and one day when they happened to collide among the shrubbery, they confessed to each other their common passion and cooked up a sordid little plan.

It was a hot afternoon, and Susanna, having first modestly dismissed her two maids and told them to be sure to latch the gate on their way out, undressed and started bathing in the garden pool. She had no idea that the two were crouching in the bushes, and as soon as she was alone, they emerged and confronted her.

It is a haunting scene—the slim girl floating like a lily under the blue sky and the two old lechers standing there at the water's edge in the rusty black gowns of their profession. Either she was to let them have their way with her then and there, they said, or they would swear under oath they'd caught her in the act with a young lover and get her stoned to death. Though the temptation must have been considerable to save her skin instead of her honor, she turned them down cold. The next day, despite her protestations of innocence, the testimony of her two accusers was believed, and she was led off to her execution. On the way, however, she said a prayer to Yahweh, and Yahweh answered it by sending to the rescue a young man named Daniel.

Daniel was no lawyer, but he had some ideas of his own about the law. First he turned to the men who were standing there at the ready with stones in their hands and called them a pack of fools. Then he got permission to interrogate the two old goats separately and asked them both the same question: Under what kind of tree had they seen Susanna and her alleged boyfriend carrying on? When one of them said it was a mastic and the other a holm, the crowd wised up to them at last and tossed them off the edge of a cliff. It was a disagreeable fate, but for one thing they'd asked for it, and for another maybe the shock of being thrown off a cliff isn't all that much worse than the torments of unsatisfied desire. At least it's over quicker.

In one sense Daniel is the hero of the tale, and in another Yahweh is for getting him there just in time. But the real hero, of course, is Susanna herself. Though she was naked as the day she was born that time at the pool and the two dirty old men decked out like Supreme Court justices on Inauguration Day, she wore her integrity like gold lamé, and her sheer guts stripped their seaminess bare. In the event that Daniel hadn't shown up when he did, you feel that even lying dead of multiple fractures under a pile of stones she would have come out the winner, and even with their reputations still intact, the two old goats would have lost, and known they'd lost, vastly more than just the tryst they'd dreamed of with a lovely girl on a summer afternoon.   *Daniel 13, Latin Vulgate*

See also Daniel.

TEARS

YOU NEVER KNOW what may cause tears. The sight of the Atlantic Ocean can do it, or a piece of music, or a face you've
never seen before. A pair of somebody's old shoes can do it. Almost
any movie made before the great sadness that came over the world
after the Second World War, a horse cantering across a meadow, the
high-school basketball team running out onto the gym floor at the
start of a game. You can never be sure. But of this you can be sure.
Whenever you find tears in your eyes, especially unexpected tears,
it is well to pay the closest attention.

They are not only telling you something about the secret of who
you are, but more often than not God is speaking to you through
them of the mystery of where you have come from and is summon-
ing you to where, if your soul is to be saved, you should go to next.

TELEVANGELISM

MAYBE IT'S ALL THE LIGHTS and cameras and having
makeup put on and their hair fussed with before the show

begins that does it, but most of the men and women who proclaim the Gospel on television come through as either phony as three-dollar bills or so simplistic and shallow and downright silly that it's hard to see how anybody can take them seriously.

Maybe they speak out of personal faith that can move mountains, but what comes through is about as inspired and inspiring as a commercial for dental adhesive.

TERRORISM

DAY 322   TERRORISTS ARE PEOPLE who seek to terrify their enemies by attacking or threatening to attack them anywhere, anytime, and in any form. The U.S.A. does not have to make such threats because, in view of its devastating might as the only surviving superpower, by its very existence it *is* such a threat. In view of recent history, it is no wonder that increasingly the rest of the world finds itself terrified.

THEODICY

DAY 323   THEODICY IS THE BRANCH OF THEOLOGY that asks the question: If God is just, why do terrible things happen to wonderful people? The Bible's best answer is the book of Job.

Job is a good man and knows it, as does everybody else, including God. Then one day his cattle are stolen, his servants are killed, and the wind blows down the house where his children happen to be whooping it up at the time, and not one of them lives to tell what it was they thought they had to whoop it up about. But being a good man he says only, "The Lord gave, and the Lord hath taken away. Blessed be the name of the Lord" (Job 1:21). Even when he comes down with a bad case of boils and his wife advises him to curse God and die, he manages to bite his tongue and say nothing. It's his friends who finally break the camel's back. They come to offer their condolences and hang around a full week. When Job finds them still there at the start of the second week, he curses the day he was born. He never quite takes his wife's advice and curses God, but he comes very close to it. He asks some unpleasant questions:

If God is all he's cracked up to be, how come houses blow down on innocent people? Why does a good woman die of cancer in her prime while an old man who can't remember his name or hold his water goes on in a nursing home forever? Why are there so many crooks riding around in Cadillacs and so many children going to bed hungry at night? Job's friends offer an assortment of theological explanations, but God doesn't offer one.

God doesn't explain. He explodes. He asks Job who he thinks he is anyway. He says that to try to explain the kinds of things Job wants explained would be like trying to explain Einstein to a little-neck clam. He also, incidentally, gets off some of the greatest poetry in the Old Testament. "Hast thou entered into the treasures of the snow? Canst thou bind the sweet influences of the Pleiades? Hast thou given the horse strength and clothed his neck with thunder?" (Job 38:31).

Maybe the reason God doesn't explain to Job why terrible things happen is that he knows what Job needs isn't an explanation. Suppose that God did explain. Suppose that God were to say to Job that the reason the cattle were stolen, the crops ruined, and the children killed was thus and so, spelling everything out right down to and including the case of boils. Job would have his explanation.

And then what?

Understanding in terms of the divine economy why his children had to die, Job would still have to face their empty chairs at breakfast every morning. Carrying in his pocket straight from the horse's mouth a complete theological justification of his boils, he would still have to scratch and burn.

God doesn't reveal his grand design. He reveals himself. He doesn't show why things are as they are. He shows his face. And Job says, "I had heard of thee by the hearing of the ear, but now my eyes see thee" (Job 42:5). Even covered with sores and ashes, he looks oddly like a man who has asked for a crust and been given the whole loaf.

At least for the moment.

See also Job.

THEOLOGY

DAY 324   THEOLOGY IS THE STUDY OF GOD and God's ways. For all we know, dung beetles may study us and our ways and call it humanology. If so, we would probably be more touched and amused than irritated. One hopes that God feels likewise.

THOMAS

DAY 325   IMAGINATION WAS NOT Thomas's long suit. He called a spade a spade. He was a realist. He didn't believe in fairy tales, and if anything else came up that he didn't believe in or couldn't understand, his questions could be pretty direct.

There was the last time he and the others had supper with Jesus, for instance. Jesus was talking about dying, and he said he would be leaving them soon, but it wouldn't be forever. He said he'd get things ready for them as soon as he got where he was going, and when their time finally came too, they'd all be together again. They knew the way he was going, he said, and some day they'd be there with him themselves.

Nobody else breathed a word, but Thomas couldn't hold back. When you got right down to it, he said, he personally had no idea where Jesus was going, and he didn't know the way to get there either. "I am the way," was what Jesus said to him (John 14:6), and although Thomas let it go at that, you can't help feeling that he found the answer less than satisfactory. Jesus wasn't a way, he was a man, and it was too bad he so often insisted on talking in riddles.

Then in the next few days all the things that everybody could see were going to happen happened, and Jesus was dead, just as he'd said he'd be. That much Thomas was sure of. He'd been on hand himself. There was no doubt about it. And then the thing that nobody had ever been quite able to believe would happen happened too.

Thomas wasn't around at the time, but all the rest of them were. They were sitting crowded together in a room with the door locked and the shades drawn, scared sick they'd be the ones to get it next, when suddenly Jesus came in. He wasn't a ghost you could see the wallpaper through, and he wasn't just a figment of their imagination because they were all too busy imagining the horrors that were all too likely in store for themselves to imagine anything much about anybody else. He said *"Shalom"* and then showed them enough of where the Romans had let him have it to convince them he was as real as they were, if not more so. He breathed the Holy Spirit on them, gave them a few instructions to go with it, and then left.

Nobody says where Thomas was at the time. One good thing about not having too much of an imagination is that you're not apt to work yourself up into quite as much of a panic as Thomas's friends had, for example, and maybe he'd gone out for a cup of coffee or just to sit in the park for a while and watch the pigeons. Anyway, when he finally returned and they told him what had happened, his reaction was just about what they might have expected. He said that unless Jesus came back again so he could not only see the nail marks for himself but actually touch them, he was afraid that, much as he hated to say so, he simply couldn't believe that what they had seen was anything more than the product of wishful thinking or a hallucination of an unusually vivid kind.

Eight days later, when Jesus did come back, Thomas was there and got his wish. Jesus let him see him and hear him and touch him, and not even Thomas could hold out against evidence like that. He had no questions left to ask and not enough energy left to ask them with even if he'd had a couple. All he could say was, "My Lord and my God!" (John 20:28), and Jesus seemed to consider that under the circumstances that was enough.

Then Jesus asked a question of his own. "Have you believed because you have seen me?" he asked and then added, addressing himself to all the generations that have come since, "Blessed are those who have not seen and yet believe" (John 20:29).

Even though he said the greater blessing is for those who can believe without seeing, it's hard to imagine that there's a believer anywhere who wouldn't have traded places with Thomas, given the chance, and seen that face and heard that voice and touched those ruined hands.　*John 14:1–7; 20:19–29*

TOBIAS

TOBIAS WAS A YOUNG MAN when he ran into the angel
Raphael and, not knowing that he was an angel at all, let alone
one of seven great ones who stand and enter before the glory of the
Lord, Tobias hired him at a drachma a day to be his traveling companion. Accompanied by Tobias's dog, they had a series of adventures that were nothing less than extraordinary.

Tobias almost lost his foot to a great fish. He discovered a cure
for his father's blindness. He picked up a large sum of money that
his father had left with a friend. And after first curing a young
woman named Sarah of a demon who had caused her first seven
husbands to perish on their wedding nights, he not only married
her himself but lived to tell the tale.

But the best part of the story is the short, no-nonsense prayer
with which he married her. "And now I take not this my sister for
lust, but in truth," he said. "Command that I and she may find
mercy and grow old together. Amen" (Tobit 8:8–9).

Never has the knot been more securely or simply or eloquently
tied, and it's small wonder that it lasted them through a long and
happy marriage that did not come to an end until Tobias died in
peace at the age of one hundred and seventeen.   *The Book of Tobit*

TODAY

IT IS A MOMENT OF LIGHT surrounded on all sides by darkness
and oblivion. In the entire history of the universe, let alone in
your own history, there has never been another just like it and there
will never be another just like it again. It is the point to which all

your yesterdays have been leading since the hour of your birth. It is the point from which all your tomorrows will proceed until the hour of your death. If you were aware of how precious it is, you could hardly live through it. Unless you are aware of how precious it is, you can hardly be said to be living at all.

"This is the day which the Lord has made," says Psalm 118. "Let us rejoice and be glad in it" (v. 24). Or weep and be sad in it for that matter. The point is to see it for what it is, because it will be gone before you know it. If you waste it, it is your life that you're wasting. If you look the other way, it may be the moment you've been waiting for always that you're missing.

All other days have either disappeared into darkness and oblivion or not yet emerged from it. Today is the only day there is.

TOLERATION

DAY 328   TOLERATION is often just indifference in disguise.

"It doesn't matter what religion you have as long as you have one" is apt to mean really, "I couldn't care less whether you have one or not."

If it means what it says, the question arises about a religion that demands, say, that firstborn children be fed to the crocodiles to ensure a good harvest. Somewhere lines have to be drawn. Sometimes it's not so easy to draw them.

Buddhism says, "Those who love a hundred have a hundred woes. Those who love ten have ten woes. Those who love one have one woe. Those who love none have no woe." Christianity says, "Whoever does not love abides in death" (1 John 3:14). The trouble is that each speaks a different kind of truth. If you choose for one as the truer and more profound of the two, then you choose against the other, granting it only a kind of proximate validity. Thus toleration must be limited in the interests of honesty.

It is sometimes argued that in our society the young should not be taught about Christianity. They should be taught about all religions. That is like saying they should be taught comparative linguistics before they have mastered English grammar.

It is sometimes argued that no religion of any kind should be taught in schools. The name of God should not be mentioned, prayers should not be prayed, religious holidays should not be observed—all of this to avoid in any way indoctrinating the young. This is itself, of course, the most powerful kind of indoctrination, because it is the most subtle and for that reason the hardest for the young or anybody else to defend themselves against. Given no reason to believe that the issue of God has any importance at all, or even exists as an issue, how can anybody make an intelligent decision either for God or against?

My wife went to a college in the fifties that was so tolerant religiously that it wouldn't allow an ordained minister to conduct an informal discussion group on the campus.

TOUCH

I HEAR YOUR WORDS. I see your face. I smell the rain in your hair, the coffee on your breath. I am inside me experiencing you as you are inside you experiencing me, but the you and the I themselves, those two insiders, don't entirely meet until something else happens.

We shake hands perhaps. We pat each other on the back. At parting or greeting, we may even go so far as to give each other a hug. And now it has happened. We discover each other to be

DAY 329

three-dimensional, solid creatures of reality as well as dimension-less, airy creators of it. We have an outside of flesh and bone as well as an inside where we live and move and have our being.

Through simply touching, more directly than in any other way, we can transmit to each other something of the power of the life we have inside us. It is no wonder that the laying on of hands has always been a traditional part of healing or that when Jesus was around, "all the crowd sought to touch him" (Luke 6:19). It is no wonder that just the touch of another human being at a dark time can be enough to save the day.

TOURIST PREACHING

DAY 330

ENGLISH-SPEAKING TOURISTS abroad are inclined to believe that if only they speak English loudly and distinctly and slowly enough, the natives will know what's being said even though they don't understand a single word of the language.

Preachers often make the same mistake. They believe that if only they speak the ancient verities loudly and distinctly and slowly enough, their congregations will understand them.

Unfortunately, the only language people really understand is their own language, and unless preachers are prepared to translate the ancient verities into it, they might as well save their breath.

TRANSFIGURATION

DAY 331

HIS FACE SHONE like the sun," Matthew says, "and his garments became white as light." Moses and Elijah were talking to him. There was a bright cloud overshadowing him and out of it a voice saying, "This is my beloved son, with whom I am well pleased; listen to him." The three disciples who witnessed the scene "fell on their faces, and were filled with awe" (Matthew 17:1–6).

It is as strange a scene as there is in the Gospels. Even without the voice from the cloud to explain it, they had no doubt what they were witnessing. It was Jesus of Nazareth all right, the man they'd tramped many a dusty mile with, whose mother and brothers they knew, the one they'd seen as hungry, tired, and footsore as the rest of them. But it was also the Messiah, the Christ, in his glory. It was the holiness of the man shining through his humanness, his face so afire with it they were almost blinded.

Even with us something like that happens once in a while. The face of a man walking with his child in the park, of a woman baking bread, of sometimes even the unlikeliest person listening to a concert, say, or standing barefoot in the sand watching the waves roll in, or just having a beer at a Saturday baseball game in July. Every once and so often, something so touching, so incandescent, so alive transfigures the human face that it's almost beyond bearing.

TRAVEL

SOMETIMES WE TRAVEL to get away and see something of the world. Sometimes we travel just to get away from ourselves. DAY 332 Sometimes we travel to convince ourselves that we are getting someplace.

The author of the Letter to the Hebrews lists a number of gadabouts like Noah and Abraham, Sarah and Jacob, and the footloose Israelites generally. He then makes the point that what they were really doing was "seeking a homeland," which they died without ever finding but never gave up seeking even so (Hebrews 11:14).

Maybe that is true of all of us. Maybe at the heart of all our traveling is the dream of someday, somehow, getting Home.

TREE

DAY 333

MY BROTHER LIKED DIGGING HOLES, and the summer before he died he dug one for an apple tree that I see every day through a window in my office. Thanks to the tree, it is the one hole he dug that has not been filled in and forgotten.

By the side of an old dirt road in the woods is a big maple tree that is so nearly hollow that three children can get into it together and still have wiggle room. Year after year it puts out a canopy of leaves even so, and a friend of mine once said, "If that tree can keep on doing that in the shape it's in, then there's hope for all of us." So we named it the Hope Tree.

Sycamore, willow, catalpa, ash—who knows what their true names are? We know only that they are most beautiful in the fall when they are dying. They are craziest when the wind is blowing. In the snow they are holiest.

Maybe what is most precious about them is their silence. Maybe what is most touching about them is the way they reach out to us as we pass.

TRINITY

DAY 334

THE MUCH MALIGNED DOCTRINE of the Trinity is an assertion that, appearances to the contrary notwithstanding, there is only one God.

Father, Son, and Holy Spirit mean that the mystery beyond us, the mystery among us, and the mystery within us are all the same mystery. Thus the Trinity is a way of saying something about us and the way we experience God.

The Trinity is also a way of saying something about God and

God's inner nature; that is, God does not need the creation in order to have something to love, because within God's being love happens. In other words, the love God is is love not as a noun, but as a verb. This verb is reflexive as well as transitive.

If the idea of God as both Three and One seems farfetched and obfuscating, look in the mirror someday.

There is (a) the interior life known only to yourself and those you choose to communicate it to (the Father). There is (b) the visible face, which in some measure reflects that inner life (the Son). And there is (c) the invisible power you have that enables you to communicate that interior life in such a way that others do not merely know *about* it, but know it in the sense of its becoming part of who they are (the Holy Spirit). Yet what you are looking at in the mirror is clearly and indivisibly the one and only you.

TRUTH

WHEN JESUS SAYS that he has come to bear witness to the truth, Pilate asks, "What is truth?" (John 18:38). Contrary to the traditional view that his question is cynical, it is possible that he asks it with a lump in his throat. Instead of truth, Pilate has only expedience. His decision to throw Jesus to the wolves is expedient. Pilate views humankind as alone in the universe with nothing but its own courage and ingenuity to see it through. That is enough to choke up anybody.

Pilate asks "What is truth?" and for years there have been politicians, scientists, theologians, philosophers, poets, and so on to tell him. The sound they make is like the sound of crickets chirping.

Jesus doesn't answer Pilate's question. He just stands there. *Stands,* and stands *there.*

DAY 335

UBIQUITY

DAY 336   E VERY AUTOMOBILE BEARS on its license plate a number that represents the number of years that have elapsed since the birth of Christ. This is a powerful symbol of the ubiquity of God and the indifference of the human race.

UGLINESS

DAY 337   W HOEVER THE SUFFERING SERVANT WAS—that mysterious figure whom Isaiah saw as destined somehow to save the world by suffering for it, and in terms of whom Jesus apparently saw himself—we know that his appearance was "marred beyond human semblance and his form beyond that of the sons of men" (Isaiah 52:14). "He had no comeliness that we should look at him, and no beauty that we should desire him," Isaiah continues, and presumably that was a large part of why "he was despised and rejected by men" (Isaiah 53:2b–3a).

You think of the grossly overweight woman struggling to get through the turnstile at the county fair, the acne-scarred teenager at the high-school prom, the skeletal AIDS victim sitting on the New York sidewalk with a Styrofoam begging cup between his ankles. They too, like the Servant, are men and women "of sorrow and acquainted with grief" (Isaiah 53:3b).

Who knows to what extent their ugliness has led them too to be despised and rejected and to despise and reject themselves? Who knows whether their acquaintance with grief will open their hearts to the grieving of others or whether it will turn their hearts to stone? But for the sake of the one who bore it before they did, we are to honor them for the sanctity of their burden. For his sake, we are called to see their terrible beauty.

UNBELIEF

U NBELIEF IS AS MUCH OF A CHOICE as belief is. What makes   DAY 338
it in many ways more appealing is that, whereas to believe in
something requires some measure of understanding and effort, not to believe doesn't require much of anything at all.

URIAH THE HITTITE

U RIAH THE HITTITE, Bathsheba's husband, was a straight ar-   DAY 339
row and a patriot, and in his eyes the king could do no
wrong. There's no reason to think he had any idea David was carrying on with Bathsheba while he was off in the army, but you suspect that even if somebody had tipped him off about it, he wouldn't have made all that much of a fuss.

When Bathsheba told David she was pregnant by him, he decided to move fast and had her husband sent back from the front on the double. His hope was that Uriah would lose no time bedding down his beautiful bride, and that way, when the time came, he'd have no reason for thinking the baby was anyone's but his. But he didn't count on Uriah's strong moral character and high sense of duty. Uriah said that as long as his troops were back there slogging it out in the trenches, he refused to live it up at home or have sex with anybody. Even after David got him all liquored up one night in an effort to lower his resistance, he still insisted on sleeping curled up on the palace floor, and Bathsheba bedded down alone.

His first trick having failed, David had Uriah bundled off to the front again with a note to General Joab saying to assign him where the fighting was fiercest. Uriah was soon shot down by the enemy, and after a long enough mourning period to make it look respectable, David married Bathsheba himself.

If Uriah could have known about the long and illustrious line that was to issue from that unseemly match, the chances are he would have considered his death none too high a price to pay. With Solomon in mind and all the mighty kings who followed him, he would probably have rejoiced in the thought that by bowing out at the right moment he had been able to give so many lives besides his own to the service of his country.   *2 Samuel 11*

See also Bathsheba, Nathan.

U.S.A.

DAY 340   THE KU KLUX KLAN and the Bill of Rights. *Moby Dick* and drugstore paperbacks. Abraham Lincoln and Richard Nixon.

The Mississippi River and Coney Island. Reinhold Niebuhr and Aimee Semple McPherson. The Vietnam War and the Peace Corps.

Out of many, one. The question, of course, is: one what? The hope of the world? The despair of the world?

Anybody who lived through the Cuban Missile Crisis of 1962 is unlikely to forget it. The U.S.S.R. refusing to call back its freighters. The U.S.A. refusing to call off its blockade. The world going to sleep at night wondering if there would be a world to wake up to in the morning.

One misstep is all it would have taken. One misstep is all it will take.

VANITY

VANITY IS FUTILITY.

According to the book of Ecclesiastes, everything is vanity because the good and the evil, the wise and the foolish, the lucky and the unlucky, the haves and the have-nots all turn to dust in the end. If you're honest about it, that's a hard point to refute.

Saint Paul puts it this way, "If Christ has not been raised, then our preaching is in vain and your faith is in vain. . . . If for this life only we have hoped in Christ, we are of all people most to be pitied" (1 Corinthians 15:14, 19). In other words, he is as honest as Ecclesiastes if not more so. But then he goes one step further.

He says Christ has been raised. In honesty he has to say that too, because on his way to the city of Damascus one day he experienced it. That being so, he suggests, not even death is futile. That being so, not even life is in vain.

VASHTI

K ING AHASUERUS OF PERSIA, better known as Xerxes, decided to throw a party that would make the Darktown Strut-
ters' Ball look like a nursery tea. He invited not only everybody who
was anybody, but everybody who was nobody in particular too,
and as far as expense went, the sky was the limit. It was to last for
seven days, and the palace was turned upside down getting ready
for it. New blue-and-white curtains were hung in all the windows,
silver couches were moved in by the cartload, and drinks were
served in goblets of pure gold. Vashti, the king's wife and queen,
decided that the boys shouldn't be the only ones to enjoy themselves, so she threw a party of her own and asked in all the girls.

DAY 342

By the time the seventh day rolled around, the king was feeling
no pain. Having shown off all his other treasures, he decided the
moment had come to show off Queen Vashti too. She was a raving
beauty, and he wanted to see the rest of the boys turn green with
envy when he paraded her around in front of them for a while. So
he sent word to her through a couple of eunuchs to get down there
in a hurry. On the grounds that she was a human being rather than
a silver couch and that a woman was as good as a man any day,
she refused to be trotted out as a sex object and turned the king
down flat.

Needless to say, the king was fit to be tied. Not only had he and
his friends been personally insulted, but if Vashti was allowed to get
away with a thing like that, who could tell what the girls would be
up to next. Maybe even asking for the vote. Therefore he divorced
her on the spot and married a lady named Esther instead.

That is how Queen Vashti lost her throne but kept her self-respect, and there seems to be absolutely no question as to which of the two she valued more highly.   *Esther 1–2*

See also Xerxes.

VIRGIN BIRTH

DAY 343   THE EARLIEST OF THE FOUR GOSPELS makes no reference to the virgin birth, and neither does Paul, who wrote earlier still. On later evidence, however, many Christians have made it an article of faith that it was the Holy Spirit rather than Joseph who got Mary pregnant. If you believe God was somehow in Christ, it shouldn't make much difference to you how he got there. If you don't believe, it should make less difference still. In either case, life is complicated enough without confusing theology and gynecology.

In one sense anyway, the doctrine of the virgin birth is demonstrably true. Whereas the villains of history can always be seen as the products of heredity and environment, the saints always seem to arrive under their own steam. Evil evolves. Holiness happens.

VIRGINITY

DAY 344   THERE IS NO SPECIAL WORD for people who have never fallen in love, or had major surgery, or learned how to swim, but virginity is the special word for people who have never had sex with another human being. They have heard about it. The chances are they have dreamed about it. If they are honest, they will probably admit there have been times when they have come close to it. But for one reason or another, they have never given it a try.

In the old days virgins were considered purer and holier than other people. In our day they are apt to be snickered at. The plain truth of the matter is that they are simply people who for one reason or another have never set forth on one of life's great adventures. Who knows where the adventure might lead them? Who can predict the dangers and delights along the way? Who can foresee the endless consequences?

Maybe uncertainties like those are among the reasons why virgins hold on to their virginity. And who can foresee the consequences of that either?

VIRTUE

NEXT TO THE SEVEN DEADLY SINS, the seven cardinal virtues are apt to look pale and unenterprising, but appearances are notoriously untrustworthy. DAY 345

Prudence and *temperance,* taken separately, may not be apt to get you to your feet cheering, but when they go together, as they almost always do, that's a different matter. The chain smoker or the junkie, for instance, who exemplifies both by managing to kick the habit, can very well have you throwing your hat in the air, especially if it happens to be somebody whom for personal reasons you'd like to have around a few years longer. And the *courage* involved isn't likely to leave you cold either. Often it's the habit kicker's variety that seems the most courageous.

If you think of *justice* as sitting blindfolded with a scale in her hand, you may have to stifle a yawn, but if you think of a black judge acquitting a white racist of a false murder charge, it can give you gooseflesh.

The *faith* of a child taking your hand in the night is as moving as the faith of Mother Teresa among the untouchables, or Bernadette facing the skeptics at Lourdes, or Abraham, age seventy-five, packing up his bags for the Promised Land. And *hope* is the glimmer on the horizon that keeps faith plugging forward, of course, the wings that keep it more or less in the air.

Maybe it's only *love* that turns things around and makes the seven deadly sins be the ones to look pale and unenterprising for a change. Greed, gluttony, lust, envy, and pride are no more than sad efforts to fill the empty place where love belongs, and anger and sloth just two things that may happen when you find that not even all seven of them at their deadliest ever can.

VOCATION

DAY 346

VOCATION COMES FROM the Latin *vocare*, "to call," and means the work a person is called to by God.

There are all different kinds of voices calling you to all different kinds of work, and the problem is to find out which is the voice of God rather than of society, say, or the superego, or self-interest.

By and large a good rule for finding out is this: The kind of work God usually calls you to is the kind of work (a) that you need to do and (b) that the world needs to have done. If you really get a kick out of your work, you've presumably met requirement (a), but if your work is writing cigarette ads, the chances are you've missed requirement (b). On the other hand, if your work is being a doctor in a leper colony, you have probably met requirement (b), but if most of the time you're bored and depressed by it, the chances are you have not only bypassed (a), but probably aren't helping your patients much either.

Neither the hair shirt nor the soft berth will do. The place God calls you to is the place where your deep gladness and the world's deep hunger meet.

WAR

WE CANNOT BE reminded too often that the largely middle-aged or elderly politicians, generalissimos, and assorted heads of state who declare war on each other take no part in the dirty business of actually waging it, but leave that instead to the young. The attempt is made to secure their participation by stirring them up into a patriotic fervor, but if that doesn't work there are laws to compel it, with the result that they find themselves faced willy-nilly with having to fight to the death if necessary for a cause that a great many of them neither understand nor in their hearts consider worth paying anything like such a price for. When their bodies start coming back in bags like rubbish, they are honored as having given their lives for their country, whereas the truth of the matter is that more often than not they did not so much give them as have them wrested from them whether that's what they had in mind or not.

Can there be any doubt that if the fighting were to be left to the leaders themselves, the story would be a very different one? It is a thought worth pursuing. Many of them are overweight. Many can't see without glasses. A few wear hearing aids or pacemakers and feel faint at the sight of blood. Even the younger ones who have kept in some kind of shape have in all likelihood never so much as punched another human being in the nose, let alone aimed a gun at one in anger. But no matter. Theirs it is to do or die, and one pictures them in their business suits and long dresses, their burnooses and caftans and saris, as they head off to do it armed with weapons they have no idea how to use and ultimatums, principles, and slogans that suddenly seem equally useless, and with their hearts in their mouths.

Can there be any question as to how long it would take them to turn around and go home? Can any crazy scenario we manage to dream up be even half as crazy as war is crazy? Can there be any doubt that Jesus was speaking only the simple truth when he said that those who live by the sword will perish by the sword?

The lucky ones are the ones who perish all at once and get it over with. The others are those who still have years and years left for remembering the handsome young men and strong young women who were once the fairest and dearest they had.

WATER

FOR NINE MONTHS we breathe in it. The sight of water in oceans, rivers, and lakes is soothing to the spirit as almost nothing else. To swim in it is to become as weightless and untrammeled as in dreams. The wake of a ship, the falling of a cataract, and the tumbling of a brook can hold us spellbound for hours, and in times of

DAY 348

drought we feel as parched in our being as the lawn that crackles beneath our feet.

Air is our element, but water is our heart's delight. "My flesh faints for thee," the Psalmist sings, "as in a dry and weary land where no water is" (63:1). And among the last things that Jesus ever said, and among the most human, were the words, "I thirst" (John 19:28).

WHALE

DAY 349 IF IT WAS ACTUALLY A WHALE that swallowed Jonah on his voyage to Tarshish, it couldn't have been the kind of right whale you find in those waters because their gullets aren't big enough. Maybe it was a sperm whale, because they can handle something the size of a prophet without batting an eye. Or maybe, since the Hebrew word means only "great fish," it wasn't a whale at all, but a people-eating shark, some of whom attain lengths as great as thirty feet. But whatever it was, this much is certain.

No matter how deep it dove and no matter how dark the inside of its belly, no depth or darkness was enough to drown out the sound of Jonah's prayer. "I am cast out from thy presence. How shall I again look upon thy holy temple?" (Jonah 2:4), the intractable and waterlogged old man called out from sixty fathoms, and Yahweh heard him, and answered him, and Jonah's relief at being delivered from the whale can hardly have been any greater than the whale's at being delivered of Jonah.

Jonah 1:17–2:10

See also Jonah.

WINE

UNFERMENTED GRAPE JUICE is a bland and pleasant drink, especially on a warm afternoon mixed half and half with ginger ale. But it is a ghastly symbol of the life blood of Jesus Christ, especially when served in individual antiseptic, thimble-sized glasses.

DAY 350

Wine is booze, which means it is dangerous and drunk-making. It makes the timid brave and the reserved amorous. It loosens the tongue and breaks the ice, especially when served in a loving cup. It kills germs. As symbols go, it is a rather splendid one.

WISDOM

IN THE BOOK OF PROVERBS, Wisdom is a woman. "The Lord created me at the beginning of his work," she says (8:22). She was there when he made the heaven, the sea, the earth. It was as if he needed a woman's imagination to help him make them, a woman's eye to tell him if he'd made them right, a woman's spirit to measure their beauty by. "I was daily his delight, rejoicing before him always," she says (8:30), as if it was her joy in what he was creating that made creation bearable, and that's why he created her first.

DAY 351

Wisdom is a matter not only of the mind but of the heart, like a woman's wisdom. It is born out of suffering, as a woman bears a child. It shows a way through the darkness the way a woman stands at the window holding a lamp. "Her ways are ways of pleasantness," says Solomon, then adding, just in case there should be any lingering question as to her gender, "and all her paths are peace" (3:17).

WISE MEN

DAY 352   THE GIFTS THAT THE THREE WISE MEN, or kings, or Magi, brought to the manger in Bethlehem cost them plenty but seem hardly appropriate to the occasion. Maybe they were all they could think of for the child who had everything. In any case, they set them down on the straw—the gold, the frankincense, the myrrh—worshiped briefly, and then returned to the East, where they had come from. It gives you pause to consider how, for all their great wisdom, they overlooked the one gift that the child would have been genuinely pleased to have someday, and that was the gift of themselves.   *Matthew 2:1–12*

See also Herod the Great.

WISHFUL THINKING

DAY 353   CHRISTIANITY IS MAINLY WISHFUL THINKING. Even the part about judgment and hell reflects the wish that somewhere the score is being kept.

Dreams are wishful thinking. Children playing at being grown-up is wishful thinking. Interplanetary travel is wishful thinking.

Sometimes wishing is the wings the truth comes true on.

Sometimes the truth is what sets us wishing for it.

WITCH OF ENDOR

DAY 354   AS SOON AS KING SAUL passed a law against witchcraft and drove all practitioners out of the land, the witch of Endor traded in her broomstick on a bicycle, changed her pointed black hat for a summer straw, flushed a great many evil-smelling concoctions down the john, and tried to go straight.

But then Saul fell on evil times. He felt so sure David was after his throne that he grew paranoid on the subject. He was convinced his own son Jonathan had sided against him too. And the Philistines were gathering for a massive attack at Gilboa. He had to know how things were going to turn out, and since he and Yahweh were no longer on speaking terms as far as he was concerned and the prophet Samuel was dead, he was forced to go elsewhere for his information.

He tried a dream book, but none of his dreams were in it. He tried things like tea leaves and Ouija boards, but they all malfunctioned. So he asked his servants whether they happened to know if anybody was still around who might be able to help, if they knew what he meant, and they told him about this old party in Endor who looked like something straight out of Charles Addams.

Saul disguised himself heavily for the visit, but as soon as he stepped through the door and said he wanted her to conjure up somebody who could foretell the future, she grew shrill and suspicious. What did he want to do, she said, get the fuzz after her? And only when he swore by Yahweh that he wouldn't breathe a word to a soul did she go so far as to ask him who exactly it was he'd like her to try to get hold of for him. As soon as he said Samuel, she knew there could be only one person in Israel who would dare face that fierce old ghost, and the cat was out of the bag.

"You are Saul," she said, and by that time he was past denying it. The next thing she knew, he'd let out a yelp that not only was enough to awaken the dead, but did. "An old man is coming up, and he is wrapped in a robe," she said, and Saul realized immediately he was the right old man and bowed so low his beard touched the carpet (1 Samuel 28:12–14).

Except on the grounds of wanting to make himself even more miserable than he already was, it's hard to explain why it was his old enemy he'd asked for. Even before Samuel opened his mouth, Saul knew what he was going to say, and sure enough he said it. Samuel told him that everybody was against him including Yahweh, and not only would the Philistines win at Gilboa, but by that time the next day Saul and all his sons would be joining him in the grave. Saul crumpled in a heap to the floor.

The witch did all she could to get him back on his feet. She tried to make him eat something, but he refused. She told him that she'd done what he'd asked her and the least he could do in return was take enough to get his strength back and go, but he didn't even seem to hear what she was saying. Finally with the help of the servants she managed to get him to where he was sitting on the edge of the bed (1 Samuel 28:23), and when she produced a little meat and some freshly baked bread, he stuffed a bit of it into his mouth and then left without saying a word.

Nobody knows what the witch did after they were gone. Probably she just sat there in a daze for a while, trying to pull herself together with the comforting smell of the bread she'd baked. Maybe she decided to get out of Endor for good in case Saul broke his word and squealed on her. But she needn't have worried about that because Saul had no time left to squeal on anybody.

On the next day he was just as dead as Samuel had risen from the grave to tell him he'd be, and, this side of paradise or anywhere else, she'd never have to worry about seeing him again. Unless she got herself talked into having another seance, of course, but the odds against that seem overwhelming.   *1 Samuel 28*

WORD

IN HEBREW THE TERM *DABAR* means both "word" and "deed." Thus to say something is to do something. "I love you." "I hate you." "I forgive you." "I am afraid of you." Who knows what such words do, but whatever it is, it can never be undone. Something that lay hidden in the heart is irrevocably released through speech into time, is given substance and tossed like a stone into the pool of history, where the concentric rings lap out endlessly.

Words are power, essentially the power of creation. By my words I both discover and create who I am. By my words I elicit a word from you. Through our converse we create each other.

When God *said*, "Let there be light," there *was* light where before there was only darkness. When I *say* I love you, there is love where before there was only ambiguous silence. In a sense I do not love you first and then speak it, but only by speaking it give it reality.

"In the beginning was the Word," says John, meaning perhaps that before the beginning there was something like Silence: not the absence of sound, because there was no sound yet to be absent, but the absence of absence: nothing nothinged: everything. Then the Word. The Deed. The Beginning. The beginning in time of time. "The Word was with God, and the Word was God," says John. By uttering himself, God makes God heard and makes God hearers.

God never seems to weary of trying to get across to us. Word after word God tries in search of the right word. When the creation itself doesn't seem to say it right—sun, moon, stars, all of it—God tries flesh and blood.

God tried saying it in Noah, but Noah was a drinking man. God tried saying it in Abraham, but Abraham was a little too Mesopotamian with all those wives and whiskers. God tried Moses, but

Moses himself was trying too hard; tried David, but David was too pretty for his own good. Toward the end of his rope, God tried saying it in John the Baptist with his locusts and honey and hellfire preaching, and you get the feeling that John might almost have worked except that he lacked something small but crucial like a sense of the ridiculous or a balanced diet.

So God tried once more. Jesus as the *mot juste* of God.

"The word became flesh," John said, of all flesh *this* flesh. Jesus as the Word made flesh means take it or leave it: in this life, death, life, God finally manages to say what God is and what human is. It means: just as your words have you in them—your breath, spirit, power, hiddenness—so Jesus has God in him.

WORK

DAY 356   I F YOU LOSE YOURSELF in your work, you find who you are. If you express the best you have in you in your work, it is more than just the best you have in you that you are expressing.

See also jobs, vocation.

WORSHIP

DAY 357   PHRASES LIKE *worship service* and *service of worship* are tautologies. To worship God *means* to serve God. Basically there are two ways to do it. One way is to do things for God that God needs to have done—run errands for God, carry messages for God, fight on God's side, feed God's lambs, and so on. The other way is to do things for God that you need to do—sing songs for God, create beautiful things for God, give things up for God, tell God what's on your mind and in your heart, in general rejoice in God and make a fool of yourself for God the way lovers have always made fools of themselves for the one they love.

A Quaker meeting, a pontifical High Mass, the family service at Zion Episcopal, a Holy Roller happening—unless there is an element of joy and foolishness in the proceedings, the time would be better spent doing something useful.

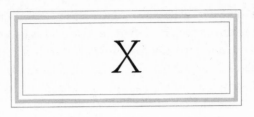

X

X IS THE GREEK LETTER CHI, which is the first letter of the word *Christ*. Thus *Xmas* is shorthand for *Christmas,* taking only about one-sixth as long to write. If you do your cards by hand, it is possible to save as much as seventy-five or eighty minutes a year.

It is tempting to say that what you do with this time that you save is your own business. Briefly stated, however, the Christian position is that there's no such thing as your own business.

XERXES

KING XERXES OF PERSIA, otherwise known as Ahasuerus, has the distinction of being the only person in the Bible whose name begins with an *X*. There's not much else you can say for him. He was a blowhard and a show-off, and anybody with an eighth-grade education could wrap him around his little finger without half trying. Or *her* little finger.

There was Haman, for example. Haman was Xerxes' right-hand man and a raging anti-Semite. There was also a Jew named Mordecai, who lived in the capital, and one day when Haman came prancing by, Mordecai refused to flatten himself out and grovel in the dust like everybody else. It was the break Haman had been waiting for. He told Xerxes about Mordecai's insubordination and rudeness and said it was a vivid illustration of how the Jews as a whole were a miserable lot. He said if you let one of them in, they brought their friends, and Persia was crawling with them. He said the only laws they respected were their own, and it was obvious they didn't give a hoot in hell about the king or anybody else. He then said that, as far as he was concerned, the only thing to do was exterminate the whole pack of them like rats and offered the king ten thousand in cash for the privilege of organizing the operation. Xerxes pocketed the cash and told him to go ahead.

But then there was also Queen Esther, a good-looking Jewish girl who was both a cousin of Mordecai's and Xerxes' second wife. As soon as she got wind of what Haman was up to, she decided to do what she could to save her people from the gas chamber. Xerxes had a rather short fuse, and you had to know how to handle him, but she planned her strategy carefully, and by the time she was through, she'd not only talked him out of letting the Jews get exterminated, but had gotten him to hang Haman from the same gallows that had been set up for Mordecai. She even managed to persuade Xerxes to give Mordecai Haman's old job.

Unfortunately, the end of the story is less edifying. Not content with having saved their people and taken care of Haman, Esther and Mordecai used their new power to orchestrate the slaughter of seventy-five thousand of their old enemies. The whole unpleasant account is contained in the book of Esther, which has the distinction of being the only book in the Bible in which the name of God isn't even mentioned. There seems every reason to believe that God considered himself well out of it.   *The Book of Esther*

See also Vashti.

X-RATED

DAY 360   THE TERMS *adult books, adult movies,* and *adult entertainment* imply that, whereas the young must be somehow protected from all those bare breasts and heaving buttocks, adults will simply take them in their stride. Possibly the reverse is closer to the truth.

The young seem to have a knack for coming through all sorts of heady experiences relatively unscathed, and paperback prurience and video venery are less apt to turn them on than to turn them elsewhere. The middle-aged, on the other hand, having fewer elsewheres, settle for what they can get.

After a while, the X-rated titillations tend to turn tawdry and tedious, but even days later, they keep on flickering away somewhere in the back of the mind to a captive audience of one.

The chances are that the loneliness and sadness of it then may leave deeper scars on a forty-five-year-old adult than the gymnastics of it on a thirteen-year-old child.

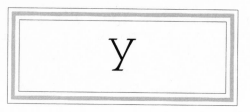

YAHWEH

Yahweh is one of God's names, and Moses was the first one he told it to. Maybe it means "I am what I am" or something along those lines, and maybe it doesn't. At other places in the Bible he is given names like Elohim, El Shaddai, and the Lord. Jesus called him mainly Abba, which is Aramaic for "father." Yahweh doesn't seem to care too much what people call him as long as the lines of communication are kept open.

He "inhabits eternity," says the prophet Isaiah (57:15). That means before there was anything, he was, and long after there's nothing much left, he still will be. But you can't apply tenses like *was* or *will be* to Yahweh literally any more than you can apply the names of colors literally to the sounds of the Royal Scots Dragoon Guards playing "Amazing Grace." He doesn't inhabit time like everybody else. He invented time.

"If I take the wings of the morning and dwell in the uttermost parts of the sea, even there thy hand shall lead me," says Psalm 139 (vv. 9–10), which means that any place you can possibly think of is a place where Yahweh is because there's no place you can possibly think of that's a place where Yahweh isn't. He no more exists in space than Norman Rockwell exists in the covers of the *Saturday Evening Post*. Space is the canvas he paints creation on.

But all this doesn't mean for one second that he doesn't keep on turning up in time and space anyway. On the contrary, that's what the whole Bible is all about. Adam and Eve heard the sound of him "walking in the garden in the cool of the day," says Genesis (3:8), and one way or another he's been down here throwing his weight around ever since. He sounds off through prophets. He raises Cain through kings. He leaves all the splendor and power of nature for his calling card and makes the whole thing fresh, like bread, every time the sun rises. He makes himself known through the best impulses and wildest longings of the human heart, and Saint Paul goes even so far as to say that when people bog down in their prayers, "that very Spirit intercedes for us with sighs too deep for words" (Romans 8:26).

The time he outdid himself, of course, was when "he so loved the world that he gave his only Son that whoever believes in him should not perish but have eternal life" (John 3:16). To put it another way, his final word to the world was the Word itself wearing flesh like a uniform and dwelling among us full of grace and truth (John 1:14). What is Yahweh all about and what do human beings have it in them at their best to be? Yahweh's answer to those formidable questions is not a theological blockbuster, but a biological human being, in a way the only real, honest-to-God human being who ever was. Jesus was his name and Christ was the title that went with his job. "He who has seen me has seen the Father," Jesus said (John 14:9), and "God is love," said John (1 John 4:8); and the basic plot of the whole True Romance of history seems to be just that Love will have us lovely before he's through or split a gut trying. He will badger us, bulldoze us, clobber and cajole us till in the end we all make it "to the measure of the stature of the fullness of Christ" (Ephesians 4:13).

Even Nebuchadnezzar, you say? Even Hiram and Herod and the queen of Sheba? Even Jacob and Jael and Judas, of all people? Is it possible that he intends to do a job on Saddam Hussein and Genghis Khan, not to mention Groucho Marx and Madame de Pompadour and Warren Gamaliel *Harding,* for Christ's sweet sake? Exactly. For Christ's sweet sake. And not the least staggering thought is that it seems he has similar plans in mind not only for the author of this outrageous compendium, but for every last Jack and Jill who read it and even the ones who don't.

Nobody ever claimed it was going to be easy, least of all Jesus, who continually said to take up our crosses and follow him, not just our picnic baskets and tickets to Disneyland. A lot of barnacles are going to have to be scraped off and a lot of horse manure shoveled out and a lot of rooms stripped bare and redecorated before the final product emerges bright as a new penny, to mix a metaphor or two. But peculiar as we are, every last one of us, for reasons best known to himself, Yahweh apparently treasures the whole three-ring circus, and every time we say "Thy kingdom come," it's home we're talking about, our best, last stop.

"I am the Alpha and the Omega," Yahweh says, "the beginning and the end" (Revelation 21:6), and he will have everybody aboard at last, because if even just a couple of stragglers fail to show up, the party simply won't be complete without them.

YHWH

I N EXODUS 3:13–14, when Moses asks God's name, God says it is YHWH, which is apparently derived from the Hebrew verb *to be* and means something like "I am what I am" or "I will be what I will be." The original text of the Old Testament didn't include vowels, so YHWH is all that appears.

DAY 362

Since it was believed that God's name was too holy to be used by just anybody, over the years it came to be used only by the high priest on special occasions. When other people ran across it in their reading, they simply substituted for it the title *Lord*. The result of this pious practice was that in time no one knew any longer what vowels belonged in between the four consonants, and thus the proper pronunciation of God's name was lost. The best guess is that it was something like YaHWeH, but there's no way of being sure.

Like the bear in Thurber's fable, sometimes the pious lean so far over backward that they fall flat on their face.

YOU

DAY 363   IN THE BOOK OF GENESIS the first word God speaks to a human being is "*You*" (2:15), and in the book of Revelation the last word a human being speaks in effect to God is "Come, Lord Jesus!" which is to say "Come, *you!*" (22:20).

It is possible that the whole miracle of creation is to bridge the immeasurable distance between Creator and creature with that one small word, and every time human beings use it to bridge the immeasurable distances between one another, something of that miracle happens again.

YOUTH

DAY 364   YOUTH ISN'T FOR SISSIES EITHER.

See also adolescence, children, old age.

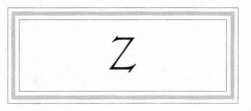

ZACCHAEUS

ZACCHAEUS APPEARS JUST ONCE in the New Testament, and his story is brief (Luke 19:1–10). It is also one of the few places in the Gospels where we're given any visual detail. Maybe that is part of what makes it stand out.

We're told that Zacchaeus was a runt, for one thing. That is why, when Jesus was reported to be en route into Jericho and the crowds gathered to see what they could see, Zacchaeus had to climb a tree to get a good look. Luke says the tree he climbed was a sycamore tree.

We're also told that Zacchaeus was a crook—a Jewish legman for the Roman IRS, who (following the practice of the day) raked in as much more than the going tax as he could get and pocketed the difference. When people saw Zacchaeus oiling down the street, they crossed to the other side.

The story goes like this. The sawed-off shyster is perched in the sycamore tree. Jesus opens his mouth to speak. All Jericho hugs itself in anticipation of hearing him give the man holy hell. "Woe unto you! Repent! Wise up!" is the least of what they expect. What

Jesus says is, "Come down on the double. I'm staying at your house." The mob points out that the man Jesus is talking to is a public disaster. Jesus' silence is deafening.

It is not reported how Zacchaeus got out of the sycamore, but the chances are good that he fell out in pure astonishment. He said, "I'm giving everything back. In spades." Maybe he even meant it. Jesus said, "Three cheers for the Irish!"

The unflagging lunacy of God. The unending seaminess of human beings. The meeting between them that is always a matter of life or death and usually both. The story of Zacchaeus is the gospel in sycamore. It is the best and oldest joke in the world.

ZERO

DAY 366   IN THE BEGINNING . . . the earth was without form and void, and darkness was upon the face of the deep" (Genesis 1:1–2). In other words, God started with nothing, zero, and out of it brought everything.

In the end, says John, "I saw a great white throne and him who sat upon it; from his presence earth and sky fled away, and no place was found for them" (Revelation 20:11). In other words, there is zero again, and out of it God brought a new heaven and a new earth.

Perhaps more than for anything else, God is famous for calling something precious out of something that doesn't even exist until God calls it. At the beginning of each one of us it happened, and at the end of each one of us maybe by God's grace it will happen again.

Index